Violence and Warfare in Social Context

Violence and Warfare in Social Context
Archaeological and Historical Studies

Rolf Fabricius Warming (Ed.)
Foreword by J. J. Widen

Södertörns högskola

Södertörns högskola
(Södertörn University)
The Library
SE-141 89 Huddinge
www.sh.se/publications

Cover illustration: Rizky Nugraha ©2025
Cover: Jonathan Robson
Graphic form: Per Lindblom & Jonathan Robson

Stockholm 2025

Stockholm Studies in Archaeology 89
ISSN 0349-4128
Södertörn Archaeological Studies 16
ISSN 1652-2559
Södertörn Academic Studies 100
ISSN 1650-433X
ISBN 978-91-89962-06-4 (print)
ISBN 978-91-89962-07-1 (digital)

For friends and colleagues in Ukraine

Acknowledgements

This anthology was compiled during my PhD at the CEMAS/Department of Archaeology and Classical Studies at Stockholm University. The book is based on the *Studies of Conflict* mini conference, which was also hosted at Stockholm University on June 3rd, 2022. I am grateful to the university for supporting both the event and this publication, particularly our head of department Professor Andrew Jones, whose backing has been invaluable As this volume continues on from *On War on Board* (Johan Rönnby, 2019) in some ways, I would also like to express my gratitude to MARIS/Södertörn University for the ongoing collaboration in researching this subject, as well as to Södertörn University Publications Committee for their support in bringing this publication to fruition.

I extend my sincere thanks to all the contributors for their thought-provoking work and their willingness to participate. I hope that another conference or seminar will be arranged soon.

I am also deeply appreciative of my PhD supervisors, Professor Mats Burström, Associate Professor Niklas Eriksson, and Professor Johan Rönnby for their patience and for allowing me the flexibility to pursue this side project alongside my primary PhD research.

My gratitude extends as well to my colleagues at the Swedish Defence University, particularly those at the Department of War Studies and my fellow PhD students there, Henrique Garbino and July Decarpentrie. I am especially thankful to Professor J. J. Widen for the engaging discussions and the stimulating War Studies seminars, where I have had the opportunity to present and refine some of my ideas. My time there has helped shape parts of this book, and I hope that they, too, will find it of interest.

I would also like to thank David Payne (International research editor, Södertörn University Publications Department) as well as the two peer reviewers for their valuable input and constructive comments. Additionally, I am grateful to Hon. associate professor John Carman for his insightful feedback, as well as to those who have read and commented on my own contributions to this volume, including

Professor Andrew Jones, adjunct professor Liliana Duica-Amaya, associate professor Peter Haldén, associate professor Lena Holmquist, Frida Espolin Norstein, Antti Ijäs and my fellow PhD students Erik Solfeldt and Fredrik Lundström. Their perspectives and suggestions have been greatly appreciated. However, any oversights or mistakes are entirely my own.

Finally, I want to express my deepest appreciation to my wife, Dianne, for her patience and unwavering support – especially in these recent months, as she has spent much time at home caring for our newborn daughter.

– Rolf Fabricius Warming

Contents

J. J. Widen

In a world that is changing rapidly on many fronts, and with wars closer to our doorstep, a drive to better understand violence and warfare is obvious. These issues are not only central in geopolitics and on a grand strategic level but so embedded in society that they intrude on everyday lives across different regions, whether in active conflict zones or more peaceful areas. With the increasing complexity, scale, variety and pace of modern warfare, there is an added need for ever more nuanced approaches and conceptualizations that look beyond traditional great power-oriented military thinking. Such theories of war and warfare are sometimes lacking when confronted with the intricate and irrational nature of many modern conflicts, particularly those of an ethnic or religious nature, which are grounded in a history of cultures.

War Studies is now an established field that explores in depth how to use, create and direct military forces, but also its causes, consequences, and wider implications for society at large. Moving beyond traditional military history and strategic theorizing, it recognizes war as a complex interplay of political, military, social and cultural forces, each exerting profound and varied influences on the dynamics of conflict. Contrary to popular belief, War Studies consists of more than narrow and command-centric strategic, operational, and tactical ideas. It also seizes on insights gained from a wide variety of disciplines, such as history, sociology, psychology and anthropology. Theoretical understandings of combat, an area of special interest in my own research, may be approached from three overarching perspectives: human-centred, social and physical. As such, War Studies recognizes the cultural dimensions of war and acknowledges a need to study them.

No doubt, War Studies and Conflict Archaeology share this viewpoint and have much to learn from one another. As is made clear in this volume, social theory and humanities can shed considerable light on the social and cultural aspects of war and violence through a historical and archaeological lens. Above all, the chapters in this book make clear that culture is an integral component of war that must be studied by paying careful attention to social and cultural interactions. Weapons cannot be reduced to mere war implements, just as warfare cannot simply be reduced to rational and instrumental military decision-making. Studying more broadly the different ways that past societies have expressed and dealt with warfare and violence gives important insights into perspectives vastly different to our own. This, in turn, improves our understanding of modern conflicts through comparison.

This volume speaks to those interested in the cultural and social dimensions of conflicts, violence and warfare, both past and present. Promoting this socio-cultural perspective remedies an overly top-down, instrumental and pragmatic perspective to which most of us fall victim. As such, it provides an important bottom-up perspective and spells out the materialistic conditions that is crucial for a more profound understanding of violence and warfare.

Professor J. J. Widen
Department of War Studies
Swedish Defence University

CHAPTER 1

Violence and Warfare in Social Context: An Introduction

Rolf Warming

The crux of this book is this: *No violence or warfare exists as an isolated phenomenon devoid of social context*. Stated so simply, why does this issue require a whole book?

The answer lies partly in addressing perspectives that have historically given insufficient attention to the social dimensions of violence and warfare. Scholarship has often treated these practices as marginal and instrumental occurrences or as mechanical processes that can be reduced to technological, biological, or political drivers, sidelining their nature as genuine social phenomena (discussed further as the 'The Three Ps' below). The emerging field of sociology of violence explicitly challenges this oversight by repositioning violence as a central social fact (Malešević, 2010; Ray, 2011; Walby, 2012; Hartmann, 2017; Kuznar, 2024). As Hartmann (2017:4) argues, 'A general sociology of violence must first and foremost take the historicity, the social construction, of its subject as its analytical starting point: the empirical forms and modalities of violence do not exist in isolation from historical forms of social (and political) organisation but are always embedded in social frameworks.' From this perspective, acts such as homicide or drone killings, as abhorrent or permissible as they may be, are not simply acts of destruction but as socially embedded as burial rites or agricultural practices (Scheper-Hughes & Bourgois, 2004:3). Building on this understanding, *social contextualisation* situates violence and warfare within broader networks of social interaction, including the society, examining how such acts (both in expression and repression) are shaped by and contribute to social life beyond their immediate physicality. Rather than treating it as a moral or political problem, this perspective conceives violence as a social fact analysed within a framework that emphasizes the dynamic relations between individual behaviour and collective social processes (Hartmann, 2017:8). By focusing on the social context, we thus gain a fuller understanding of how violence and warfare operate not only on an individual level but also as mechanisms that reflect and reshape the societies in which they occur. This volume focuses on social context in its broadest sense, extending its scope to encompass cultural context, thereby exploring the sociocultural processes through which violence and warfare are socialized and enculturated.

Furthermore, the value of the opening statement lies in the exploration of its many manifestations, to which this book contributes from an archaeological and historical perspective. By exploring violence and warfare in their diverse cultural expressions, we gain a deeper understanding of the social factors involved. Here, the many available case studies of the past warrant attention. Crucially, archaeology and history offer more than interesting cases for the history nerd; they provide means of defamiliarization, compelling us to reconsider our fundamental assumptions about conflict and security. As Carman & Carman (2020:6ff.) argue, drawing on Michael Shapiro (1997:xi), such assumptions are often shaped by a Western functional rationality that normalizes state-centric perspectives and obscures alternative ways of conceptualizing conflict. However, as they also highlight, even the recent past is less familiar than it appears to be in reality (West 1992:2), underscoring the necessity of approaching historical cases without the biases of contemporary perspectives. Archaeology and history, by contrast, challenge these assumptions by revealing how past societies engaged with violence in ways that defy modern expectations. Moreover, a key benefit of archaeological and historical approaches is the ability to situate violence and warfare within their historical contexts – that is, to analyse their temporal specificity by considering how occurrences and sociopolitical factors are interwoven with the dynamics of particular times (see also the afterword in this volume). This (pre)historical lens not only enriches our understanding of how violence and warfare operated in specific periods; it also reveals patterns of continuity and change, which can challenge modern assumptions, such as the idea that modernity has brought a decline in violence (e.g., Pinker, 2011; cf. Malešević 2010:89–174). By investigating these dimensions across diverse cultural and historical contexts, where societal conditions may be more distinctly observable than in our own, we gain a broader perspective on similar processes at work in today's world.

This overarching thematic inquiry is especially urgent in light of the Russian invasion of Ukraine in 2014 and 2022, which has brought war back to Europe with devastating humanitarian and geopolitical consequences. The impacts of this conflict extend beyond the battlefield, reshaping global defence policies, disrupting economic stability and influencing everyday lives, from household finances to public discourse. More recently, the geopolitical landscape and world security has shifted further. Donald Trump's second presidency from 2025 marks a pivotal moment in global security. His administration's aggressive policies and transactional approach to international relations are damaging traditional alliances and intensifying uncertainty in an already volatile world order. In these times, the study of conflict must not be reduced to strategic and economic calculations alone. A humanistic approach is essential – not only to understand warfare as a complex historical and social phenomenon but to ensure that the lived experiences of those affected by violence remain central to our analyses. These studies cultivate necessary compassion for human life and illuminate, on a material level, those impacted by war, the perpetrators, and the means. By centring the human element, conflict studies serve not only as an academic pursuit but as a critical lens through which we recognize the patterns of suffering and power projection – past and present (e.g., Cipolla, Crellin & Harris, 2024). The need for such studies is becoming increasingly critical.

Evoked partly by the current geopolitical climate and a growing multidisciplinary interest in conflict studies at Stockholm University, this anthology is grounded in the seminar *Studies of Conflict: Bridging the Gap*, held on June 3rd, 2022, at the Department of Archaeology and Classical Studies (Warming, 2022). Originally envisioned as a modest academic gathering, the seminar aimed to foster dialogue between researchers in the humanities interested in conflict studies. However, it quickly evolved into a full-day hybrid event featuring 11 papers from early-career and senior scholars across archaeology, history, and philology. The seminar addressed the fragmented nature of conflict studies and explored how an increased focus on social contextualisation could bridge gaps separating disciplines.

The seminar presentations covered an array of subjects, ranging from Mesolithic violence to Early Modern naval warfare. Despite the diversity, a shared interest in broader social questions, particularly the complex relationships between past societies and violence and warfare, unified the discourse. Key discussions focused on how material cultures reflect different attitudes towards violence and warfare, the dynamics of civil-military relations, the ontology of war in different cultures, the influence of material culture on violent practices, and culturally dependent responses to different sets of conditions in periods of conflict and security. If the right questions are asked, such studies can make valuable contributions to our understanding of violence and warfare and their wider social context.

This book seeks to explore the following question: *What insights can the social context reveal about violence and warfare in the past, and how can these aspects be approached?* The core purpose is not to present a radically novel idea, or to settle on an answer, but simply to advocate more socially focused approaches to the study of violence and warfare in the past. This perspective, previously advocated by scholars like Ian Armit (Armit et al., 2006) and John Carman (1997a, 1999, 2013; see also Carman & Carman, 2020), who partly inspired the seminar, has yet to gain widespread adoption but holds significant potential for enriching archaeological research on topics pertaining to conflicts.[1] It is thus particularly pertinent to the subdiscipline of Conflict Archaeology. Here, it could could foster greater cooperation as well as more engagement with other fields, especially (modern) War Studies, which still awaits substantial contributions from archaeological theory and methodologies (see the afterword in this volume).

To summarize, the specific aims of this book are:

1. To promote a socially focused perspective in the study of violence and warfare within archaeology.

---

[1] As has also been emphasized in several issues and editorials in the *Journal of Conflict Archaeology* (e.g., Banks & Pollard 2013).

2. To disseminate the findings of the seminar 'Studies of Conflict: Bridging the Gap', highlighting its discussions and extending its themes to wider audiences.
3. To foster greater collaboration within the fragmented field of Conflict Archaeology as well as interdisciplinary engagement between different fields dealing with the social context of violence and warfare.

By encouraging socially aware approaches, this volume should stimulate further discussions and investigations into conflict studies as social phenomena and enable more comprehensive debates and research that transcend historically bound physicalities.

Conflict Archaeology and the Social Approach

Conflict Archaeology

While aspects of this volume branch out to more historical and philological subjects, it primarily falls into the subdiscipline of 'Conflict Archaeology', answering a call for the further development in this field.

Here, Conflict Archaeology may be broadly defined as *the (re)contextualisation of human-related material culture associated with interpersonal violence and conflict.* Unlike historical approaches that prioritise written sources, Conflict Archaeology centres around material sources, undertaking studies of material culture and seeking out the contexts – both the physical and social relationships – that pertain to interpersonal violence. Often operating alongside other umbrella terms that distinguish archaeological research into violent subject matters, such as Battlefield Archaeology, Combat Archaeology and Military Archaeology, Conflict Archaeology is generally accepted as a more encompassing subdiscipline for all archaeological studies relating to conflict and interpersonal violence. 'Combat Archaeology', for instance, is sometimes used synonymously but typically emphasizes fighting practices and acts of interpersonal violence, rather than more overarching conflict-related issues (Figure 1).[2] Conflict Archaeology

---

[2] These distinctions are somewhat blurred. For example, while the Society for Combat Archaeology highlights the practice of interpersonal violence, it also engages with more general conflict-related topics in much the same way as Conflict Archaeology does.

thus includes a variety of different studies like investigations of battlefield sites, material culture studies (particularly of arms and armour), experimental trials with weaponry replicas, osteological analyses, analyses of gendered violence etc. As summarized by Armit et al. (2006), the data strands available for addressing conflict archaeological enquiries are (1) skeletal material, (2) iconographic sources, (3) artefacts, (4) architecture and (5) written sources. To this we might add (6) experimental archaeology, which can generate new data for interpretation based on the above.

Conflict Archaeology is a relatively recent strand of archaeological research, only formalized in the past three decades, and is best understood as a response to certain disciplinary challenges within the archaeology. A full review of its development is not feasible here, but it should be noted that the study of violence in archaeology underwent something of a revival in the 1990s after a long period influenced by post-WWII anti-militarism (for discussion, see Carman 2013; Holmquist, this volume). Partly accelerated by methodological advancements in battlefield research (Scott et al., 1989) and several important initiatives of the 1990s, which were to some extent stimulated by the Yugoslav Wars (1991-2001), archaeologist and anthropologists began to address problematic attitudes and interpretations that had seriously downplayed, neglected and sanitized our violent past in major areas of the discipline.

Much of the rightful criticism came in the wake of Lawrence Keeley's *War Before Civilization* (1996), in which cogent arguments directed against archaeological narratives depicting a 'pacified past'. However, as pointed out by later authors in their revisionist readings of this discursive field (Ferguson, 2006; Carman, 2013:23ff.; Vandkilde, 2014; Fernández-Götz & Roymans, 2018:3), the past never was entirely as pacified as is sometimes suggested. For instance, in American anthropology, where archaeology is considered a subdiscipline, the subject of warfare was more frequently featured from the 1960s onwards. Nonetheless, society was often the main concern of early studies dealing with the subject of warfare, resulting in a social but rather bloodless reading of warfare (Childe, 1941; Arnold 1982; Vencl 1984; Hedeager & Kristiansen 1985; Nordbladh 1989).

Figure 1: An example of Combat Archaeology in action: Experimental trials with the author testing the durability of a reconstruction of Viking Age round shield in simulated combat scenarios at the Trelleborg Viking Fortress (National Museum of Denmark). Photo: Jacob Nyborg Andreassen (Society for Combat Archaeology).

Another conflict-related genre of literature that is commonly overlooked is the early work on weaponry in museum collections which, although often heavily reliant on written sources, have contributed to a better understanding of the manufacturing, use and role of historical weaponry (e.g., Hoffmeyer, 1954; Oakeshott, 1960). Notwithstanding such early studies, Keeley (1996) and subsequent authors correctly identified and addressed an existing problem in archaeological discourse involving a severe neglect and marginalization of violence in archaeological research.

Although diminished, these problematic attitudes persist in certain areas of archaeological research and geographical regions. For instance, according to recent quantitative assessments, conflict-related studies remain underrepresented in Sweden (Bornfalk Back,

2016; 2023:49ff.).[3] It is particularly notable that the main Swedish journal for archaeological research, *Current Swedish Archaeology*, has only published six articles focused on aspects pertaining to violence, conflict or weaponry from its first publication in 1993 until now, with only one on the actual practice of violence (Horn, 2013). Recently, these problematic attitudes have been linked by feminist critique, dismissing such subjects as being too focused on 'masculine-encoded activities.' Needless to say, conflicts and their multivarious interactions with society affects us all, regardless of gender (for gendered approaches, see Matić & Jensen, 2017). These challenges should be understood as major factors in the emergence of Conflict Archaeology as a subdiscipline that recognizes conflict as a legitimate area of specialization, providing opportunities for more developed discourses and synthesized studies about violence and coercive power.

At present, Conflict Archaeology is a thriving field of research. For the past three decades, a commitment has been made to un-pacify the 'pacified past': the subdiscipline now boasts of, among other things, two international conference series (*Fields of Conflict* and *Archaeology of Conflicts Conference*)[4], a regularly peer-reviewed journal (*Journal of Conflict Archaeology*, established 2005), research centres (e.g., *Scottish Centre for War Studies and Conflict Archaeology* at the University of Glasgow), societies (e.g., *Society for Combat Archaeology*, www.combatarchaeology.org), and, more generally, a renewed research interest expressed in the form of various fieldwork efforts and scholarly publications. The growing number and diversity of conflict studies signal a revived importance of this research field, let alone the demise of a previous taboo to deal with such subjects within certain branches of archaeology. Much of this is owed to the successful combination of appropriate tools, methodology and theoretical approaches (Scott & McFeaters, 2011). Accordingly, Conflict Archaeology enjoys a firmly

---

[3] However, several important conflict archaeology projects and publications have emerged in Sweden in recent years, no doubt partly owing to the current geopolitical climate and Sweden's admittance into NATO (e.g., Rönnby, 2019; Bornfalk Back, 2023; Lidén et al., 2024; Lingström, 2025; see also Holmquist, this volume).

[4] To this might be added The Roman Military Equipment Conference (ROMEC), which is more multidisciplinary in nature and focused on Roman military, as the name implied.

established status within archaeology at large but is not without its share of disciplinary challenges.

The Call for Social Approaches: Towards Disciplinary Cohesion?

Despite the success in becoming a legitimate field of archaeological research, the current fragmented state of conflict studies poses a challenge. As both Ferguson (2006) and Carman (2013) make clear, there are disciplinary divisions between three periods of interest, each with distinct scholarly traditions and influences. The three divisions in question are (1) prehistoric conflict, (2) historic battlefield archaeology, and (3) the archaeology of 20th-century conflict. The study of prehistoric conflict often intersects with anthropological approaches, which is particularly true in the North American tradition where archaeology is a sub-field of the four-field discipline of anthropology (together with physical anthropology, cultural anthropology and linguistics). In these studies, archaeological interpretation often draws on anthropological understanding of the warfare of traditional small-scale societies and focuses on socially oriented questions. In contrast, historic battlefield archaeology is closely linked to military history, with research centring on battlefield reconstruction and recovering the successes and failures of strategic and tactical elements of warfare from Ancient Greece to the late nineteenth century. Meanwhile, the archaeology of 20th-century conflict is predominantly driven by heritage management concerns, particularly the preservation and interpretation of sites related to the World Wars and other modern conflicts. However, recently, this branch of Conflict Archaeology has developed a strand of material culture studies, often concentrated on the theme of commemoration and difficult heritage (Arnshav, 2020; Burström et al., 2009; Burström & Gelderblom, 2011; Saunders, 2004, 2012; Damlund, 2021; Saunders & Cornish, 2021). This separation is both evident in the specialized literature of each tradition and the organisation of academic conferences and professional communities, which, by and large, tend to remain siloed within these three distinct periods. The different origins and intellectual agendas of each division underscore their separation, highlighting the need for more integrated approaches to the archaeological study of war and conflict.

The fragmented nature of Conflict Archaeology has prompted calls for more socially focused and anthropological approaches within the field. John Carman is a key advocate of this perspective, suggesting that Conflict Archaeology, in all its varieties, should not only examine the practice of warfare but also its broader social context, consequences, and symbolic dimensions (Carman, 1997:225; 2013; Carman & Carman 2020). He argues that drawing on anthropological insights, rather than restricting the discipline to a narrow military history perspective, can open new and intriguing questions for archaeological investigation and bring cohesion to the otherwise splintered field. Carman nonetheless clarifies that this approach is not about subsuming Conflict Archaeology under the heading of an 'anthropology of conflict', but rather about leveraging existing disciplinary connections to benefit all branches of the field, regardless of their specific focus or time period. Supporting this view, Armit et al. (2006) criticise the lack of cultural consideration in studies of violence, advocating for more socially oriented approaches, especially in research on prehistoric conflict. They warn that without understanding the social or cultural contexts, there is a risk of imposing an ethnocentric view on past societies or reducing the work to simple descriptions of (pre)-historical instances of violence. Highlighting a problematic divide between archaeology and osteology, the authors emphasize the need for an integrated social approach to overcome partitions along traditional disciplinary borders. Their anthology calls for a framework that treats conflict as socially and historically contextualized, rather than as a 'natural' universal phenomenon. Echoing these viewpoints, Fernández-Götz and Roymans (2018) underscore the heterogenous domain of Conflict Archaeology and advocate a deeper level of social interpretation that proceeds from a historical-anthropological perspective. For this purpose, they suggest a broad, multidimensional approach that attempts to integrate elements from different research agendas (Figure 2).

These discussions highlight a shared recognition of the untapped potential within the disparate field of Conflict Archaeology and suggest that adopting more socially oriented approaches could offer a unifying solution.

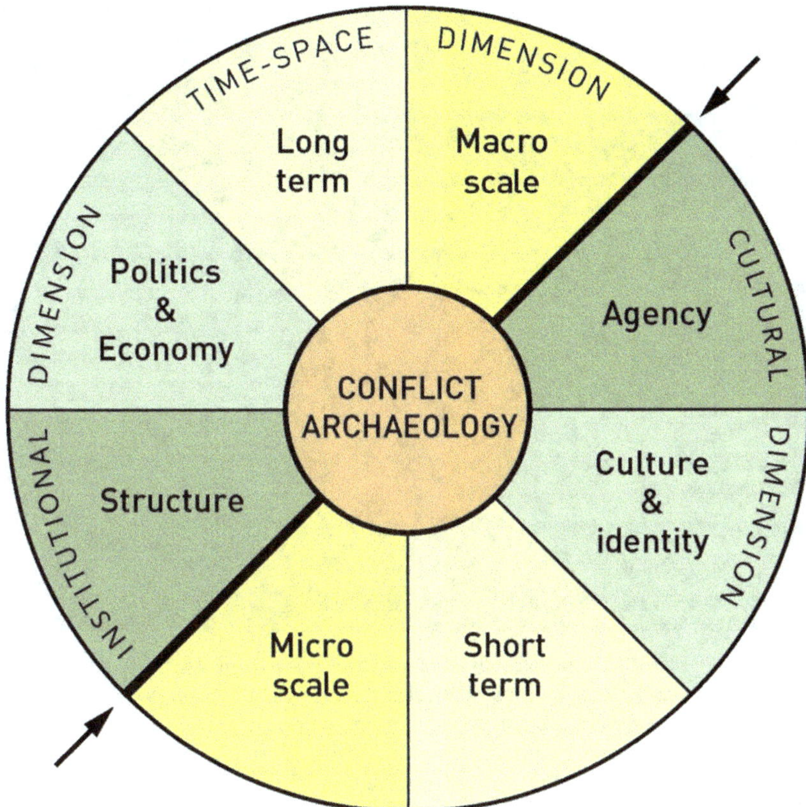

Figure 2: Model of a multidimensional approach to Conflict Archaeology from a historical-anthropological perspective (from Roymans & Fernández-Götz, 2018:9, fig. 1.3, inspired by Slofstra, 2002:20). The model serves as a useful hermeneutic reminder about the many dimensions and aspects that can be explored through conflict-related material.

The same social emphasis has been advocated in the field of maritime archaeology to counterbalance an overly techno-functional and empirical focus on specific cases of shipwreck (Gould, 1981; Adams, 2003, 2013; Adams & Rönnby, 2013).

Curiously, maritime archaeological topics are seldom featured in broader conflict archaeological research, despite their frequent focus on conflict-related material, especially warships (Figure 2). This divide

Figure 3: The wreck of the Swedish warship *Mars*, which sank off the coast of Öland after a fierce battle against a Dano-Lübeckian fleet in 1564. A diver with white cylinders may be observed in the upper right corner. Scorched by fire and penetrated by cannon balls, the wreck and the surrounding debris, which is located at a depth of c. 80 m, practically constitutes a sunken battlefield of the Early Modern Period (Rönnby, 2019). While often confined to the subdiscipline of maritime archaeology, warships and other conflict-related topics with connection to waterways also fall into the purview of conflict archaeology. Photomosaic: Tomasz Stachura/Ocean Discovery.

likely stems from maritime archaeology's well-established status as an independent field and the fact that warship finds often fall under historical archaeology, which tends to align more closely with military history than with anthropological approaches when it comes to conflict studies.

One notable exception to this general tendency is the anthology *On War on Board* (Johan Rönnby, 2019). Containing a selection of historical and archaeological papers about warships and naval battles in the Early Modern Period, the anthology seeks to explore the human organisation and attitudes towards systematic violence and warfare, raising important humanistic questions about such topics in the process. Thus, the book extends beyond the typical scope of maritime studies, connecting to broader social issues commonly addressed in Conflict Archaeology, such as the cultural aspects of war and the human experience in warfare. *On War on Board*, as well as Rönnby's chapter (7) in this volume, illustrate that maritime archaeology has the potential to engage more robustly in conflict archaeological discourses and make substantial contributions. From a broader Conflict Archaeology perspective, the unique socio-technological dynamics aboard warships – characterized by their specialized, shipborne societies and highly structured environments functioning as 'maritime battlefields' – offer a promising yet underexplored area for research. This setting provides rich opportunities for scholars interested in examining conflict-related social questions, highlighting the need for further scholarly attention in this domain – from both inside and outside the field of maritime archaeology.

The importance of a socially and culturally contextualised approach to interpersonal violence and conflict has been widely recognised. Nikolaidou and Kokkinidou (1997:175) argue violent behaviour is best understood within the context of human relations in a given society, noting that 'it manifests itself in a variety of ways and is characterized by a multiplicity of meanings and purposes that can be explained only by reference to a specific cultural discourse.' This perspective aligns with several key scholarly works that aim to forge stronger connections between anthropology and archaeology. The anthology *Warfare and Society: Archaeological and Social Anthropological Perspectives* (Otto et al., 2006) is central in this regard, as it integrates archaeological and anthropological approaches to explore the intricate relationships between society and warfare, maintaining that war is a social practice that is 'always based upon a cultural logic' (Otto et al., 2006:15). Similarly, Pérez (2012:14ff.) also views violence as 'a complex expression of cultural performance', emphasizing that 'violent acts often exemplify intricate social and cultural dimensions and are frequently defined by these same social contexts.' Some scholars take this further arguing that the practice of warfare inherently involves the subjectivity of fighters, bringing attention to the fact that fighters are not uniform and thus their embodiment of bodily/material culture should be a focus (e.g., Warnier, 2011). These reflections resonate with Conflict Archaeology research that adopts a practice approach to the study of violence and warfare, i.e., that examine such actions in terms of recursive relationships between agents and social structures (Nielsen & Walker, 2009; Warming, 2018). Frameworks from related fields, such as sociology, have also been effectively combined with archaeological research on violence to allow for interpretations that surpass the physical evidence (e.g., Bill et al., 2024).

In many ways, these sentiments reflect a theoretical foundation very much in line with 'contextual archaeology', emphasizing the uniqueness of individual cultures and the social relationships contained therein (Hodder, 1982). In other words, violent acts can be regarded in terms of an 'ecological' framework (see Lundström, this volume). In essence, the approach that is forwarded here is one that seeks to understand how violence and warfare is socialized and enculturated.

Opposing Perspectives: The Three Ps

The value of a social approach in conflict studies is evident. However, which opposing viewpoints on violence and warfare might lead to less socially oriented studies? While scholars rarely overlook the social dimensions of conflicts entirely, they may, consciously or unconsciously, adhere to certain perspectives that if fully adopted can simply relegate these aspects to footnotes of archaeological studies. In treating violence and warfare as cultural and social expressions, this anthology gets to grips with certain influential perspectives that primarily treat such actions as isolated phenomena outside of their social contexts.

These perspectives may be subsumed under three main headings: 'The Pathological', 'The Primitive', and 'The Pragmatic', or the Three Ps. *Pathological* refers to a position where violence is understood as irrational social pathologies, standing in contrast to the instrumental violence of state societies that have evident social functions, such as maintaining order or protecting citizens (Armit et al., 2006:1; Blok, 2000). From this logic follows the problematic position that such pathologies do not need to be factored in when considering the 'normal' aspects of society, where issues like conflicts and security often are overlooked in archaeological research (Armit et al., 2006; Brothwell 1999:34f.; James 2013:100f.; Warming 2018). *Primitive* refers to a set of similar preconceptions that dismiss violence and warfare as primitive aggression, either deficient in or devoid of culture or, whereby culture is otherwise seen as a secondary phenomenon. On this understanding, violence and warfare are primarily ruled by biological predispositions and materialist interests, where culture is rendered irrelevant, and the primary task becomes one of identifying environmental factors in the causes of war, such as population pressure or resource scarcity (e.g., Ferguson, 1984; Haas, 1990; for related discussions, see Carman 2013:34ff.). Without serious consideration of cultural discourse, this position amounts to deterministic interpretations grounded in evolutionary psychology or ecology where the agentic powers of individuals and societies are neglected, assuming instead that a common logic is followed within certain socio-environmental parameters (e.g., Lorenz, 1966; for discussion, see Brothwell 1999:26;). *Pragmatic* concerns instrumental violence, referring to the position that organized violence such as battles are rationally carried out by the most efficient means possible to attain some functional end. It is most poignantly expressed through the Clausewitzian notion that 'War is merely the continuation of policy by other means' but is also characteristic of idealized interpretations of combat technique based on martial effectiveness. Violence is thus explained through a modern conception of effective functionality, often with reference to technology and resources as well as the successes and failures of commanders in terms of their rationale (Carman, 1999; Lynn, 2003; Sipilä & Lahelma, 2006). The tropes of technological determinism and instrumentalism also fall into this general category. Committing to any of the 'Three Ps' is problematic as it entails imposing an a priori ethnocentric perspective on warfare and violence that detracts from their social contexts, thus 'reducing our work to, at best, simple description and at worst, a decontextualized voyeuristic sensationalism of broken heads, mutilated limbs, and cannibalism.' (Armit et al., 2006:1).

With the above considerations in mind, the theoretical starting point of this book acknowledges the sociocultural dimensions of violence and warfare and pays careful attention to underlying preconceptions that relegate such acts to a social vacuum. 'The Three Ps' establish some of the prevailing views in this regard and are from a social or cultural reading of warfare, if not unsatisfactory, then highly impartial, as the contents of this book demonstrate in various ways.

The Contents of this Book

The contributions to this volume cover an array of subjects, ranging from the Mesolithic to the Modern Period. Despite their diversity, the papers are unified by a common theme, namely the sociocultural context of (pre)historical cases of violence and warfare. This interconnectedness between violent acts and society and culture is explored by the contributing authors to varying degrees: some are explicitly concerned with such questions throughout while others tackle them more tangentially in their efforts to understand specific practices or historical circumstances. The contributions also vary in their emphasis on theory, methodology and empirics. Attentive readers will also notice differences in terms of disciplinary traditions, reflecting the archaeological and historical as well as linguistic backgrounds of the authors who, in addition, comprise both early-career and senior researchers. The papers not only reflect the multifaceted nature of conflict studies but also showcase the numerous ways the social contexts of violence and warfare may be investigated.

Overall, the approach taken in this volume demonstrates the value of examining conflicts through broader social questions as well as its ability to inform studies across different time periods, disciplines and otherwise disparate studies. Indeed, by seeking out issues beyond specific historically bound physicalities, and instead exploring broader social issues, it provides scholars opportunities to engage in conflict-studies on more equal footing and on a higher level of abstraction, making the work relevant to a broader academic audience beyond those with specialized interests in particular historical events (e.g., specific battles) or particular lines of empirical data (e.g., specific weaponry types). By bringing together these varied studies, we aim to promote a socially focused approach towards the study of conflicts within archaeology and, more generally, the humanities that should facilitate a valuable exchange of knowledge and stimulate further discussions regarding conflict and society.

While not a novel perspective, it is crucial to continue fostering this approach and engaging in discussions rather than relegating these aspects to footnotes. Through dedicated discussions these studies can significantly strengthen our understanding of violent practices and their broader social contexts, including the complex relationships that underlie conflicts, how conflicts relate to the structure and development of culture as well as how humans respond under different sets of conditions in periods of conflict and security.

While such themes are discernible in the contributions, the chapters are organized more-or-less chronologically, highlighting the applicability of socially focused perspectives on conflict and society throughout the ages. What follows is a presentation of these chapters with my own brief commentaries that are intended to stress the broader social implications and their thematic relevance for modern discourses.

Chapter 2: Headhunting as Ritualised Violence in Prehistory and the Recent Past

Beginning with a particular form of recurrent ritualized violence in both prehistory and the modern period, Ian Armit's chapter investigates the phenomenon of headhunting and explores its occurrence across different and distant societies and periods in time. He examines ethnographic records to understand the cultural beliefs and societal functions surrounding headhunting, and how these practices facilitated and conceptualized inter-societal violence.

While seemingly far-removed from our own world, in which such practices are now regarded as morbid and obscene, the chapter poses important questions about the legitimization and role(s) of violence, questions that remain as pertinent today as they have throughout history and will continue to be in the future. At the heart of these ethical enquiries are the timeless questions: 'What is legitimate violence?' and 'Do the ends justify the means?'. By examining so seemingly far-removed practices, which highlight just how culturally dependent the answers to these questions might be, we can approach the social conditions that shape radically different understandings of appropriate responses, not least uncover possible innate inclinations towards violence and their more symbolic manifestations. Conversely, it is crucial to recognize that physically similar expressions of violence may carry vastly different meanings. Going further, and adopting a Wittgensteinean perspective, we might find that similar practices and even enduring concepts – such as war and peace – might obscure their actual underlying meanings if we are not attuned to their discursive histories. For instance, while the states of 'war' and 'peace' are still widely used today, their meanings have become increasingly blurred in modern geopolitics (sometimes to the point of being meaningless), even as they remain instrumental for domestic and international affairs (Bartelson, 2016; Stoker & Whiteside, 2020). By investigating practices as seemingly alien as headhunting, we are compelled to reflect on aspects of violence and warfare that we leave unquestioned a priori – elements so ingrained in our worldview that they escape our critical attention.

Chapter 3: An Ethnohistory of Souls and Violence: On the Animation of Humans among the Recent Past Animists of Northwestern Siberia and Animism in Hunter-gatherer Archaeology

In this chapter, Erik Solfeldt challenges the perception of animism and shamanism as purely peaceful ideologies by examining ethnographic and ethnohistorical data from northwestern Siberia. He argues that these belief systems also legitimized violence and warfare, and urges archaeologists to reconsider Western ideological biases, particularly the uncritical application of western thought to hunter-gatherer cultures. With this as a basis, the contribution highlights the complexities of animism and illustrates that prehistoric animistic practices can have included both peaceful and violent dimensions.

Above all, the chapter sheds light on the theme of the ontology of war, showing how different underlying ideologies can significantly shape the understanding and conduct of warfare. The act of killing is not always as simple as ending a physical life but may also require tackling its consequences, which in some animistic practices entailed avoiding harmful immaterial continuations in the form of vengeful spirits. An equally important aspect discussed in Solfeld's chapter is that of Othering, relevant to all societies defined by the necessary distinction between an in-group and out-group (Khrebtan-Hörhager, 2023). Various cultural elements – including folklore, language and material culture – can express and contribute to certain attitudes and inclinations, either positive or negative, towards peoples outside of our immediate society. However, as seen in the ongoing Russo–Ukraine War and Israeli–Palestinian Conflict, Othering is perhaps most pronounced when war crimes and atrocities are committed, actions that starkly violate our shared ethical understandings. Such actions rightfully bring out the strongest feelings of condemnation and highlight that not all subscribe to the same humanistic values. Othering is effectively used as a political tool to control narratives, especially when enhanced by powerful technologies such as social media. In its fullest form, Othering defines who our enemies are and why they deserve to be the subject of violence, to large extent making the act of killing possible (Ibid; Molloy & Grossman, 2007; Grossman, 1996; Delori & Ware, 2019; McIntosh, 2021). Given the often-subtle nature of Othering, it is crucial that we look to historical and archaeological examples for a better awareness of such processes and for informed decision-making in modern conflicts and diplomacy.

Chapter 4: Beneath the Military Horizon: Measuring Stone Age Hunter Weapon Point Technology at the Ecological Scale

In Chapter 4, Frederik Lundström addresses the study of Stone Age weaponry, particularly projectile points, within the context of hunter-gatherer warfare. He identifies challenges in defining violent activities and functional roles of these weapons, proposing instead a more holistic approached inspired by ecological psychology and dynamic systems theory.

In so doing, Lundström re-visits the challenging task of identifying weaponry in the archaeological record, an endeavour often complicated by the persistent permeability and blurred distinction between weapons and tools (Chapman, 1999). Whereas highly specialized artefacts such as swords, which are widely recognized as the first true weapons, are more easily identifiable, other items – such clubs, axes, spearheads and projectile points – may be harder to distinguish from hunting or working tools. Accurate identification of these artefacts is crucial for understanding prehistoric modes of warfare and elucidating the role of the warrior as a social category in ancient societies. As John Carman (2013:31) points out, the warrior is one of the most easily identifiable figures, being highly gendered (typically male) and associated with distinctive forms of material culture, especially weapons. Identifying the warrior, moreover, more easily allows for the distinction of other social roles. However, as Lundström explains, realizing just what it is that makes something a weapon and its role in conflict necessitates deep contextualisation that takes into consideration societal influences, the user, task goals and the environment. As such, the ecological perspective outlined by Lundström underscores the intricate interactions between conflict/violence and society, even at the level of small weapon components.

Chapter 5: On Conflict and Cooperation: Dimensions of Warfare during the Nordic Bronze Age

In Chapter 5, Christian Horn and Barry Molloy explore the dual nature of warfare during the Nordic Bronze Age, acknowledging its destructive impacts while also highlighting its role in fostering cooperation. Drawing on data primarily from bronze weaponry and rock art, the authors contend that small-scale warfare practices, such as raiding, contributed to a dynamic network of conflict and cooperation. This network, in turn, shaped the cultural homogeneity observed in the Nordic Bronze Age.

Instead of viewing conflict as a destructive social force and an 'event', the authors emphasize conflict as a 'process' that comprised both war- and peace-making processes. This perspective aligns with debates within international relations (IR) in which war has both been regarded as a productive and destructive force for sociopolitical order, with the former view informing the conditions under which the very concept of war became intelligible (Bartelson, 2016). An important observation by Horn and Molloy, which is perhaps sometimes overshadowed in prehistoric studies by the pervasive notion of war as an 'event', is that societies must constantly address the threat of violence. This necessitates, among other things, investments in resources, training, fortification, surveillance as well as social measures such as diplomacy to avert violence and mitigate tensions. It is owing to the societal entanglement in such structures that some political science scholars even regard war to be a 'chronic' condition (Grove, 2019:59ff.), thus echoing similar worrisome conclusions in archaeological literature that highlight how war reshapes society in its own image (Ferguson, 1999; Allen & Arkush, 2006:6). As Ferguson (1999:427) puts it, 'A society in a system evolved for war is ready, even waiting, for war…. [I]n many cases war is so woven into the fabric of social life that a given polity could not survive without it.' From this perspective, might the pervasive presence of weaponry and other conspicuous martial elements in the Nordic Bronze Age reflect a sort of militarization of society and deterrence efforts? As also made clear by the authors, cooperative violent activities – such as raiding – could simultaneously be a form of peace-making. Upon further reflection, the role of raiding in fostering cooperation is curiously reminiscent of group-level cooperation in chimpanzee communities where males form strong bonds through group hunting and sharing of meat, something which reportedly increases in intensity with social complexity and the need for greater sociopolitical cohesion (Mitani & Watts, 1999, 2001). While these intricate forms of violent cooperation may indeed have primal roots, it is crucial to recognize that the sociocultural context plays a significant role in shaping these behaviours. As this chapter makes clear, there is much to explore on the theme of conflict and cooperation, particularly its long-term cultural consequences into which archaeology is uniquely positioned to make important enquiries.

Chapter 6: Written Sources on Medieval Fighting Practices

Here, Antti Ijäs presents an analysis of medieval fighting practices based on various written sources, including treatises and fight books by Geoffroi de Charny, Hans Talhoffer, and Paulus Kal. The chapter discusses judicial duels and other forms of combat, revealing the technical knowledge and social significance behind these practices. Ijäs examines how these historical texts reflect the conventions and realities of medieval martial culture.

In so doing, the author cogently demonstrates that combat techniques described in fight books and other written sources must be interpreted in relation to literary context but also as socially and historically contextualized actions (Nielsen & Walker, 2009). In other words, these actions are not carried out in a social vacuum, and the means of transmitting such knowledge are similarly embedded in sociocultural frameworks. As Ijäs observes, the writings about practices may very well be more revealing of the perceptions and attitudes of the authors and their respective societies than what happened in combat or training. The study simultaneously underscores how explicit technical knowledge can also shape fighting practices and combat by providing a structured framework for understanding and executing violent actions in what might otherwise be chaotic conditions. However, it is equally important to realize that conceptualizing combat through technical knowledge can obscure the very chaos that it seeks to make sense of, risking an overly technically focused and romanticized view of violence where the brutal realities and unpredictability of combat are glossed over (see Keegan, 1976; Grossman & Christensen 2004). Conceptualizations, although invaluable, can thus create unrealistic expectations and attitudes towards violence and warfare, both in historical studies and contemporary practice. Understanding the consequences of this conceptualization helps ensure that scholars maintain a realistic and adaptable approach to combat, acknowledging both its structured yet chaotic nature. The contents of sources on fighting reveal much about the conceptualization of technique – i.e., the attempt to create order in that ultimate chaos of human affairs, combat – as well as actual practices, complementing the study of material sources. While the author's focus is on fight books and other written sources, these observations are equally important to consider in relation to material culture, which may be said to embody both practices and body techniques (Mauss, 1992; Horn, 2013).

Chapter 7: Ships or People?
On Material Agency and the New Early Modern Warships

In Chapter 7, Johan Rönnby delves into the role of technology, specifically warships, in the societal changes of the Early Modern Period. He contextualizes the development of heavily armed ships in the fifteenth and sixteenth centuries, discussing their impact on global exploration and European power dynamics. Rönnby argues for a dialectical relationship between technology and society, asserting that material innovations both shape and are shaped by the historical contexts and power structures from which they emerge. Rönnby acknowledges the agentic powers of material things as well as human agency, stressing that the interaction between these takes places in a historically determined context.

By taking an approach that both appreciates the agency of individuals and societal structures, Rönnby avoids falling victim to the pervasive trap of simple technological determinism and technocratic explanations, instead acknowledging the important role of material conditions from a bottom-up perspective. While the choices and actions of rulers and influential figures have traditionally garnered substantial scholarly attention, studies into the agentic capacities of objects are something that has been promulgated much more recently with perspectives influenced by new materialism. This perspective is increasingly explored within War Studies and Security Studies, where researchers have drawn on new materialism to better understand how culturally dependent object–human relationships influence the ontology of war and actions in conflict (e.g., Bourne, 2012; Meiches, 2017; see also the afterword, this volume). Across these studies and disciplines, there is widespread agreement that weapons are not just passive instruments of violence but pluripotential entities that act in ways surpassing human intentions. As pointed out by Rönnby, however, it is equally important that we do not go overboard with an anti-anthropocentric perspective and depreciate human agency in human–thing relationships. Archaeology, being a discipline focused on material culture and historical processes, is well-suited to contribute to these debates without losing sight of the importance of material conditions (see the afterword, this volume).

Chapter 8: Money and War: The Contribution of Numismatics and Monetary History to the Study of Conflict

Jens Christian Moesgaard directs his attention to the intersection of numismatics and warfare in Chapter 8, delving into various topics that illustrate the interwoven nature of money and war. Drawing on a wide range of evidence from archaeology, history and numismatics, the paper provides examples primarily from France and Scandinavia during the Middle Ages and Early Modern Period, exploring themes such as coinage debasement to finance wars, the destabilization of enemy economies, war-induced monetary disorders, logistical problems of transporting money in connection with war. With these examples, among others, the paper aims to illustrate the complex relationship between money and conflict, providing a broad overview to inspire future research in these interconnected fields.

The significance of researching the role of money in conflict is reinforced by contemporary examples such as the ongoing Russo–Ukraine War. In this modern conflict, economic sanctions have been a critical tool used by the international community to exert pressure. These sanctions target key sectors of the Russian economy, aiming to destabilize its financial stability and limit its ability to fund military operations. The economic impact is profound, affecting everything from the value of the Russian ruble to the broader global financial markets. Ukraine, on the other hand, relies heavily on international financial aid and military assistance, emphasizing the importance of monetary support in sustaining defence capabilities. Understanding the historical context of money and war provides valuable insights into these modern dynamics. The debasement of coinage in the past to fund wars mirrors contemporary practices of economic manipulation and financial warfare. By studying these historical precedents, researchers can better comprehend the long-term effects of economic strategies in wartime, offering lessons that are pertinent to today's conflicts. With the ongoing trade war recently launched by President Trump's administration, there is a pressing incentive to explore the topic of money and warfare in the pursuit for solutions and a clearer understanding of possible outcomes. The interplay between financial strategies and military outcomes remains a critical area of study, demonstrating that the power of money in shaping the course of wars is as relevant today as it was centuries ago.

Chapter 9: Concluding Remarks: Reflections on Research into Conflict Archaeology

In the concluding remarks, Lena Holmquist summarizes the developments in conflict studies within archaeology and centres on Swedish and Scandinavian scholarship, reflecting on the historical shifts in research focus and paradigms since the 1990s. Holmquist's review of conflict in archaeological studies brings to light long-held assumptions and biases that have influenced the understanding of violence in historical contexts, illustrating, among other things, how past attitudes often downplayed or neglected the presence of violence and armed conflict in ancient societies. Furthermore, by bringing attention to previously neglected aspects – such as the roles of women and children in conflicts – Holmquist calls for more nuanced and inclusive narratives within conflict archaeological research (see also Matić & Jensen, 2017). Having witnessed several developments within conflict archaeological research in course of her career, Holmquist's review brings clarity to the way such studies have been influenced by certain research paradigms over the years, providing an important basis for discussing future directions in the field. There is ample evidence that conflict archaeological research has developed in a positive direction in the past three decades. However, as pointed out by Holmquist, there is also a necessity to advance the field further in a direction that will allow a more mature theoretical foundation and interdisciplinary dialogue that transcends individual case studies and chronological boundaries. Undoubtedly, contemporary issues and research paradigms will continue to influence conflict archaeological research in the future, necessitating a certain degree of self-awareness about how current issues and attitudes shape scholarship.

Afterword: The Archaeological Contribution to the Study of War and Future Directions

This volume concludes with the editor's afterword, which takes a broader perspective on archaeology's contributions to the study of war. The chapter highlights the largely untapped potential of Conflict

Archaeology to engage in interdisciplinary research with modern conflict and war studies. Despite archaeology's rich methodological and theoretical frameworks, its integration into contemporary War Studies remains limited. This point is also emphasized by Carman and Carman (2020), who likewise argue that archaeology is well-suited to contribute to Critical Military and Security Studies through its capacity to challenge and deconstruct entrenched narratives. The general lack of interdisciplinary engagement is especially striking given that related disciplines, such as military history and anthropology, regularly contribute to these discussions.

Drawing on my experience as a visiting fellow at the Swedish Defence University in Stockholm, I argue that a greater collaboration between archaeology and War Studies would be mutually beneficial. Archaeological insights have the potential to deepen understandings of conflict by situating it within long-term historical processes, while modern War Studies offer valuable theoretical perspectives that can refine archaeological interpretations of past conflicts. As highlighted in the afterword, there are significant thematic overlaps between modern War Studies and Conflict Archaeology that warrant further exploration. To this end, the Department of Archaeology and Classical Studies at Stockholm University, in collaboration with the Swedish Defence University, plans to hold a multidisciplinary panel discussion ('Materialities of War') and a PhD workshop ('Researching the Thing') 9–10th April 2025. By fostering greater interdisciplinary dialogue, we can bridge existing gaps between these fields and enhance our understanding of warfare as a deeply embedded social and cultural phenomenon across both historical and contemporary contexts.

Through the diverse chapters within this anthology we emphasize the value of a socially focused approach to studying violence and warfare. The wide chronological scope of these contributions underscores the applicability and insights that this approach can bring to archaeological and historical studies. In putting this volume together, our intention is to promote inquiries into the enculturation and socialization of violent acts, building on similar calls from other scholars (e.g., Armit et al., 2006; Carman 1997b, 1999, 2013; Dolfini et al., 2018; Carman & Carman 2020; Cipolla, Crellin & Harris, 2024), and to encourage dialogue across traditional chronological and (sub)-disciplinary boundaries. This anthology thus invites further exploration of socially focused inquiries within Conflict Archaeology, encouraging scholars to frame their research with mature social questions and avoid falling victim to 'The Three Ps' (discussed above). We encourage practitioners in prehistoric, historic, and contemporary archaeology to join this endeavour, recognizing that Conflict Archaeology, as a social and cultural inquiry into violence and warfare, has much to contribute to the ongoing discussions in the study of war (see the afterword, this volume).

To conclude, exploring the material realities of war and violence can be unsettling. As James (2013:99) asserts, this process not only involves confronting harsh realities but also demands an examination of the perspectives of those who sanctioned and inflicted violent acts. Expressing interest in these subjects can provoke suspicion or even hostility from those who perceive such inquiries as morally fraught or politically charged. However, a critical and ethical commitment to historical inquiry demands confronting these very complexities. These inquiries do not equate endorsing the actions of belligerents; rather, they seek to understand them, thereby fostering a deeper awareness of the causes, consequences and human experiences of conflict. Here, it is fitting to quote British military historian John Ellis (1986:1):

> ...if one is unable to regard war as a function of particular forms of social and political organisation and particular stages of historical developments, one will not be able to conceive of even the possibility of a world without war.

References

Adams, J. (2003). *Ships, Innovation and Social Change: Aspects of Carvel Shipbuilding in Northern Europe 1450–1850*. PhD Dissertation. Stockholm University.

Adams, J. & Rönnby, J. (Eds.). (2013). *Interpreting shipwrecks: maritime archaeological approaches*. Southampton: Highfield Press.

Adams, J. (2013). *A Maritime Archaeology of Ships: Innovation and Social Change in Medieval and Early Modern Europe*. Oxbow Books.

Arkush, E. N. & Allen, M. W. (2008). *The Archaeology of Warfare: Prehistories of Raiding and Conquest*. Gainesville, FL: University Press of Florida.

Armit, I., Knüsel, C., Robb, J. & Schulting, R. (2006). Warfare and Violence in Prehistoric Europe: An Introduction. *Journal of Conflict Archaeology*, 2(1), 1–11.

Arnshav, M. (2020). *De små båtarna och den stora flykten: Arkeologi i spåren av andra världskrigets baltiska flyktbåtar*. PhD dissertation. Department of Archaeology and Classical Studies, Stockholm University. Lind: Nordic Academic Press.

Arnold, Christopher J. (1982). *Stress As a Stimulus for Socio-Economic Change: Anglo-Saxon England in the Seventh Century. In Ranking, Resources, and Exchange*. Massachusetts: University of Cambridge.

Banks, I. & Pollard, T. (2013). Arms and Armour: The Nuts and Bolts of Conflict Archaeology. *Journal of Conflict Archaeology*, 8(1), 1–2.

Bartelson, J. (2016). Blasts from the Past: War and Fracture in the International System. *International Political Sociology*, 10(4), 352–368.

Bill, J., Jacobson, D., Nagel, S. & Strand, M. S. (2024). Violence as a lens to Viking societies: A comparison of Norway and Denmark. *Journal of Anthropological Archaeology, 75*.

Blok, Anton. (2000). The Enigma of Senseless Violence. In G. Aijmer & J. Abbink (Eds.), *Meanings of Violence* (pp. 23–37). Oxford: Berg.

Bornfalk Back, A. (2016). Konflikt i den arkeologiska rekonstruktionen: en pacificerad förhistoria? *Fornvännen, 111*(3), 184–19.

Bornfalk Back, A. (2023). *Från stenkrigare till borgjarl. Befästningskonsten i östra Sverige, 375–750 e.Kr*. Aun 54. Uppsala: Institutionen för arkeologi och antik historia, Uppsala University.

Bourne, M. (2012). Guns Don't Kill People, Cyborgs Do: A Latourian Provocation for Transformatory Arms Control and Disarmament. *Global Change, Peace & Security*, 24(1), 141–63.

Brothwell, D. (1999). Biosocial and Bioarchaeological Aspects of Conflict and Warfare. In J. Carman, & A. F. Harding (Eds.), *Ancient Warfare: Archaeological Perspectives* (pp. 25–38). Stroud: Sutton.

Burström, M., Diez Acosta, T., González Noriega, E., Gustafsson, A., Hernández, I., Karlsson, H., Pajón, J. M., Robaina Jaramillo, J. R. & Westergaard, B. (2009). Memories of a world crisis: The archaeology of a former Soviet nuclear missile site in Cuba. *Journal of Social Archaeology*, 9(3), 295–318.

Burström, M. & Gelderblom, B. (2011). Dealing with difficult heritage: The case of Bückeberg, site of the Third Reich Harvest Festival. *Journal of Social Archaeology, 11*(3), 266–282.

Carman, J. (Ed.). (1997a). *Material Harm: Archaeological Studies of War and Violence*. Glasgow: Cruithne Press.

Carman, J. (1997b). Giving Archaeology a Moral Voice. In J. Carman (Ed.), *Material Harm: Archaeological studies of war and violence* (pp. 220–239). Glasgow: Cruithne Press.

Carman, J. (1997c). Introduction: Approaches to Violence. In J. Carman (Ed.), *Material Harm: Archaeological studies of war and violence* (pp. 1–23). Glasgow: Cruithne Press.

Carman, J. (1999). Beyond the western way of war: ancient battlefields in comparative perspective. In J. Carman & A. Harding (Eds.), *Ancient warfare: archaeological perspectives* (pp. 39–55). Stroud: Sutton.

Carman, J. (2013). *Archaeologies of Conflict*. London: Bloomsbury Academic, an imprint of Bloomsbury Publishing Plc.

Carman, J. & Carman, P. (2020). *Battlfields: fromt Event to Heritage*. Oxford: Oxford University Press.

Chapman, J. (1999). The Origins of Warfare in the Prehistory of Central and Eastern Europe. In J. Carman, & Harding, A.F. (Eds.), *Ancient Warfare: Archaeological Perspectives* (pp. 101–142). History Press Limited.

Childe, V. G. (1941). War in prehistoric societies. *Sociological Review, 33*, 126–39.

Cipolla, C. N., Crellin, R. J., Harris, O. J. T. (2024). Violence across the human/non-human divide: the virtual and the actual. In *Archaeology for Today and Tomorrow* (pp. 71–88). New York: Routledge.

Damlund, C. (2021). Concrete Reminders: Changing Perspectives on WWII Defences in Denmark. *Journal of Conflict Archaeology, 16*(2), 28–45.

Delori, M. & Ware, V. 2019. The faces of enmity in international relations. An introduction. *Critical Military Studies, 5*(4), 299–303.

Dolfini, A., Crellin, R. J., Horn, C. & Uckelmann, M. (Eds.). (2018). *Prehistoric Warfare and Violence: Quantitative and Qualitative Approaches*. London & New York: Springer.

Ferguson, R. B. (Ed.). (1984). *Warfare, Culture, and Environment*. Orlando, FL: Academic Press.

Ferguson, B. R. (1999). A Paradigm for the Study of War and Society. In K. Raaflaub & N. Rosenstein (Eds.), *War and Society in the Ancient and Medieval Worlds: Asia, The Mediterranean, Europe and Mesoamerica* (pp. 389–437). Cambridge: Harvard University Press.

Ferguson, R. B. (2006). Archaeology, cultural anthropology and the origin and intensification of war. In E. N. Arkush & M. W. Allen (Eds.), *The Archaeology of Warfare: Prehistories of Raiding and Conquest* (pp. 469–523). Gainesville, FL: University of Florida Press.

Fernández-Götz, M. & Roymans, N. (Eds.). (2018). *Conflict archaeology: materialities of collective violence from prehistory to Late Antiquity*. London: Routledge.

Gould, R. A. (Ed.). (1983). *Shipwreck Anthropology*. School of American Research Advanced Seminar Series 45. Albuquerque: University of New Mexico Press.

Grossman, D. (1996). *On Killing: The Psychological Cost of Learning to Kill in War and Society*. New York: Little, Brown, and Company.

Grossman, D. & Christensen, L. (2004). *On Combat: The Psychology and Physiology of Deadly Conflict in War and in Peace*. PPCT Research Publications.

Grove, J. V. (2019). *Savage Ecology: War and Geopolitics at the End of the World*. New York, USA: Duke University Press.

Haas, J. (Ed.). (1990). *The Anthropology of War*. Cambridge; New York: Cambridge University Press.

Hartmann, E. (2017). Violence: Constructing an Emerging Field of Sociology. *International Journal of Conflict and Violence, 11*, 1–9.

Hedeager, L. & Kristiansen, K. (1985). Krig og samfund i Danmarks Oldtid. *Den jyske historiker*, 9–25.

Hodder, I. (1982). *Symbols in action: ethnoarchaeological studies of material culture*. Cambridge: Cambridge University Press.

Hoffmeyer, A. B. (1954). *Middelalderens Tvææggede Svaerd: En Undersøgelse Af Dets Udviklingshistorie, Kronologi Og Nationalitet, Dets Stilling i Den Almindelige Våbenhistoriske Udvikling Og Dets Krigsmæssige Betydning*. University of Copenhagen: Tøjhusmuseet.

Horn, C. (2013). Harm's Way: An Approach to Change and Continuity in Prehistoric Combat. *Current Swedish Archaeology, 21*, 93–116.

James, S. (2010). The Point of the Sword. What Roman-Era Weapons Could Do to Bodies – and Why They Often Didn't. In M. Müller and H. J. Schalles (Eds.), *Waffen in Aktion. Akten der 16. Roman Military Equipment Conference* (pp. 41–54). Xanten: Xantener Berichte 16.

Keegan, J. (1976). *The Face of Battle: A Study of Agincourt, Waterloo and the Somme*. New York: Viking Press.

Keeley, L. H. (1996). *War Before Civilization: The Myth of the Peaceful Savage*. Oxford: Oxford University Press.

Khrebtan-Hörhager, J. (2023). *Communicating the Other Across Cultures: From Othering as Equipment for Living to Communicating Other/Wise*. Ann Arbor: Michigan University Press.

Kuznar, A. B. (2024). Understanding war: The sociological perspective revisited. *European Journal of Social Theory*, 1–25.

Lidén, K., Eriksson, G., Isaksson, S., Kalmring, S., Papmehl-Dufay, L. & Victor, H. (2024). New Research Programme: Crisis, Conflict and Climate: Societal Change in Scnadinavia 300–700 CE. *Current Swedish Archaeology, 31*, 213–218. DOI: 10.37718/CSA.2023.19.

Lingström, M. (2025). *Mästerby, 1361: Battlefield Archaeological Perspectives on the Danish Invasion of Gotland*. PhD thesis. Uppsala: Department of Archaeology and Ancient History, Uppsala University.

Lorenz, K. (1966). *On Aggression*. New York: A Helen and Kurt Wolff Book/ Harcourt, Brace and World, Inc.

Lynn, J. (2003). *Battle: A Cultural History of Combat and Culture*. Boulder: Westview Press.

Malešević, S. (2010). *The Sociology of War and Violence*. Cambridge: Cambridge University Press.

Mauss, M. (1992). Techniques of the Body. In J. Crary & S. Kwinter (Eds.), *Incorporations* (pp. 455–477). New York: Zone Press.

McIntosh, J. (2021). 'Because it's easier to kill that way': Dehumanizing epithets, militarized subjectivity, and American necropolitics. *Language in Society, 50*(4), 583–603.

Meiches, B. (2017). Weapons, Desire, and the Making of War. *Critical Studies on Security, 5*(1), 9–27.

Mitani, J. C. & Watts, D. P. (1999). Demographic influences on the hunting behavior of chimpanzees. *American Journal of Physical Anthropology, 109*(4), 439–54.

Mitani, J. C. & Watts, D. P. (2001). Why do chimpanzees hunt and share meat? *Animal Behaviour, 61*, 915–924.

Molloy, B. & Grossman, D. (2007). Why can't Johnny Kill? The Psychology and Physiology of Interpersonal Combat. In B. Molloy (Ed.), *The Cutting Edge: Studies in Ancient and Medieval Combat* (pp. 188–202). Stroud: Tempus Publishing Ltd.

Nielsen, A. E. & Walker, W. H. (Eds.). (2009). *Warfare in Cultural Context: Practice, Agency, and the Archaeology of Violence*. Tucson: The University of Arizona Press.

Nikolaidou, M. & Kokkinidou, D. (1997). The symbolism of violence in Late Bronze Age palatial societies of the Aegean: a gender approach. In J. Carman (Ed.), *Material Harm: Archaeological Studies of War and Violence*, 174–197. Glasgow: Cruithne Press.

Nordbladh, J. (1989). Armour and fighting in the south Scandinavian Bronze Age, especially in view of rock art representations. In T. B. Larson & H. Lundmark (Eds.), *Approaches to Swedish Prehistory: A Spectrum of Problems and Perspectives in Contemporary Research* (pp. 323–33). Oxford: Archaeopress.

Matić, U. & Jensen, B. (Eds.). (2017). *Archaeologies of gender and violence*. Oxford & Philadelphia (PA): Oxbow.

Oakeshott, E. (1960). *The Archaeology of Weapons: Arms and armour from Prehistory to the Age of Chivalry*. London: Lutterworth Press.

Otto, T., Thrane, H. & Vandkilde, H. (Eds.). (2006). *Warfare and Society: Archaeological and Social Anthropological Perspectives*. Aarhus: Aarhus University Press.

Pérez, V. (2012). The Politicization of the Dead: Violence as Performance, Politics as Usual. In D. Martin, R. Harrod & V. Pérez (Eds.), *The Bioarchaeology of Violence* (pp. 13–28). Gainesville: University Press of Florida.

Pinker, S. (2012). *The Better Angels of Our Nature: A History of Violence and Humanity*. London: Penguin.

Ray, L. (2011). Violence and Society. London: Sage Publications Ltd.

Rönnby, J. (Ed.). (2019). *On War on Board. Archaeological and Historical perspectives on Early Modern Maritime Violence and Warfare*. Södertörn Academic Studies 78 & Södertörn Archaeological Studies 15. Huddinge: Södertörn University.

Saunders, N. J. (2004). *Matters of Conflict: Material Culture, Memory and the First World War*. London: Taylor & Francis Group.

Saunders, N. J. (Ed.). (2012). *Beyond the Dead Horizon: Studies in Modern Conflict Archaeology*. Oxbow Books.

Saunders, N. J. & Cornish, P. (Eds.). (2021). *Conflict Landscapes: Materiality and Meaning in Contested Places*. Routledge.

Scheper-Hughes, N. & Bourgois, P. (2004). Introduction: Making Sense of Violence. In N. Scheper-Hughes & P. Bourgois (Eds.), *Violence in War and Peace: An Anthology* (pp. 1–27). Oxford: Blackwell.

Scott, D., Fox, R. A., Connor, M. A. & Harmon, D. (1989). Archaeological Perspectives on the Battle of the Little Big Horn. Norman O and London: University of Oklahoma Press.

Scott, D. D. & McFeaters, A. P. (2011). The Archaeology of Historic Battlefields: A History and Theoretical Development in Conflict Archaeology. *Journal of Archaeological Research*, *19*(1), 103–132.

Shapiro, M. J. (1997). *Violent Cartographies: mapping cultures of war*. Minneapolis MI: University of Minnesota Press.

Sipilä, J. & Lahelma, A. (2006). War as a Paradigmatic Phenomenon: Endemic Violence and the Finnish Subneolithic. *Journal of Conflict Archaeology*, *2*(1),189–209.

Slofstra, J. (2002). Batavians and Romans on the Lower Rhine: The Romanisation of a Frontier Area. *Archaeological Dialogues*, *9*, 16–38, 55–57.

Stoker, D. & Whiteside, C. (2020). Blurred Lines: Gray-Zone Conflict and Hybrid War – Two Failures of American Strategic Thinking. *Naval War College Review*, *73*(1), 1–37.

Vandkilde, H. (2014). Archaeology, theory, and war-related violence: theoretical perspectives on the archaeology of warfare and warriorhood. In A. Gardner, M. Lake & U. Sommer (Eds.), *The Oxford handbook of archaeological theory*. Oxford University Press.

Vencl, S. (1984). War and warfare in archaeology. *Journal of Anthropological Archaeology*, *3*, 116–32.

West, S. (1999). Introduction. In S. Tarlow & S. West (Eds.), *The Familiar Past? Archaeologies of later historical Britain* (pp. 1–15). London: Routledge.

Walby, S. (2012). Violence and society: Introduction to an emerging field of sociology. *Current Sociology*, *61*(2): 95–111.

Warming, R. (2018). Praksistilgangen i kamparkæologi: 'The Practice Approach' og vikingetidens krigeriske praksisser. *Arkæologisk Forum, 38,* 15–23.

Warming, R. (2022). Studies of Conflict: Bridging the Gap. Conference report. *The European Archaeologist*, *73*, 43–47. Link (accessed 04.08.2024): https://www.e-a-a.org/EAA/Publications/TEA/TEA_73/ Navigation_Publications/TEA_73.aspx.

Warming, R. (in prep.). *Soldiers at sea: Close Quarter Combat at Sea in the Fleets of Northern Europe, c.1450–1650*. PhD thesis. Stockholm: Stockholm University.

CHAPTER 2

Headhunting as Ritualised Violence in Prehistory and the Recent Past

Ian Armit

The practice of headhunting is remarkably recurrent in ethnographic literature. Many sources, dating principally from the late eighteenth to the first half of the 20th century, document the taking of enemy heads and frequently also their curation and even veneration (e.g., Duncan, 1847; Walsh, 1884; Davis, 1891; Tremearne, 1912; Up de Graff, 1923; Mills, 1926). As products of their time, such accounts are highly variable in quality, detail and trustworthiness (for discussion of the biases inherent in the ethnographic sources, see Armit 2012:45–68). Nonetheless, they are so geographically, culturally and chronologically diverse, ranging across New Zealand (Vayda, 1960), south-east Asia (Hocart, 1931), northern India (Jacobs, 1990), North America (Chacon and Dye, 2007), South America (Harner, 1973), Africa (Law, 1989) and beyond, that they clearly attest to practices that emerged independently at many different times and places (Armit, 2012). It is also evident that headhunting was not limited to small-scale tribal communities; it could in fact be central to the performance and display of power in complex, hierarchical societies, such as those of pre-Columbian Mesoamerica (Moser 1973, 1974; Mendoza 2007) or nineteenth century West Africa (Adeyinka, 1974). These latter contexts are discussed at length in *Headhunting and the body in Iron Age Europe* (Armit, 2012), but this paper will focus on those communities with less hierarchical social ordering.

Headhunting can also be inferred from archaeological evidence, which frequently attests to the removal, curation and display of human heads. Evidence for such practices can come directly from deposits of human remains, or indirectly through iconographic representations and cases can be identified in many unconnected periods and regions ranging from the European Mesolithic (Orschiedt, 2002;

Armit, 2006) to Shang China (Wolin, 2022). Some appear relatively unambiguous, such as the Swedish Mesolithic wetland site of Kanaljorden (Gummesson et al., 2018) where both male and female crania showing clear signs of perimortem trauma were mounted on stakes for display. Similarly, the remains of several hundred headless warriors at the La Tène Iron Age site of Ribemont-sur-Ancre, Picardy (Brunaux, 2018), leave little room for doubt over the violent context of head taking in that region. Several millennia later, and much more ambiguous in its meaning, however, is a perforated cranial fragment from Ribe, Denmark, dating to the Viking Age, and inscribed with complex apotropaic runes (Larsen, 2004). While this fragment may well derive from a trophy-head, it is equally possible that it was a curated relic of a venerated ancestor. While the first two cases offer *prima facie* evidence for predatory headhunting, the Ribe fragment reminds us of the difficulties inherent in working with archaeological evidence and the need for broad contextual study.

In this paper, I will briefly examine the ritualisation of headhunting practices as part of a broader consideration of the ways in which violence can become embedded within cultural and cosmological structures. I will draw upon evidence both from ethnographies of relatively recent societies, as well as wide-ranging archaeological evidence, to argue that headhunting was intrinsic to the construction of identity within many prehistoric societies.

Theorising Headhunting

Among these spectacles I was arrested by the ghastly appearance of a once human head. In mere derision it had been boiled, stripped of the skin and hair, and put on a post with a raw kumara [sweet potato] placed in the mouth. (John Alexander, nineteenth century New Zealand missionary, cited in Vayda, 1960:95)

Headhunting, along with other practices, described (as above) in outraged prose by colonial writers, such as cannibalism and human sacrifice, has been paid relatively little serious anthropological attention. Indeed, for understandable reasons, this 'savage package' has been actively avoided by most working in the field (Armit, 2012). Most of the earliest first-hand accounts, like that from which the preceding quotation is taken, were written by Christian missionaries, administrators, soldiers or adventurers, quick to emphasise the brutality of headhunting and their own disgust at the practice. Indeed, as Shankar Aswani succinctly puts it (2000a:4): "in writing about head-hunting we risk evoking images of the savage other". Even the terms 'headhunting' and 'trophy head' themselves derive from a colonial mindset, since both seem to reference the practice of animal hunting and trophy-taking common among the European elite. Implicit here is the perception that headhunting was no more than a primitive and murderous 'sport.' (cf. Tinyi, 2017).

Aside from its problematic associations with western perceptions of the 'primitive', the paucity of modern scholarly attention has partly also been the result of the early suppression of headhunting practices by colonial administrations. In most of the regions where it was formerly practised, this prohibition occurred before the establishment of anthropology as a mature discipline. Thus, with some notable exceptions, such as Christoph von Fürer-Haimendorf's fieldwork among the Nagas of northern India (1938, 1969), and Renato Rosaldo's work in Borneo (1980), there are few anthropologically-informed, first-hand accounts of headhunting.

Given this dearth of high-quality field data, there have been correspondingly few attempts to theorise or even define headhunting as a social practice. Most important have been anthropologists such as Hoskins (1996a, 1996b) and Renato Rosaldo (1980, 1984) in southeast Asia, Aswani and colleagues in the Solomon Islands (2000a, 2000b, 2000c), and Arnold and Hastorf (2008) in South America. In terms of definitions, perhaps the most useful is that given by Janet Hoskins (1996b:2) who defines headhunting as "an organised, coherent form of violence in which the severed head is given a specific ritual meaning and the act of head taking is consecrated and commemorated in some form". Importantly, this definition foregrounds the recognition that headhunting is not simply about violence or denigration of outsiders. Almost always (perhaps even universally) it is embedded within wider belief structures and its practice is highly ritualised, whether in the taking of the head itself or, more commonly, in its subsequent processing, curation and/or display. The motivation for these ritualised behaviours may be religious, as Hoskins' use of the term 'consecration' implies, but they might equally relate more broadly to areas of cosmology and ideology (Armit, 2012:12–14). The distinction between religion, as a codified body of belief relating to the supernatural world, and cosmology, as a more generalised understanding of how the world works is neatly summarised in the following quotation:

> If we do not get a head every year, the crops will be bad, the pigs and cattle will not increase, our children will get ill… We cannot say why this should be. It has always been like that. (attributed to Konyak Naga informant, from private notes of W. G. Archer, 1940s, cited by Jacobs, 1990:120)

For the Konyak Nagas, as for many other groups, headhunting was not a formalised religious practice, but rather a set of heavily ritualised actions bound by tradition and cosmological understandings of the world. More importantly, in the present context, it demonstrates how the extreme violence perpetrated on outsiders was core to the Nagas' understanding of the cosmological principles governing their own survival and security (although of course this dichotomy of violence versus non-violence is an etic rather than emic interpretation). This ritualisation of headhunting and its deep entanglements with cosmology and social practice can also be seen archaeologically, for example, in the Iron Age societies of southern France, where headhunting practices shifted through time as the scale and hierarchisation of society itself changed (Armit, 2010, 2011a, 2012).

Archaeological Correlates of Headhunting: the Problem of Deposition and the Prevalence of Headhunting in Prehistory

The preceding discussion has indicated how widespread headhunting was as a social practice in recent centuries and has also given some indication of the frequency with which it has been detected archaeologically. Archaeologists, however, deal principally with the products of deposition – material which has, either deliberately or accidentally, become incorporated into the ground at some time in the past. The degree to which we can attribute intentionality to the deposition of various materials, and our ability to reconstruct the complexity of pre-depositional practices is of course highly debated and patently problematic. In relation to headhunting, we find very few accounts of deposition in the ethnographic literature. Instead, we have often meticulously detailed descriptions of the ritualised activities that accompanied headhunting raids, the reception of the heads and successful headhunters by their community, and the post-mortem treatment and curation (rather than disposal) of trophy heads themselves.

By way of illustration, headhunting for the Konyak Nagas, as we have seen, was related to fertility, understood here in its broadest sense in terms of the health and reproduction of the community. In simplified terms, Figure 1 depicts the *chaîne opératoire* of predatory headhunting within this community during the 1930s, recorded in scrupulous detail during first-hand observations by Christoph von Fürer-Haimendorf (1938, 1969). These practices become even more complex if we elaborate on just one stage of the operation (Table 1). None of this highly ritualised activity, however, was related directly to the deposition of human remains in any archaeologically recoverable context. Any remains that might have entered the archaeological record would have done so inadvertently, as decayed fragments, perhaps swept onto a midden or unwittingly embedded in occupation debris.

In many cases, despite the centrality of headhunting within the Nagas social world, there would be no direct material trace in the archaeological record, at least in the form of discarded or deliberately deposited human remains (although we might infer the importance of the head from its frequent representation in brass pendants and wooden hairpins).

Given that most headhunting activity in the remote past will likely have left virtually no direct archaeological trace, the ubiquity of cranial fragments that we do find in archaeological deposits in so many diverse geographical and chronological contexts, many with overt signs of violence, strongly suggests that headhunting was practised just as commonly in prehistory as it was around the fringes of the colonial world in the last few centuries.

Table 1: This table describes the sequence of events associated with the reception of a trophy head in a Konyak Naga village, based on commentaries produced by Christoph von Fürer-Haimendorf (1969).

	Activity
1	returning head hunters welcomed by the village elders and other men of the community
2	head taken to area outside village, close to where heads of ancestors were kept in stone 'cists'
3	head pelted with raw eggs to 'blind the kinsmen of the dead foe'
4	Rice beer poured into mouth of head, accompanied by invocations to the victim's kin to come and surrender themselves
5	head taken into village, dancing in front of cult-house (the 'morung'), head hunters ritually washed
6	head tied to log gong
7	head placed on a post in front of the 'morung', accompanied by dancing
8	head taken in procession by the men of the village in body paint and ceremonial costume, to a ritual area
10	ritualist cuts off parts of the ears and tongue, calling on victim's kinsmen
11	sacrifice of a chicken and reading of its entrails
12	head hung from a tree and, for a period of a day, dancing and feasting
13	one month later, further feast
14	head given rice beer to 'drink'
15	head placed in the 'morung'

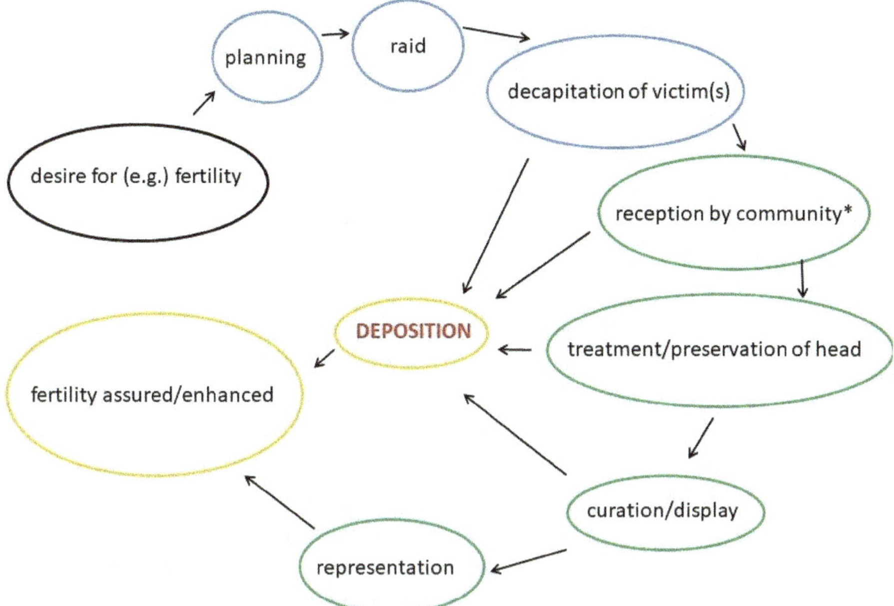

Figure 1: This diagram presents the *chaîne opératoire* of headhunting among the Konyak Nagas, as described by Christoph von Fürer-Haimendorff (1969). Deposition, where the practice of headhunting might become observable archaeologically, might occur at several points in the process, but in many cases will not occur (at least deliberately) at all.

Souls in Suspension

The marked cultural diversity displayed by headhunting communities over the past few centuries demonstrates that it would be unwise to seek any universally applicable explanations for the practice. Nonetheless, underlying the enormous variability of cultural expression evident in ethnographic descriptions of headhunting practices, certain themes emerge that might usefully inform our approach to understanding headhunting in various archaeological contexts (Armit, 2012).

The frequent association between heads and fertility, as mentioned above, is perhaps the most dominant theme amongst headhunting communities globally. This should be no surprise when dealing with societies operating within subsistence farming regimes, where resources could be fragile and insecure. Yet the concept of fertility here is broad, perhaps better expressed in terms of success or bounty, affecting every element of the well-being of the community, as the following quotations illustrate:

> If no heads are brought in there will be much illness, poor harvest, little fruit, fish will not come up the river as far as our kampong [village], and the dogs will not care to pursue pigs. (Lumholtz, 1920:155)

> when we took heads all the time, there was no illness. (M. Rosaldo, 1977:168)

This association between headhunting and the perceived well-being of the community was recognised by writers from at least the end of the nineteenth century. Rather than simply the product of barbarous trophy-taking, it began to be understood that the taking of enemy heads was somehow seen as conferring spiritual benefits on the community. Early ethnographers, notably the Dutch Calvinist missionary Albert Kruyt, active in Indonesia during the 1890s, initially conceptualised this as occurring through the transfer of some form of incorporeal 'life-fluid', or 'soul-substance' (Needham, 1976). This idea formed the basis for much writing about headhunting during the early 20th century and is expressed, for example, in John Henry Hutton's work on the Nagas, where he understood this 'soul-substance' as:

> a supply of life-fertilizer which exudes into the sacred stones of [the Naga head hunter's] village, to pass into the cycle of life of its crops, its livestock, and its human population. (Hutton, 1938:12)

Such ideas have subsequently been dismissed as essentially an etic rationalisation of indigenous beliefs, to render them more readily digestible to a western mindset and perhaps more compatible with post-Enlightenment ideas of causation (cf. Jacobs, 1990:124). In indigenous cosmologies, however, human actions in the physical world could have effects in the spirit world without the need for any intermediate quasi-physical 'fluid' or 'substance' to do the necessary work. Instead, severed heads themselves simply mediated between the two realms, whose boundaries were fluid and permeable. Thus, in Sumba, scalps were hung alongside ears of corn to ensure a good harvest (Hoskins, 1996c:230), while in Borneo, severed trophy heads were placed between the thighs of infertile women to promote conception (Freeman, 1979:237). The accumulation, appropriate treatment, and display of heads could thus enable spiritual interventions to the benefit of the community.

Trophy heads are well-suited to this liminal role. When preserved with the flesh intact, the head signifies the suspension of an individual in a state between life and death; physically dead but prevented from undergoing the funerary rites that translate the non-corporeal soul (or souls) to the world beyond. They are evidence of souls in suspension; neither alive nor fully dead, neither person nor object. Their embodiment of ambiguity and transition makes them peculiarly appropriate as mediators with the otherworld. Cross-culturally, the taking of a head has been associated with rites of passage, such as the assumption of adult male status among the Asmat of New Guinea (Zegwaard, 1959) and the Ilongot of Luzon in the Philippines (R. Rosaldo, 1980). Trophy heads have also been employed in other liminal contexts, such as the foundation or inauguration rituals for war canoes (Hocart, 1931:303), log-gongs (Jacobs, 1990:120), and house-poles (Zegwaard, 1959:1028).

Most of the societies described above are characterised by relatively egalitarian social structures based around principles of kinship. As has been mentioned, however, headhunting is by no means limited to such groups. Studies of both recent and ancient societies have demonstrated how the role of headhunting changed with the increasing hierarchisation of society. In Indonesia, for example, Janet Hoskins (1996c) has examined the different historical trajectories of the east and west parts of the island of Sumba during the nineteenth and early 20th century. In West Sumba, relatively egalitarian societies practised headhunting as part of an ongoing cycle of reciprocal revenge killings between small-scale communities. In neighbouring East Sumba, however, where contact with Dutch trading partners had led to the establishment of an increasingly powerful noble class, headhunting became much more targeted at political display and an 'ideology of encompassment' of smaller neighbours, promoted by expansionist elites (Hoskins, 1996c:

225). Similarly, in the Solomon Islands the development of increasingly powerful chiefdoms from the sixteenth to nineteenth centuries altered the emphasis of headhunting practice to a targeted focus on the acquisition and display of the heads of chiefs and prominent warriors (Aswani, 2000a, 2000b, 2000c).

For prehistoric periods, it is harder to reconstruct such detailed trajectories of headhunting practice. Nonetheless, in the Iron Age societies of southern France, from around 700 BC–AD 100, a remarkable constellation of archaeological, osteological and iconographic material, complemented (towards the end of the period) by some descriptive accounts by classical writers, enables a similar level of interpretation (Armit, 2012). In the earlier centuries of this period, a conceptual link between severed human heads and fertility is obvious, paralleling much of what we can see in the ethnographic record.

Evidence for this association includes the remarkable carved stone known as the *bloc aux épis*, from the site of Entremont, two sides of which display highly stylised images of human heads, while a third bears a depiction of ears of wheat; the latter being rendered in such a way as to make them visually cognate with the heads (Armit 2012:93, Figure 2). Other iconographic evidence from the period focuses on the accumulation and ordering of repetitive and anonymous severed heads, with no depictions of the head hunters themselves. As power becomes more centralised in the region and hierarchical structures establish themselves in the third century BC, the iconography of headhunting changes markedly, with depictions of carefully individualised warriors presented holding or sitting with collections of (again individualised) severed heads (Armit, 2012, Figure 3). In this region it would appear that a headhunting tradition associated with fertility and community success was ultimately appropriated by an emergent militarised elite who displayed and embedded their own power through situating themselves at the centre of headhunting performance and ritual (Armit, 2012). The social, cultural and cosmological role of headhunting was thus, in this archaeological context, considerably more complex and fluid than the somewhat sensationalized accounts of early ethnographic sources describe.

Figure 2: The *bloc aux épis*, from the oppidum of Entremont, built into the remains of a first century BC fortification wall, but probably derived from a much earlier sanctuary on the hill. The upper photograph shows the face depicting ears of wheat which give the stone its name. The lower drawing shows the two other faces, bearing images of human heads, identified during conservation works on the site in 1996 (photo: Ian Armit; illustration drawn by Dan Bashford).

Figure 3: Reconstruction of one of the warrior statues from Entremont, dating to the third century BC (illustration drawn by Libby Mulqueeny).

Conclusion: headhunting, violence and society

This brief consideration of headhunting in both the remote and the recent past illustrates something of the wider relationship between violence and society (Armit, 2011b). Debates around this subject in archaeology have frequently coalesced around binary issues, such as whether sites like hillforts, or objects like elaborately decorated weapons, should be viewed as functional or symbolic. They are of course usually both; violence is frequently highly ritualised, and ritual (as the headhunting literature clearly demonstrates) can often be very bloody (e.g., Armit, 2007). The study of violence in past human societies should not, therefore, be consigned to a specialist subdiscipline of conflict archaeology but should be fully considered as an intrinsic part of social life and societal reproduction.

Violence, or the fear of violence, encroaches on all areas of social life in past societies, from domestic abuse and slavery, through feuding between neighbours and predatory raiding, to outright inter-communal warfare. In all cases it is implicated in wider social dynamics. As examples we might consider the development of metal-working technology in Bronze Age Europe, which was spurred on in large measure by the desire to produce longer, heavier and generally more efficient swords and spearheads, or the impact of slave-raiding on demographic structures and power relations around the fringes of the Roman Empire. Economic organisation and landscape exploitation (for example through the creation of 'no-man's lands') must also necessarily involve negotiations around potentially contested resources. Human societies do not exist in a vacuum; they evolve mechanisms and strategies to deal with internal tensions and the potential of conflict with their neighbours.

With headhunting we see violence used strategically to reinforce the solidarity and identity of the in-group (often also structuring gender roles and identities within), while also dehumanising the out-group, turning the latter into a resource to be used for the spiritual benefit of the community. As such, it forms a stark illustration of the instrumental role of violence in past social life.

References

Adeyinka, A. A. (1974). King Gezo of Dahomey, 1818–1858: a reassessment of a west African monarch in the nineteenth century, *African Studies Review, 17*(3), 541–548.

Armit, I. (2006). Inside Kurtz's compound: headhunting and the human body in prehistoric Europe. In M. Bonogofsky (Ed.), *Skull collection, modification and decoration* (pp. 1–14). British Archaeological Reports International Series. Archaeopress: Oxford.

Armit, I. (2007). Hillforts at war: from Maiden Castle to Taniwaha Pā. *Proceedings of the Prehistoric Society, 73*, 25–38.

Armit, I. (2010). Porticos, pillars and severed heads: the display and curation of human remains in the southern French Iron Age. In K. Rebay-Salisbury, M.-L. Stig Sørensen & J. Hughes (Eds.), *Body parts and bodies whole* (pp. 89–99). Oxford: Oxbow.

Armit, I. (2011a). Headhunting and social power in Iron Age Europe. In T. Moore & X. L. Armada (Eds.), *Atlantic Europe in the first millennium BC: Crossing the Divide* (pp. 590–607). Oxford: Oxford University Press.

Armit, I. (2011b). Violence and society in the deep human past. *British Journal of Criminology, 51*(3), 499–517.

Armit, I. (2012). *Headhunting and the body in Iron Age Europe.* Cambridge University Press: Cambridge.

Armit, I. (2017). Les Demoiselles d'Entremont: violence, gender and headhunting in Iron Age Europe. In U. Matić & B. Jensen (Eds.), *Archaeologies of gender and violence* (pp. 122–132). Oxford: Oxbow.

Arnold, D. Y. & Hastorf, C. A. (2008). *Heads of state: icons, power and politics in the ancient and modern Andes.* Walnut Creek: Left Coast Press.

Aswani, S. (2000a). Preface: on head-hunting in the Western Solomons. In *Essays on head-hunting in the Western Solomon Islands* (pp. 4–9). (Special Issue of the *Journal of the Polynesian Society 109*). Auckland: Polynesian Society.

Aswani, S. (Ed.) (2000b). *Essays on head-hunting in the Western Solomon Islands.* (Special Issue of the *Journal of the Polynesian Society 109*). Auckland: Polynesian Society.

Aswani, S. (2000c). Changing identities: the ethnohistory of Roviana predatory head-hunting. In *Essays on head-hunting in the Western Solomon Islands* (pp. 39–70). (Special Issue of the *Journal of the Polynesian Society 109*). Auckland: Polynesian Society.

Brunaux, J.-L. (2018). A battle between Gauls in Picardy: the *tropaion* of Ribemont-sur-Ancre. In M. Fernández-Götz & N. Roymans (Eds.), *Conflict Archaeology: Materialities of Collective Violence from Prehistory to Late Antiquity* (pp. 79–88). London: Taylor and Francis.

Chacon, R. J. & Dye, D. H. (2007). Introduction to human trophy taking: an ancient and widespread practice. In R. J. Chacon & D. H. Dye (Eds.), *The taking and displaying of human body parts as trophies by Amerindians* (pp. 5–31). New York: Springer.

Davis, A. (1891). Naga tribes. In *Assam Census Report, 1891, Vol. 1* (pp. 237–251). Shillong: Government Press.

Duncan, J. (1847). *Travels in West Africa in 1845 and 1846: Volume II,* London: Bentley.

Freeman, D. (1979). Severed heads that germinate. In R. H. Hook (Ed.), *Fantasy and symbol: studies in anthropological interpretation* (pp. 233–246). New York: Academic Press.

Fürer-Haimendorf, C. von. (1938). The head-hunting ceremonies of the Konyak Nagas of Assam. *Man, 38,* 25.

Fürer-Haimendorf, C. von (1969). *The Konyak Nagas: an Indian frontier tribe.* New York: Holt, Rinehart & Winston.

Gummesson, S., Hallgren, F. & Kjellström, A. (2018). Keep your head high: Skulls on stakes and cranial trauma in Mesolithic Sweden. *Antiquity, 92*(361), 74–90.

Harner, M. J. (1973). *The Jivaro: people of the sacred waterfalls.* London: Robert Hale.

Hocart, A. M. (1931). Warfare in Eddystone of the Solomon Islands. *Journal of the Royal Anthropological Institute, 61,* 301–324.

Hoskins, J. (Ed.) (1996a). *Headhunting and the social imagination in Southeast Asia.* Stanford University Press: California.

Hoskins, J. (1996b). Introduction: headhunting as practice and as trope. In J. Hoskins (Ed.), *Headhunting and the social imagination in Southeast Asia* (pp. 1–49). Stanford University Press: California.

Hoskins, J. (1996c). The heritage of headhunting: history, ideology and violence on Sumba 1890–1990. In Hoskins, J. (Ed.), *Headhunting and the social imagination in Southeast Asia* (pp. 216–48). California: Stanford University Press.

Hutton, J. H. (1938). *A primitive philosophy of life (Frazer Lecture).* Oxford: Oxford University Press.

Jacobs, J. (1990). *The Nagas: society, culture and the colonial encounter.* London: Thames and Hudson.

Larsen, E. B. (2004). The Ribe skull fragment. Toolmarks and surface textures. In M. Bencard, L. Bender Jørgensen & H. Brinch Madsen (Eds.), *Ribe. The excavations 1970–1976* (pp. 43–59). Esbjerg: Sydjysk Universitetsforlag.

Law, R. (1989). 'My head belongs to the king': On the political and ritual significance of decapitation in pre-colonial Dahomey. *Journal of African History, 30*(3), 399–415.

Lumholtz, C. S. (1920). *Through Central Borneo. An account of two years travel in the land of the head-hunters Between the years 1913 and 1917.* Montana: Kessinger.

McKinley, R. (1976). Human and proud of it! A structural treatment of head-hunting rites and the social definition of enemies. In G. N. Appell (Ed.), *Studies in Borneo societies: social process and anthropological explanation (Special Report no. 12).* Illinois: DeKalb, Northern Illinois University.

Mendoza, R. G. (2007). The divine gourd tree: tzompantli skull racks, decapitation rituals, and human trophies in ancient Mesoamerica. In R. Chacon & D. H. Dye (Eds.), *The taking and displaying of human body parts as trophies by Amerindians* (pp. 400–443). New York: Springer.

Mills, J. P. (1926). *The Ao Nagas.* London: Macmillan and Co.

Moser, C. (1973). *Human decapitation in Ancient Mesoamerica.* Dumbarton Oaks: Washington.

Moser, C. (1974). Ritual decapitation in Moche art. *Archaeology, 27,* 30–7.

Needham, R. (1976). Skulls and causality. *Man, 11*(1), 71–88.

Orschiedt, J. A. (2002). Die kopfbestattungen der Ofnet-Höhle: ein beleg für kriegerische auseinandersetzungen im Mesolithikum. *Archäologische Informationen, 24,* 199–207.

Rosaldo, M. (1977). Skulls and causality, *Man, 12*(1), 168–170.

Rosaldo, R. (1980). *Ilongot headhunting 1883–1974: a Study in Society and History.* Stanford University Press: California.

Rosaldo, R. (1984). Grief and a headhunter's rage: on the cultural force of emotions. In E. W. Bruner (Ed.), *Text, play and story: the construction and reconstruction of self and society* (pp. 178–195). Proceedings of the American Ethnological Society. Washington DC: American Ethnological Society.

Tinyi, V. (2017). The headhunting culture of the Nagas: reinterpreting the self. *The South Asianist, 5*(1): 83–98.

Tremearne, A. J. N. (1912). *The tailed head-hunters of Nigeria: an account of an official's seven years' experiences in the northern Nigerian pagan belt, and a description of the manners, habits, and customs of the native tribes.* London: Seeley.

Up De Graff, F. (1923). *Head hunters of the Amazon: seven years of exploration and adventure.* New York: Duffield.

Vayda, A. P. (1960). *Maori warfare.* Polynesian Society Maori Monographs 2: Wellington.

Walsh, P. (1894). Maori preserved heads. *Transactions and Proceedings of the Royal Society of New Zealand, 27,* 610–616.

Wolin, D. (2022). Decapitated heads as elite visual culture in Late Shang China. *Cambridge Archaeological Journal, 32*(2), 189–204.

Zegwaard, G. A. (1959). Headhunting practices of the Asmat of Netherlands New Guinea. *American Anthropologist, 61,* 1020–1041.

An Ethnohistory of Souls and Violence: On the Animation of Humans among the Recent Past Animists of Northwestern Siberia and Animism in Hunter-gatherer Archaeology

Erik Solfeldt

Since the mid-1990s, a spate of different so-called new animist approaches have emerged (Harvey, 2017), and have been developed and applied both in the fields of anthropology and archaeology (Bird-David, 1999; Conneller, 2004, 2011; Herva & Lahelma, 2019; Ingold, 2011b, 2011a; Solfeldt, 2021, 2024; Viveiros de Castro, 1998; Walker, 2009; Willerslev, 2007). These approaches reject the Victorian anthropologist Edward B. Tylor's notion of animism as "…the doctrine of all men who believe in active spiritual beings…" (Tylor, 1869:567), which, Tylor argued, is the result of the absence of modern (Victorian) science (Segal, 2014) and, therefore, constitutes a failed epistemology (Bird-David, 1999). These approaches equally reject trends and tendencies that followed Victorian unilinear evolutionism: modernity and postmodernity, including functionalism, structuralism, constructivism, and poststructuralism – all of which rely on defining and ordering things and phenomena based on dichotomies, e.g., humanity and nature, intelligence and instinct, immaterial and material, and so on (Ingold 2011b:6). Such a dualistic view of reality characterises the 'Western way' of perceiving reality (Bird-David, 1999; Descola 2014; Ingold, 2011b; Viveiros de Castro, 1998) – a dualistic perspective evolving from Aristotle's hylomorphism, Christian theology, and Cartesian metaphysics (see Descola, 2014; Dika, 2020; Ingold, 2011b; Marenbon, 2016; Simondon, 2020; Willerslev, 2007:13–15). A further important notion to add to this Western dualistic perception of reality is anthropocentrism – a notion that, since the writing of Aristotle, has held a key position in the Western tradition, placing the rational human above other co-inhabitants of environments, such as animals and plants (Coccia, 2019). The pre-eminence of this assumption has arguably remained unquestioned up to the development of the recent, so-called 'ontological turn', new materialism and new animism. These developments are critical towards Western dualisms and the assumption that this perspective is supposed to be universal through both space and time (Bird-David, 1999; Conneller, 2004, 2011; Holbraad & Pedersen, 2017; Ingold, 2011b, 2011a; Willerslev, 2007).

New animistic approaches instead emphasise relations between all things, living and non-living, and thus seek to investigate what relations lie in between the dichotomies of the West (Bird-David, 1999; Conneller, 2004, 2011; Ingold, 2011b, 2011a; Willerslev, 2007). Viewing empirical material from an animist's perspective is about creating the conditions under which new ideas can be thought, thoughts previously deemed unimaginable (see Holbraad & Pedersen, 2017). The purpose is to give both life and agency to the non-human.

While these new animistic approaches have contributed much to understandings of animism(s) and human–animal relations among the distant past, recent past and contemporary animists – often focusing on hunter-fisher-gatherers and pastoralists – they share a problem: the assumption that the animation, i.e., the recognition of agency and life-giving, of *humans* works in the same way, regardless of ontological and cultural differences. The focus on non-anthropocentrism within these approaches has resulted in an overcompensation, insofar as emphases placed on the animation of non-human animals have ended up neglecting human animations. While anthropologists have touched upon differences within human animation (Descola, 2014: 288; Viveiros de Castro, 1998:479), archaeologists seem to have ignored this aspect, and how it relates to perceptions of violence and warfare within animistic ontologies.

Avoiding this discussion of human animation, and its implications in relation to violence and warfare among animist hunter-fisher-gathers and pastoralists goes hand in hand with the thoughts of the eighteenth-century philosopher Jean-Jacques Rousseau (2009) and, specifically, his notion of the 'noble savage' that puts onus on the peace and tranquillity of the lives of prehistoric hunter-fisher-gatherer animists and animism(s) – an oversimplification that still echoes today in hunter-gatherer and pastoralist research drawing on new animism and shamanism as theoretical frameworks. For example, historian Andrei Znamenski (2021:225) has pointed out that archaeologists who study shamanism and prehistoric cave art, and argue that such art was made by shamans, tend to assume that it was produced for altogether noble reasons. Znamenski asks:

> Why should we exclude so-called black magic and assume that the shamans of old always painted those images in order to heal people or somehow benefit their communities? Anthropologists know well that in tribal societies shamans cannot only heal but also harm and kill. (Znamenski, 2021:225)

Assumptions like this further contribute to a reproduction of Rousseau's (2009) notion of the 'noble savage' in understanding the archaeological past, while ethnographic and ethnohistorical materials and studies show another picture (Forsyth, 1992; Golovnev, 2000; Riboli & Torri, 2016; Znamenski, 2021:225).

The aim of this chapter is twofold. Firstly, I explore human animation and its relations to the justification of violence and warfare among the recent past animists of northwestern Siberia (c. 1600–1900), specifically focusing on the ethnography and ethnohistory of the Nenets, Nganasan, Enets, Khanty, Mansi, Selkup, and Kets. Secondly, I relate these ethnohistorical results of human animation to some examples of archaeological interpretations of the hunter-fisher-gatherers of the distant past and discuss how, when applying theories of new animism to archaeological materials, archaeologists need to consider human animations and violence and warfare as part of the prehistoric animism(s) of the distant past hunter-fisher-gatherers.

Animisms in Northwestern Siberia

The Indigenous peoples of northwestern Siberia had already been in contact with outsiders, whether directly or indirectly, before the start of the Russian imperial colonisation during the fifteenth century. This resulted in their animisms being further affected by the Russian colonisers and missionaries and marked the beginning of a syncretism between Indigenous traditional animisms, Tatar Islamic paganisms and Russian orthodoxy (Forsyth, 1992) – a syncretism that still can be seen in contemporary ethnographic materials of northwestern Siberia. Elements of traditional animisms still exist among these groups today. The study of animisms of the recent past should, however, be carried out on the premise that the process of these syncretisms had already begun at the start of colonisation and that syncretisms have evolved ever since. It must also be stressed that syncretisms between different kinds of animisms existed long before the colonisation, given not only that the animists of southern Siberia migrated to the north during prehistoric times, but also that these peoples, categorised as ethnic groups, have never been isolated from one another (cf. Forsyth, 1992).

A major difference between the contemporary syncretic animisms of northwestern Siberia and the tradition of Western dualisms is that the ontologies of the animists are relational and such relational ontologies are generated by close relations with specific environments (taiga and tundra) and their non-human co-inhabitants (Berkes, 2008; Bird-David, 1990; Bird-David, 1999; Ingold, 2011b, 2011a). Their animisms are generally based on immanentism, in contradistinction to the transcendentalism that characterises the Western dualistic perspective, meaning that the Siberian spirits, gods and ancestors are not separated from the material world as they are in the West in the form of representations – which is to say, the material represents an image of Jesus on the cross, the image is not Jesus himself (Castrén 1853:197; Solfeldt & Naglaya 2024).

Social anthropologist Tim Ingold defines animism as "A complex network of reciprocal interdependence, based on the give and take of substance, care and vital force… [that] extends throughout cosmos, linking human, animal and all other forms of life." (Ingold, 2011b, p. 133). Within animistic ontologies, the notion of the soul (or some kind of vital force comprehensively understood but not fully comparable to the Western concept of the soul) can therefore extend beyond the material body and is not exclusive to humans (Ingold, 2022: 56–57). Certain non-human animals, plants, hills, mountains, rivers, lakes, stones and artefacts can have a soul. Moreover, in contrast to the Western equation of one soul per individual, most living beings, human as well as non-human, have several souls that relate to the material body and its properties or, in the case of landscape features and things, its form and material presence in the world (Ingold, 2022; see also Armit, this volume). These are the most basic premises for the various kinds of animistic syncretisms existing worldwide, and how this network of reciprocal interdependence, or correspondences, as Ingold (2011a, 2022) terms it in his later publications, works and how they are ontologically and culturally understood will vary between different groups of animists.

While different animisms of northwestern Siberia exhibit many similarities, they differ in some important respects. As Ingold argues (Ingold, 2022:56), souls in northwestern Siberia are not exclusive to humans and they are not only housed within the material body (Castrén, 1853:200–201; Jordan, 2003:217–218; Kharyuchi, 2004:161; Vallikivi, 2011:88).

Among the Khanty (formerly known as the Ostyaks), for example, humans consist of a body and several souls. Men have five souls, where-as women have four souls. These are: shadow soul, bird soul, dream soul, breath soul and strength soul – the latter is exclusive for men (Jordan, 2003:217). All these souls must be considered an immaterial continuation of the material since they always relate to the material world. The Western dualism between the immaterial soul and the material body does not apply within these ontologies, as others have argued (Descola, 2014:287–288; Willerslev, 2007:57–58).

The shadow soul relates to the shadow of a human being. If light is present, this soul never leaves; it remains as a shadow cast, persisting through death, even after the body has been reduced to a pile of bones (Jordan, 2003:217–218). The bird soul resides either in the head or in clothes. It has the potential to fly away for a short while, in the form of a bird, but being without a soul for a longer time will result in illness and death. When this soul is considered to reside in a person's clothes it is important to treat the clothing with respect, and not shake them too hard or leave them lying around (Jordan, 2003:218). The dream soul is a wood grouse, or a black cock, that roams freely in the forest. It visits a person during sleep. An inability to sleep means the soul has flown away (Jordan, 2003:218). When awake, the dream soul is out in the forest in the form of a wood grouse or a black cock and it can potentially be killed by a hunter – it is even possible that a hunter kills his or her own dream soul (Jordan, 2003:219). The breath soul resides in the hair of a person and this soul is the only one that reincarnates from the dead person into a new-born from the same clan. It persists through death and stays in the cemetery until it is possible to reincarnate (Jordan, 2003:219).

While this description of the Khanty souls provides a way to approach the concept of the soul(s) in northwestern Siberia, it should be noted that the souls are understood differently among the other peoples of northwestern Siberia. It should also be mentioned that even among the Khanty it may differ depending on how the animistic syncretism plays out on a local level (cf. Jordan, 2003:39). However, similarities can be found.

The Nenets, the Nganasan, the Enets, and the Selkup (formerly known as the Samoyeds and Ostyak-Samoyeds) mainly relate the concept of the soul(s) with breathing but, like the Khanty, they have several souls (Kim, 2000:461). For the Nganasan, the breath soul lives in the heart and has the form of strings (like sunbeams) while the Enets consider the breath soul to reside in the chest (Kim, 2000:462). Ethnolinguist Alexandra A. Kim (2000:462) has suggested that the concept of the breath soul among the Samoyedic-speaking peoples should be understood as a person's vapor rather than in Western terms of an immaterial soul housed within the material body. Breathing must be understood in terms of a relational environmental correspondence, as there is no clear limit between the breath soul and the air. Based on earlier linguistic and ethnographic studies, Kim's (2000) analysis of the Selkup soul(s) concept shows many similarities with the Khanty souls. The male strength soul appears here too and when it is lost the male turns female. It is common that shamans lose this soul during rituals and become non-binary (Kim, 2000:468). The shadow soul, or the living shadow, is however only for the living and when one dies the shadow roams the forest, slowly turning into a spirit (Kim, 2000:471). The life soul is like the Khanty breath soul and is the source of life. For some Selkup, when a person dies, this soul turns into a spider. Other Selkup believe instead that this soul wanders the forest, later turning into a wood goblin (Kim, 2000:463). Kim's (2000) study shows that some Selkup groups have up to seven different souls that constitute the vital elements of life. Like the Selkup, the northern Kets also have seven souls that constitute life (Avdeeva et al., 2019:741). The concept of the Kets soul(s) is reminiscent of the Khanty and the Selkup. A major difference, however, is that with the Kets, the bones, or the skeleton, *are* one of the souls (Avdeeva et al., 2019:741; cf. Donner, 1922:130, 1933:239).

It is important to stress that some of these souls are not exclusive to humans; as mentioned above, animals also have many of these souls but, as I have mentioned, so do landscape features and things (Avdeeva et al., 2019; Castrén, 1853:197–198; Donner, 1922:129; Jordan, 2003:103). For example, the Nenets humanoid *material spirits*, commonly referred to as 'idols' in earlier ethnography, (Figure 1) have both a shadow soul and a breath soul (Vallikivi, 2011:88).

This brief overview of the northwestern Siberian animists' understanding of the soul(s) provides a complex abstraction of what life is and how and where someone or something can be alive and live. Being alive within animistic ontologies is not an enclosed embodied process but is relational; the body is not only surrounded by the environment, it is a part of it (cf. Ingold, 1992). The material reality is in direct correspondence with the immaterial reality – an immaterial reality as real as the material reality. The immaterial spirits – e.g., former shadow souls amid turning spirits, or breath souls that are waiting to reincarnate – live next to the material souls and spirits, e.g., the wood grouse, the river, the wooden material spirits, clothes, non-human animals and their fellow humans, etc. The souls both reside in materials and are materials, and their forms are fluid and changeable.

This worldview seems at first sight to be a peaceful, environmentally friendly ontology, where animations extend beyond the human and create a social bond between humans and non-humans. While in many cases true, the animation of other humans does not always work in the same way as the animation of humans belonging to the same group. 'The Other' is animated differently.

Figure 1: Nenets household material spirit/ancestral image (13,5 x 4 cm) inv. nr. 1880.04.0093. Photo: Världskulturmuseumerna: Etnografiska (CC-BY).

The Animation of 'The Others'

Eduardo Viveiros de Castro provides an example of human animation from the colonisation of the Americas, which shows that humans are not always human in the same way:

> For the Europeans, the issue was to decide whether the others possessed a soul… The Europeans never doubted the Indians had bodies: the Indians never doubted that the Europeans had souls (animals and spirits have them too). What the Indians wanted to know was whether the bodies of those "souls" were capable of the same affects as their own – whether they had bodies of humans or bodies of spirits… (Viveiros de Castro, 1998:479)

Philippe Descola, who partly draws on Viveiros de Castro, provides a further example of human animation:

> The soul of the members of neighboring tribes makes them subjects, just like me, but their bodies objectivize them as different from me. They are decorated, painted, and tattooed differently; the weapons, tools, and utensils that are extensions of their bodies differ from mine (as do the forms of the jaws, beaks, and claws or talons of animals); the houses that shelter those bodies are not the same as the one in which I live; and the language by means of which they act upon the world is not the one that I speak... (Descola, 2014:288)

The animation of 'the Other' plays as great a role within animistic ontologies as the animation of the non-human. As shown below, the recent past animisms of northwestern Siberia were no exception.

Both the historical and the ethnohistorical materials – the latter of which includes folklore and archaeology – speak of war tactics, fortifications, armour and weapons, that is, things that are typically not related to hunter-fishers and hunter-herders (Golovnev, 2000). Western dualistic thought tends to separate the hunter from the warrior and the weapon from the hunting tool. But these distinctions do not in most cases apply here (see also Lundström, this volume). The weapons used for conflict were the same as those used for hunting: bows and arrows, spears, axes and traps – except for the Khanty and the Mansi princes who sometimes wore swords and sabres (Forsyth, 1992:11, 19; Golovnev, 2000:134; Hatto, 2017:195–213). The armour consisted of everything from furs to studded leather, mail shirts and helmets (Forsyth, 1992:11; Hatto, 2017:195–213). Recent archaeological excavations show that fortifications were used from the Neolithic period until the area was fully colonised by the Russians at the end of the eighteenth century (Schreiber et al., 2022).

Tales of war and heroes can be said to characterise northwestern Siberian folklore (Chindina, 2000:78; Golovnev, 2000:126; Hatto, 2017:172). The reasons for conflict and war, both clan wars and wars between peoples, in these tales are territorial claims, women, religion and reindeer (Golovnev, 2000:126; Golovnev & Osherenko, 1999:54–

55). Territorial claims were mainly because of hunting, fishing and reindeer herding grounds and the conflicts most likely increased as the Russians seized Siberian lands. Women were captured and were kept either as hostages or for marriage (Chindina, 2000:78; Golovnev, 2000:126, 131). Religious wars had to do with traditional animists, especially those in the north, who saw their neighbours' conversion to Christianity as a betrayal and therefore declared war on them (Golovnev & Osherenko, 1999:54–55). Reindeer were stolen as a way of sabotaging the enemy. Not only did the Nenets, the Nganasan and the Enets use reindeer and sleighs when migrating, they also used them in raids and in war (Golovnev, 2000:131). The Nenets' war tactics involved quickly attacking at night, using sleighs during the winter and skin boats in the summer so as to escape as fast and efficiently as they had arrived. This tactic was especially successful when attacking the Khanty and the Selkup living along the tundra-taiga border. They could not, however, follow the Nenets out onto the tundra, since they were not as skilled in sleigh building and made use of much heavier wooden boats compared to the Nenets' skin boats (Golovnev, 2000:131).

While this kind of raiding was common in different forms among all the northwestern Siberian hunter-fishers and hunter-herders, there are also examples of organised warfare where clans decided in advance where and when to meet in battle (Golovnev, 2000:133). This violence, raiding and warfare, does not stand separate from the animistic ontologies. They are to be understood as being constituted by relations between the material and the immaterial.

The Nenets, for example, believed that powerful enemies could only be killed with the use of magic (Golovnev, 2000:134). Since souls were not only housed within the material body, it was often not enough to kill the material body (Golovnev, 2000:134). The Nenets also believed that it was not sufficient to cut off a shaman's head, as it had the potential to grow back again (Golovnev, 2000:134–135). For some Nenets the most effective method for killing a person was to give the whole body to the water spirit, otherwise parts of it, for example, the heart, might escape into the ground and later return and cause harm (Golovnev, 2000:135). According to Khanty and Mansi folklore, enemies needed to be scalped to be completely dead (Golovnev, 2000:145). To die a slow death was also preferred, for in that way some of the souls would have time to leave the body (Hatto, 2017:178–180). When, however, an enemy was scalped, or beheaded, the result was a violent expulsion for some of the souls, thereby making reincarnation impossible (Hatto, 2017:180). Early ethnographic studies also describe how enemy hearts were eaten to gain their desirable qualities (Donner, 1922:145, 1933:239–242; Golovnev, 2000:145). The ethnographer Andrei V. Golovnev describes the rituals related to the killings of other humans in the following terms:

> An enemy was treated as a "nonhuman" who deserved brutality. Probably this was a ritual rule rather than "the nature" of fighters. In order to conceive an enemy (and oneself) that he was "nonhuman", it was necessary to kill him in a "nonhuman" way. (Golovnev, 2000:144).

To contrast this with the killing of reindeer – a non-human animal the Nenets regard as sacred (cf. Sundström, 2008) – a Nenets' legend tells of how a tundra warrior, armed with a bow and arrows, targets an enemy who is fleeing in a sleigh. However, the tundra warrior is unable to shoot without possibly hitting the reindeer pulling the sleigh (Golovnev, 2000:132). To kill in a "non-human way", as Golovnev (2000:144) puts it, or in a dehumanising way is here a misleading expression. Rather, the legend tells us more about how the killing of a human is ontologically and culturally understood from an animistic perspective.

Among most Indigenous peoples, it is common to call themselves 'human' or 'person' in their local Indigenous language (Golovnev & Osherenko, 1999:1). *Nenets* means 'people' (Golovnev & Osherenko, 1999), *Enets* means 'human' (Eidlitz Kuoljok, 1993:22) and *Kets* means 'a man' (Avdeeva et al., 2019:735), and so on. The Nenets also called themselves 'Nenei Nenets', meaning 'real people', which is related to the legend telling of how they went from being hunters to reindeer herders – herders are the real people of the land (Golovnev, 2000:131; Golovnev & Osherenko, 1999:29). The 'Others' are everyone who is not them, regardless of whether they are hostile or friendly (Golovnev

& Osherenko, 1999:1). In the legends, the close neighbours are considered friendly while the neighbours living further away consist of mysterious foes (Golovnev & Osherenko, 1999:1). In a similar way as, they call themselves a 'human' or 'person', the 'Others' are called something else. For example, the Khanty and the Mansi called the Nenets, and other Samoyedic speaking groups, 'the ones that eat raw meat' while the forest Nenets called some of the Khanty 'blacks' (Castrén, 1860; Patkanov, 1891, in Golovnev, 2000:145), and the tundra Nenets considered some of the forest people – the Selkup, the Kets and the Evenki – to be savages from a different world (Golovnev, 2000:131).

This shows that language expresses the animation of the 'other' and marks out who is considered human in the same way as one's own kin. As both Viveiros de Castro (1998:479) and Descola (2014:288) argue, the Western dualism between human and non-human does not apply, since material bodies and material cultures correspond differently to the immaterial concept of the soul, or souls.

Material Culture and Immaterial Continuance of Enemies

The animation of the 'Other' can also be seen in the use of material culture and how different clans and peoples corresponded in terms of rituals and rules with their animated surroundings before the raiding or battle had begun.

The tundra Nenets, for example, considered the forest peoples to be savages, since they wore non-processed fur as clothing (Golovnev, 2000:131). The Khanty and the Mansi did not touch Nenets, Nganasan and Enets clothes and possessions, and if they needed to take anything they did so by passing it across a cleansing fire (Golovnev, 2000:145). This must be seen in relation to the Khanty bird soul that resides in a person's clothes. The traditional clothing of the peoples of north-western Siberia looks different in terms of design and decorative patterns, though all are characterised by the animist perspective. For example, fur clothes are often made from the corresponding parts of the animal – shoes and gloves are made of paws while the fur from heads are used as hoods (Golovnev, 2020:131). Traditional clothing must then be understood as more than its practical function, especially in those cases where one of the souls relates to the clothes of a person. To fully kill an enemy might then have included the destruction of the enemy's clothes and armour.

Other sacred rituals and ceremonies were conducted when first approaching the enemy camp or the battlefield. The eighteenth-century ethnographer and naturalist Gerhard F. Müller describes how the Khanty and the Mansi created and put wooden humanoid material spirits, similar to the household material spirits, or ancestral images, common throughout Siberia (Figure 1), in trees where they had a view of the enemy camp or the battlefield. Sacrifices were made to the material spirits for spiritual protection during a raid or battle (Golovnev, 2000:143).

Spiritual protection was also needed after the battle to protect the survivors and the fallen of their own clan from spiritual enemies seeking revenge. Both archaeological and ethnographic studies describe how the practice of sticking sharp things – such as arrows, spears, knives and axes, close to animist graves – was common throughout northwestern Siberia, from at least the eleventh century to modern times (Kardash & Sokolkov, 2015; Ozheredov, 2016:133–134). To stick something sharp into someone's shadow would cause harm to the person and his or her shadow soul (Jordan, 2003:220). This means that if a shadow soul can be harmed, so can the spirits of the dead who reside in the cemeteries. To offer another example, hunters among the Khanty, the Mansi and the Selkup, kept sacred arrows with copper heads in their quivers (Figure 2); they were saved for when protection was needed against evil spirits (Ozheredov, 2016:133). This shows that hunting weapons cannot be reduced to their material functions alone; they, too, must be understood as a correspondence between the material and the immaterial reality (cf. Ozheredov, 1999:77).

Northwestern Siberian folklore does not state exactly when the hunter-warriors use specific sacred weapons (cf. Ozheredov, 1999:78), since material culture is seldom in focus in both the folklore and the non-archaeological ethnography (cf. Jordan, 2003:2). Nonetheless, it is reasonable to think that in such a case where magic was needed to kill a powerful enemy, as the Nenets believed (Golovnev, 2000:134), such spiritual and sacred hunting weapons were used.

Figure 2: Khanty arrow with lanceolate copper head
(83 cm). Inv. nr. SU3904:403. Illustration: U. T. Sire-
lius, The National Museum of Finland (CC-BY).

To kill an enemy was not only to end the life of a material body, it was
also a process of separating the souls from the body. An enemy was
removed but at the same time, a potential enemy in the form of a soul
turning spirit was created – a spirit that potentially could cause harm
to both the living and the dead. The material culture – including
humanoid material spirits, armours, arrows and other sharp things –
was needed for protection against both material and immaterial
threats. There are even ethnohistorical materials speaking of war
against dead people (Golovnev, 2000:145).

'The Othering', as seen in the folklore, ethnolinguistics and material culture, was not about making violence, warfare and killing easier for the hunter-warriors in the form of distancing and not facing the direct consequences of the violent act (Grossman 2009:87; Chapa 2018:265), nor was it a form of xenophobia or dehumanisation. It was about the ontological perception of killing and the cultural rules that one had to follow to kill another kind of human, following a similar logic to the Viveiros de Castro and Descola quotations above, and how safely to do this to avoid harmful immaterial continuations in the form of spirits seeking revenge.

Approaching Animisms and Human Animation in the Distant Past

The syncretic animisms of northwestern Siberia are relational ontologies wherein human souls extend beyond material bodies and constitute parts of the environments (taiga and tundra) and some of its non-human inhabitants. Non-human souls belonging to all kinds – e.g., non-human animals, plants, landscape features, celestials, ancestors, and things – share these environments with humans and are therefore considered as co-inhabitants.

Based on the ethnohistory of the area, the category of 'non-human' also included other humans not considered to belong to the same clan or people. To truly be defined as human rested on a shared ontological perception, cultural expression, and material culture with the community at large – all others, not sharing the ontology, cultural expressions and material culture, were considered non-human or human in a different way.

Engaging in violent activities and practices – such as war and raiding, but also the hunting of non-human animals, fishing, herding and gathering – was a way of corresponding with other souls. To kill a human was more complex than ending the life of a material body, along with some of its souls. Such an act also involved continuing immaterial hostilities with the enemy – a continuation by immaterial means that could seek revenge on both the living and the dead.

A range of things – such as humanoid material spirits, sharp things and certain weapons and materials – were therefore needed as protection both from the living and the dead that sought to harm living or dead relatives, clan members, friends and allies. What this ethno-historical analysis has shown is that violent practices, such as war and raiding, were not only incorporated into the northwestern Siberian hunter-fishers' and hunter-herders' societies and cultures but it was also part of the syncretic animist ontologies.

What then does this mean for archaeological studies applying new animism to hunter-gatherer communities from the distant past? If animisms and animations are generated by the corresponding rela-tions with environments and their non-human co-inhabitants, as can be argued based on the works of Ingold and others (Bird-David, 1990, 1999; Descola, 2014; Ingold, 2011a, 2011a, 2013; Viveiros de Castro, 1998), then it is more likely that the hunter-fisher-gatherers of the distant past perceived their environments and their non-human co-inhabitations in similar ways as reflected in the ethnographic materials of northwestern Siberia rather than the dualistic premises of Western thought. They too, like the hunter-fisher-herders of northwestern Siberia, made their living based on the tasks of hunting, fishing and gathering –namely, the very material relations that most likely con-tinued in some form of animation. This means, in relation to the ontological turn and new animism, that ethnographic analogies can be used to think the unimaginable from a Western perspective and to think new thoughts that do not rest upon Western perceptions of reality by default (cf. Holbraad & Pedersen, 2017; see also Günter, 2022). The ethnographic analogies are used to rethink and to decon-struct, as well as to construct, possible ways the hunter-fisher-gatherers of the past animated their reality, *humans* ('the Self' and 'the Other'), and other co-inhabitants of the environment.

What can be concluded from all this is, firstly, that the dualisms present in Western thought are not to be taken for granted as somehow universal in both time and space, especially the oppositions between the 'human' and 'non-human', 'life' and 'death', and 'materiality' and 'im-materiality'. The 'human' is a fluid category rather than a fixed position, the dichotomic other of which is the 'non-human' animal. Secondly, traces of violence found among prehistoric hunter-fisher-gatherers – from the Middle Palaeolithic period onwards (Orschiedt, 2020) – can potentially be a result of ontological perceptions and understandings that differ from Western dualistic understandings of not only how to end the life of a body, but also the existence of some kind of vital force comparable to the modern Western notion of the soul and souls. What archaeologists have interpreted as traces of human violence was potentially not perceived in this way by past hunter-fisher-gatherers. Based on this analysis it is likely that the projectiles found in prehistoric hunter-fisher-gatherer bodies (Thorpe, 2003) were caused, if not by hunting accidents, then because the victim was considered, ontologically and culturally, as someone not human. The same can be argued for those who caused harm to the Late Mesolithic and Neolithic hunter-fisher-gathers buried in cemeteries around the Baltic Sea (Ahlström & Molnar, 2012; Jankauskas, 2012) and the potential traces of cannibalism among prehistoric hunter-fisher-gatherers (Thorpe, 2003; Villa, 1992). Furthermore, differences in human animation must especially be considered at those sites where traces of violence relating to rituals have occurred, such as the skulls attached to wooden poles at the Mesolithic site of Kanaljorden in Motala on the Scandinavian peninsula (Hallgren, 2011; Hallgren et al., 2021). It is a possibility that the non-human animals found at the site, such as deer and boar, were considered 'more human' than the humans whose skulls were put on the wooden poles.

Conclusion

Based on this study, I argue that archaeologists studying hunter-fisher-gatherers, and early pastoralists, in general need to reconsider the difference between Western ontological perceptions of reality and animistic ontological perceptions of reality (see Walker, 2009). More importantly, archaeologists applying theories of new animism must reconsider human animation and the complexities of recent past and contemporary animistic ontologies. This is especially important to rethink when studying traces of violence and warfare among animists of the distant past. Human and 'the Othering' of humans are fluid categories that depend on ontological perceptions of reality, and that moreover have implications for the study of conflicts among animists, their socialites, cultures and ontologies. To do otherwise is to reproduce the Western perception of reality, including conflict, violence and warfare, to be universal in both time and space – a reduction and simplification of both past, recent past and contemporary animist hunter-fisher-gatherers and hunter-herders.

Acknowledgements

I would like to thank the editor of this volume Rolf Warming for the invitation to present at the conference Studies of Conflict: Bridging the Gap and to contribute to the conference proceedings. I also wish to thank my supervisors, Professor Andrew Meirion Jones and Professor Peter Jordan, for commenting on this paper.

References

Ahlström, T. & Molnar, P. (2012). The placement of the feathers: Violence among Sub-boreal foragers from Gotland, central Baltic Sea. In R. Schulting & L. Fibiger (Eds.), *Sticks, Stones, and Broken Bones. Neolithic Violence in a European Perspective* (pp. 17–33). Oxford University Press.

Avdeeva, Y. N., Degtyarenko, K. A., Pchelkina, D. S., Shimanskaya, K. I., Koptseva, N. P. & Shpak, A. A. (2019). Religion of the Selkup and the Kets in the historical and cultural genesis. *Journal of Siberian Federal University. Humanities & Social Sciences*, 5(12), 726–751.

Berkes, Fikret. (2008). *Sacred ecology*. London: Routledge.

Bird-David, N. (1990). The Giving Environment: Another Perspective on the Economic System of Gatherer-Hunters. *Current Anthropology*, *31*(2), 189–196.

Bird-David, N. (1999). Animism Revisited: Personhood, Environment, and Relational Epistemology 1. *Current Anthropology*, *40*(1), 67–91.

Castrén, M. A. (1853). *Nordiska resor och forskning. Föresäsningar i Finsk mytologi*. Helsinki: Finska Litteratur-Sällskapet.

Chapa, J. O. (2018). Remotely piloted aircraft, risk, and killing as sacrifice: The cost of remote warfare. *Journal of Military Ethnics*, 16(3–4), 256–271.

Chindina, L. A. (2000). Warfare among the hunter and fishermen of Western Siberia. In P. P. Schweitzer, M. Biesele, & R. K. Hitchcock (Eds.), *Hunter and Gatherers in the Modern World. Conflicts, Resistance, and self-Determination* (pp. 77–93). Berghahn Books.

Coccia, E. (2019). *The Life of Plants. A Metaphysics of Mixture*. Cambridge: Polity Press.

Conneller, C. (2004). Becoming deer. Corporeal transformations at Star Carr. *Archaeological Dialogues*, *11*(1), 37–56.

Conneller, C. (2011). *An archaeology of materials: Substantial transformations in early prehistoric Europe*. Routledge.

Descola, P. (2014). *Beyond Nature and Culture* (J. Lloyd, Trans.). Chicago: The University of Chicago Press.

Dika, T. R. (2020). The Origins of Cartesian Dualism. *Journal of the American Philosophical Association, 6*(3), 335–352.

Donner, K. (1922). *Bland Samojeder i Sibirien. Åren 1911–1913, 1914.* Stockholm: Söderström & Co.

Donner, K. (1933). *Sibirien. Folk och Forntid.* Stockholm: Natur och Kultur.

Eidlitz Kuoljok, K. (1993). *Nordsamojediska folk.* Finsk-ugriska institutionen.

Forsyth, J. (1992). *A History of the Peoples of Siberia: Russia's North Asian Colony 1581–1990.* Cambridge Univ. Press.

Golovnev, A. V. (2000). Wars and chiefs among the Samoyeds and Ugrians of Western Siberia. In P. P. Schweitzer, M. Biesele, & R. K. Hitchcock (Eds.), *Hunter and Gatherers in the Modern World. Conflict, Resistance, and Self-Determination* (pp. 125–150). Berghahn Books.

Golovnev, A. V. (2020). Arctic nomadic design (the Nenets case). *Nomadic Peoples, 24,* 111–142.

Golovnev, A. V. & Osherenko, G. (1999). *Siberian Survival. The Nenets and Their Story.* Cornell University Press.

Grossman, D. (2009). *On Killing: The Psychological Cost of Learning to Kill in War and Society.* New York: Back Bay Books.

Günter, H. (2022). *The rhythm of rock art animals: Picturing reindeer, elk and bear around the seasonal cycle in Stone Age Alta.* Stockholm: Stockholm University.

Hallgren, F. (2011). Mesolithic skull depositions at Kanaljorden, Motala, Sweden. *Current Swedish Archaeology, 19,* 244–246.

Hallgren, F., Berggren, K., Arnberg, A., Hartzell, L. & Larsson, B. (2021). *Kanaljorden, Motala. Rituella våtmarksdepositioner och boplatslämningar från äldre stenålder, yngre stenålder och järnålder.* Stiftelsen Kulturmiljövård.

Harvey, G. (2017). If Not all Stones Are Alive…: Radical Relationality in Animism Studies. *Journal for the Study of Religion, Nature & Culture, 11*(4), 481–497.

Hatto, A. T. (2017). *The World of the Khanty Epic Hero-princes: An Exploration of a Siberian Oral Tradition.* Cambridge University Press.

Herva, V.-P. & Lahelma, A. (2019). *Northern Archaeology and Cosmology: A Relational View.* Routledge.

Holbraad, M. & Pedersen, M. Axel. (2017). *The Ontological Turn. An Anthropological Exposition.* Cambridge: Cambridge University Press.

Holmberg, U. (1964). *The mythology of all races. Finno-ugric, Siberian IV.*

Ingold, T. (1992). Culture and the perception of the environment. In Croll, E. & Parkin, D. (Eds.), *Bush base, forest farm. Culture, environment and development* (pp. 38–56). Routledge.

Ingold, T. (2011a). *Being alive: Essays on movement, knowledge and description*. London: Routledge.

Ingold, T. (2011b). *Perception of the environment: Essays on livelihood, dwelling and skill*. London: Routledge.

Ingold, T. (2013). *Making: Anthropology, archaeology, art and architecture*. London: Routledge.

Ingold, T. (2022). *Imagining for Real: Essays on Creation, Attention and Correspondence*. London: Routledge.

Jankauskas, R. (2012). Violence in the Stone Age from an eastern Baltic perspective. In R. Schulting & L. Fibiger (Eds.), *Sticks, Stones, and Broken Bones. Neolithic Violence in a European Perspective* (pp. 36–49). Oxford University Press.

Jordan, P. (2003). *Material culture and sacred landscape: The anthropology of the Siberian Khanty*. Lanham, MD: Rowman Altamira.

Kardash, O. V. & Sokolkov, A. V. (2015). Kholyato-1 Ritual Complex on the Yamal Peninsula. *Archaeology, Ethnology and Anthropology of Eurasia, 43*(1), 81–91.

Kharyuchi, G. P. (2004). Nenets sacred sites as ethnographic landscape. In I. Krupnik, R. Mason, & T. Horton (Eds.), *Northern Ethnographic Landscapes: Perspectives From Circumpolar Nations* (pp. 155–176.). Artic Studies Centre: Washington, D.C.

Kim, A. A. (2000). Lexicon as a source for understanding Sel'kup knowledge of religion. In P. P. Schweitzer, M. Biesele, & R. K. Hitchcock (Eds.), *Hunter and Gatherers in the Modern World. Conflict, Resistance, and Self-Determination* (pp. 460–474). Berghahn Books.

Marenbon, J. (2016). *Medieval Philosophy. A Very Short Introduction*. Oxford: Oxford University Press.

Orschiedt, J. (2020). Violence in Palaeolithic and Mesolithic hunter-gatherer communities. In G. G. Fagan, L. Fibiger, M. Hudson, & M. Trundle (Eds.), *The Cambridge World History of Violence: Volume 1: The Prehistoric and Ancient Worlds* (pp. 58–78). Cambridge University Press.

Ozheredov, Y. I. (1999). Sakral'nye strely yuzhnykh sel'kupov [Sacred arrows of the southern Selkups]. In E. I. Chernyak (Ed.), *Priob'e glazami arkheologov i etnografov. Materialy i issledovaniya k 'Entsiklopedii Tomskoi oblasti'* [Priobye through the eyes of archaeologists and ethnographers. Materials and research for the 'Encyclopaedia of the Tomsk Region'] (pp. 77–119). Izdatel'stvo Tomskogo universiteta.

Ozheredov, Y. I. (2016). Ritu-al'noe vtykanie oruzhiya u sel'kupov i drevnie traditsii narodov Evrazii. *Vestnik Tomskogo Gosudarstvennogo Universiteta. Istoriya, 5*(43), 133–137.

Riboli, D. & Torri, D. (2016). *Shamanism and violence: Power, repression and suffering in indigenous religious conflicts*. London: Routledge.

Rousseau, J.-J. 1712–1778. (2009). *Discourse on Inequality on the Origin and Basis of Inequality among Men*. Auckland: Floating Press.

Schreiber, T., Piezonka, H., Chairkina, N., Dubovtseva, E. N. & Kosinskaya, L. L. (2022). Towards territoriality and inequality? Examining prehistoric hunter-gatherer fortifications in the Siberian taiga. In T. Ibsen, K. Ilves, B. Maixner, S. Messal, & J. Schneeweiß (Eds.), *Fortifications in their Natural and Cultural Landscape: From Organising Space to the Creation of Power* (pp. 51–68). Habelt-Verlag.

Segal, R. A. (2014). Animism for Tylor. In Harvey, G, (Ed.) *The Handbook of Contemporary Animism* (pp. 53–62). Routledge.

Simondon, G. 2020. *Individuation in Light of Notions of Form and Information*. Minneapolis: University of Minnesota Press.

Solfeldt, E. (2021). *En arkeologi av det animistiska: Om den mesolitiska ornamentiken i Östersjöområdet*. Stockholm: Stockholm University.

Solfeldt, E. (2024). An archaeology of animism: On the Mesolithic 'portable art' of the Baltic Sea. Highly commended, Master's thesis prize. *Hunter Gatherer Research*, 9(1–2), 95–123.

Solfeldt, E. & Naglaya, A. 2024. Rethinking representation and animation. A visual ethnoarchaeology of material spirits in northwestern Siberia. *Current Swedish Archaeology*, 34, 135–158.

Sundström, O. (2008). *'Vildrenen är själv detsamma som en gud': 'gudar' och 'andar' i sovjetiska etnografers beskrivningar av samojediska världsåskådningar*. Umeå: Umeå University.

Thorpe, I. J. (2003). Anthropology, archaeology, and the origin of warfare. *World Archaeology*, 35(1), 145–165.

Tylor, E. (1869). On the survival of savage thought in modern civilization, part I. *Appletons' Journal*, 1(18), 566–568.

Vallikivi, L. (2011). What Does Matter?: Idols and Icons in the Nenets Tundra. *Journal of Ethnology and Folkloristics*, 5(1), 75–95.

Villa, P. (1992). Cannibalism in prehistoric Europe. *Evolutionary Anthropology: Issues, News, and Reviews*, 1(3), 93–104.

Viveiros de Castro, E. (1998). Cosmological Deixis and Amerindian Perspectivism. *The Journal of the Royal Anthropological Institute*, 4(3), 469–488.

Walker, W. H. (2009). Warfare and the practice of supernatural agents. In A. E. Nielsen (Ed.), *Warfare in Cultural Context. Practice, Agency, and the Archaeology of Violence* (pp. 109–138). The University of Arizona Press.

Willerslev, R. (2007). *Soul hunters: Hunting, animism, and personhood among the Siberian Yukaghirs*. Berkeley, CA: University of California Press.

Znamenski, A. (2021). Mind in the cave: Archaeology meets shamanism. *Journal of Arctic Studies*, 4, 195–226.

Beneath the Military Horizon: Measuring Stone Age Hunter Weapon Point Technology at the Ecological Scale

Fredrik Lundström

The main controversies surrounding one of the most famous burials in Sweden, the Mesolithic Barum grave in Scania, revolves around two value imbued activities, hunting and conflict. Since the burial contains a slotted bone point, it was originally assumed that the grave contained a male with his hunting weapon. However, subsequent examinations revealed that the person buried was a woman (Sten et al., 2000). The notion of the person's social role as a hunter, hinging upon the body's relationship to the bone point, has since also come into question. Moreover, the prospect has been raised that the bone point instead indicates that the woman was a victim of inter-human violence, a conflict in which she was shot by the slotted bone point. In that aspect, the burial has been compared with another Mesolithic burial, the grave of a man from Stora Bjers, Gotland, Sweden (Hanlon and Nilsson, 2004). In that example, however, the violent action is less ambiguous since the point was fragmented and found lodged in the hip bone (Gejvall, 1979; Bornfalk Back, 2017; Günther et al., 2018). Regardless of interpretation, the Barum woman's relation to both hunting and conflict is crucial for the discussions surrounding it. Why is this topic ambiguous and difficult to address?

The challenge of interpreting hunting and conflict in cases such as the Barum woman and the Stora Bjers man does not stem from a lack of available material, interest or analytical techniques. Within Stone Age archaeology, no other weapon category exemplifies universalism and temporal depth better than the weapon point, the durable ends of weapon systems, that were once launched as projectiles or thrust as spears. (e.g., Knecht, 1997; Iovita & Sano, 2016; Shott 2020; Pétillon & Cattelain, 2022). Point trauma has been found on Mesolithic human bone and as evident by several works (e.g., Keeley, 1997; Chapman, 1999; Thorpe, 2003, 2005; Roksandic, 2004; Guilaine & Zammit, 2008; Schulting & Fibiger, 2012; Allen & Jones, 2014; Hutton Estrabrook, 2014; Heath, 2017), interest in Stone Age and hunter-gatherer conflict has grown in recent decades. Simultaneously, there has been a renewed interest in Stone Age weapon functionality and recent developments in geometric analysis, experimental archaeology and digital simulations (e.g., Iovita et al., 2016; Sholts et al., 2017; MacLeod, 2018; Lundström, 2019a; Salili-James et al., 2022) offer techniques that accurately and quantitively measure weapon point properties. Despite growing archaeological interest and new techniques, the study of weapon points as conflict implements is far from straightforward. From an archaeological perspective, two major challenges obstruct research development in this field.

First, identifying and defining Stone Age violence is particularly difficult. A lack of historical sources, fragmented archaeological remains and uncertainties about which circumstances of making contributed to the production of these remnants make warfare a problematic subject to address (Roksandic, 2004; Waller, 2017; Orschiedt, 2020). In addition, ethnography and ethnohistory reveal that certain violent activities in hunter-gatherer societies defy the modern military theoretical concepts researchers are equipped with. In fact, when first analysed from that perspective, these societies were described as lacking the institutions and the logic that a modern society associate with war, i.e., as having not passed the "military horizon" (Turney-High, 1949:21–38). Later, these were also envisioned as beyond the ethnographically known, that which exists beyond the "tribal zone" (Ferguson & Whitehead, 1992). Irrespective of how these societies have been labelled, it is evident that understanding war therein relates to questions of historicity, as well as historical, cultural and societal specificity, i.e., the historical processes and the specific practices behind the emergence of particular weapon points and violent phenomena. The confusion of the historical perspective in studies of non-Western societies is problematic and has been raised by both anthropologists (e.g., Ferguson & Whitehead, 2000, 1992:xii–xvii; Whitehead, 2000) and Stone Age archaeologists (e.g., Roksandic, 2004). The goal to address the cultural and societal specificity of warfare through the study of actual practice has also been raised by proponents of the "practice approach to war" (Nielsen and Walker, 2009). In fact, a quick review of primarily South American ethnographical material discloses cultural and societal specificity in the deluge of violent inter-human practices that modern military theory would find difficult to describe and define. Anthropological studies of hunter-gatherers and horticulturalists exemplify how much analysis is required to understand indigenous perspectives and knowledge. These perspectives often rely on dynamic ontogenetic processes that include both how humans interact with their environments and the implements they use (Rival, 1996, 2012; Fausto, 2007:507; González-Ruibal et al., 2011; Bechelany, 2019, for a non-Amazonian comparison see e.g., Evans-Pritchard, 1953). By standard scientific classification, although grounded in physical relations, the notions that emerge because of these processes have psychological, physiological or social aspects. Consequently, classification can be rooted in abilities, for example, "patience" and "accuracy" (Rival, 1996), psychophysiological states, such as "hot" and "cold" (Whitehead, 2002:92f) or low-energy weapon effects, for instance sound (Bechelany, 2019:12f). Such processes may also affect the aspects addressed here, the demarcation between hunting and warfare. Hence, activities may be defined by how they are carried out rather than what is killed (e.g., Rival, 1996, 2012; Fausto, 2007). Additionally, taxonomies may not depend on strong human–animal divisions (Rival, 1996; Solfeldt, this volume), non-humans may turn a hunting episode into conflict, by adopting a reciprocal role (Fausto, 2007:500ff.; cf. Kwon, 1998:119) and important targets may be immaterial (Solfeldt, this volume). Consequently, hunter-warrior behaviour and cognition can be related to weapon effects while military theoretical definitions and modern taxonomy may be a hindrance if the goal of a conflict archaeological research project is to understand the original social world through a fragmented archaeological material (cf. Roksandic, 2004; Waller, 2017; Orschiedt, 2020). Identifying and defining violence, conflict and warfare in Stone Age hunter-gatherer societies hence requires a readiness to relinquish familiar concepts from military theory, i.e., a readiness go beneath the *military horizon.*

Second, the study of weapon point functionality is a separate archaeological sub-field with a particular research history and distinct problems. In effect, identifying the role of weapon points in conflict or warfare relates to the broader challenge of identifying the functional aspects and possibilities of a weapon point and what weapon point morphological variation means from a functional perspective (cf. Iovita & Sano, 2016; Shott, 2020). From a conflict perspective, the functional aspects and specific properties of a weapon point are important since it is through the actual use of the point (i.e., its position in interactions) that acts can be linked to practices in a specific society. In absence of detailed evidence from use-wear, organic residues or find context, the properties of the weapon point, especially its material and its form, are what remain as sources for knowledge. Unlike a double-edged sword, a shield or a morning star, a weapon point cannot unambiguously be regarded as intended for human targets, i.e., for combat use (cf. Chapman, 1999). Instead, weapon points from hunter-gatherer societies can be assumed to be multi-functional (cf. Greaves, 1997) or, at the very least, be crafted based on diverse experiences. As such, they also provide valuable insights into hunting and subsistence strategies (e.g., studies in Peterkin et al., 1993; Knecht, 1997). Developing the analysis beyond ambiguous categories, i.e., identifying specialized war point types or differentiating aspects of war from hunting in weapon points remains a daunting task (cf. Choyke and Bartosiewicz, 2004; Darmangeat, 2019; Lundström, 2019b). Researchers have addressed the issue of war point specialization by using ethnohistorical or historical weapon point form analogies (e.g., Lowrey, 1999; Loendorf et al., 2015; Iversen, 2016) and levels of point standardization (Brill, 2014) as hypotheses. However, such approaches require material to test hypotheses against. Confidently interpreting the possible functions of archaeological point types is very difficult since there are no known universal war or hunting point types made from stone or organic material (Ellis, 1997; Nelson, 1997; Lundström, 2019b). There are ethnographical and historical indications (Ellis, 1997) that a war and hunting point type scheme is more common than other form taxonomies. However, due to representativity issues, especially an underrepresentation of some point types in the ethnographical material, the link between weapon point form variation and functionality has remained a largely unexplored topic (Shott, 2020:250f). It is unclear how different types of targets and activities affect the properties of a weapon and how those activities are perceived, performed and judged in relation to the properties of the weapon.

From a conflict perspective, the challenge of Stone Age weapon point archaeology is: If both Stone Age hunter violence and object classes are a priori indeterminate, how can warfare and conflict – concepts that require historicity, knowledge of actual practice and social relations, i.e., "other programmes of violence" (Armit et al., 2006) be approached through quantitative studies of weapon point properties? The thesis of this paper is that by turning to the "ecological scale", the epistemology and ontology that Ecological Psychology and Dynamic Systems Theory (EP DST) entails, such a project is conceivable. By using EP DST approaches to build models for weapon point research, the paper will reveal that prehistoric hunting, warfare and conflict may be illuminated through the exploratory and empirical research that quantitative studies offer and less related to preconceived classes of weapon points and violence.

The benefits of such an approach will be demonstrated in three steps. First, some basic concepts used by proponents of ecological approaches will be introduced and related to point property measurement techniques. Second, experimental approaches of EP DST to organism(human)-weapon-point-environment interaction is presented as potential principles for experimental archaeology. Finally, the example of the Northern Eurasian inset point will be used to concretize the argumentation.

Ecological Psychology and Dynamic Systems Theory (EP DST)

A quantitative study of weapon points properties in relation to unknown culturally specific concepts of violence and war requires consideration of physical, biological, physiological, psychological and sociological aspects. Furthermore, it is necessary to also address coordination between humans and their surroundings. Preferably, a suitable theoretical approach would combine as many of these prerequisites as possible. A framework that considers these criteria is *Ecological Psychology and (Complex) Dynamic Systems Theory* (EP DST). As implied by the name of the approach, EP DST has largely developed through operationalising the ecological psychology of James J. and Eleanor Gibson (Gibson, 1979). Since behavioural organisation is not regarded as centrally controlled in ecological psychology, the behavioural stability and regularity of an organism has come to be viewed as originating from the *dynamism* of the agent-environment system (cf. Warren, 2006). Hence, a general quality of EP DST research is that it is directed towards how behavioural patterns emerge from relational processes, specifically the dynamic coordination between organisms and their environments (Richardson et al., 2008; Chemero, 2009; Lobo et al., 2018; Turvey, 2018). The approaches entail studying the *informational connection* between organism and environment. Besides applying models from other disciplines, such as physics, the direction of this kind of research has involved an approach that integrates ecological psychology with ideas and models from other theoretical frameworks, such as anticipatory systems theory (Latash & Turvey, 1996; Turvey, 2018:16ff., 38ff., 408–418), robotics (Chemero, 2009: 17–44) and enactivism (e.g., Chemero, 2009:183–205; Baggs and Chemero, 2021). Above all, and as implied, modelling and quantitatively studying behaviour in the dynamic way, ecological psychologist envision has required a thorough integration of that theoretical frame with (complex) and dynamic systems theory. Subsequently, it is primarily through that avenue experimental researchers have quantitatively demonstrated emergent, lawful patterns between organism, task and environment (Haken et al., 1985; Kelso, 1994; Kugler et al., 1980; Kugler & Turvey, 1987; cf. Richardson et al., 2014; Warren, 2006). From a physics perspective EP DST is a research tradition that has come to develop "an ontology motivated by nature's *ecological scale*" (Turvey, 2018:341; cf. Smith, 1996; Richardson et al., 2008:167) rather than one motivated by atomic or cosmic scales (cf. Gibson, 1979:4ff.; Baggs & Chemero, 2021). Evidently, the ecological scale is the appropriate level of analysis for both weapon points and the organisms that use them and are targeted by them.

Given the influence of ecological psychology on archaeological and anthropological theory (e.g., Ingold, 2000, 2007; Knappett, 2004; Olsen, 2010; Young-Wolfe, 2015; Jung, 2020) perspectives similar to those found in EP DST have been attractive to archaeology. Furthermore, since EP DST physics is relational and relies on dynamic systems theory, it shares important aspects with relational archaeological schools of thought and those that rely on other dynamic systems theory philosophy (e.g., works inspired by DeLanda, 2016). Indeed, works by EP DST authors have been referenced by archaeologists and anthropologists. Particular EP DST concepts connected to dynamic touch (Turvey, 1996; Turvey & Carello, 2011) have been used in lithic studies with psychological approaches (Fedato et al., 2020; Silva-Gago et al., 2022) and in psychological archaeological studies (Wilson et al., 2016b) and archaeological artefact commentary (Wagman, 2002) by ecological psychologists. Also, embodied approaches to cognitive evolutionary archaeology sometimes reference EP DST scholars (e.g., Garofoli, 2019). However, the specific quality of EP DST approaches, namely the observation and quantification of information detection in organism-environment systems, in particular goal-oriented activities, could be further exploited in archaeology. I will try to demonstrate the benefits of an EP DST approach to illuminate the possible relation between weapon points and violence. This approach is advantageous since:

1. It offers a coherent quantitative approach to investigate weapon point property variation, covariation, hypothetical functional roles and emergent phenomena in human-weapon-point-environmental interaction.
2. It includes a research program for quantitative experiments with tools and sporting equipment that can offer guiding principles for weapon point experimental archaeology.

Relational Property Measurements

To demonstrate how organisms and environments affect the properties of an object, a chemical warfare agent (CWA) analogy will be presented as an example. Thereafter, an EP DST perspective to object properties that corroborates the analogy will be introduced. The example can be compared to and contrasted with the perspectives and analogies in De Landa (2016:68–74).

Historian Edmund Russell's *War and Nature. Fighting Humans and Insects with Chemicals from World War I to Silent Spring* (2001) traces the mid-20th century development of chemical warfare agents and insecticides. In the text, chemical agent properties are described in relation to their historical role. During World War I, industrially manufactured, aerially dispersed chemicals were used widely on the battlefield for the first time (Spiers, 2010:27). Their use prompted an arms race, a search for suitable chemical agents and methods of dispersal that continued throughout the 20th century. Russell (2001) outlines how the search for technological solutions to the challenges of chemical warfare developed in harmony with technical answers to pest control problems. Above all, chemical warfare agent research benefitted from entomology and physiological tests on insects (e.g., Russell, 2001:136, 180, 193). In his analysis, a largely non-lethal laboratory obscurity, chloropicrin, proved successful both on the battlefield and as a fumigant (2001:49, 81), the most lethal nerve agents were developed and synthesized as part of insecticide research (2001:87, 199), CWA and insecticide dispersal systems were interchangeable (2001:154, 167, 176ff.) and an insecticide (DDT), arguably played a more important strategical role than any CWAs in 20th century warfare (2001:233).

Hence, in Russel's text (2001), types are commonly produced and used in one activity, only to be transferred to another and delivery systems are often interchangeable. CWA properties depend on the size and anatomy of the organisms, as well as local and global environmental parameters such as wind, humidity and air-pressure. The deadliness of organophosphates made them undesirable as insectcides since uncontrolled dispersion, especially in confined environments, made the risks to humans too high. Instead, these were considered appropriate for chemical warfare. However, chloropicrin worked well both as CWA and fumigant but for different reasons. It was primarily not the physiological effects on humans that made it an agent of choice during World War I but its ability to penetrate gas masks and cause vomiting. DDT, on the other hand, was important for success in specific environments where insects were bearers of certain diseases. A CWA analogy to weapon points is suitable as introduction to EP DST perspectives. In that case, organisms and environments are explicit components of the analysis and all properties and measurements are relational. Properties not only specifically guide functional roles, they also explicitly depend on, for example, organismal scale, local environmental conditions, such as wind and humidity, as well as global forces like gravity. Bellow follows how such a perspective is outlined and motivated among EP DST researchers.

From the perspective of EP DST, measurable properties of a thing are impredicative (Turvey, 2018; cf. Rosen, 2012:429–436) and non-linear (Richardson et al., 2008:256f), i.e., they are defined by the entirety of the organism-environment interactions. The impredicativity of a thing can be explained using quantum mechanics as analogy (Turvey, 2018:54; cf. Gomatam, 1999; Barad, 2007:140). Accordingly, a thing does not have a pre-existing state (i.e., qualities outside of a system) and if one intends to measure its qualities the measurement becomes part of that system. This stance is common sense when applied to an action-focused description of reality: a property of an object only exists in relation to an instrument of measurement. Specifically, when a single property is revealed by a measurement, a particular relation must exist between the components involved. Despite appearing ominously relativistic, properties that manifest through these relations are not illusory but lawful (Turvey, 2018:338). In classical scientific experiments, certain properties may appear constant because these are not expressed or actualised in the specific experience of a living organism. Instead, properties are isolated and represented as attributes or predicates, for example, mass and experiments are designed to test how such metrics affect linear causal chains (Turvey 2018:70ff.). That requires both a hypothesis and that the predicates remain predicates throughout the experiments, i.e., all other variables are controlled (cf. Turvey 2018:34). From an EP DST perspective, such weapon point property data lacks a relation to the relevant spatiotemporal configuration, the dynamic environment that produced the archaeological context. A weapon point, although in isolation hard-assembled, is created to be part of a softly assembled system, like a human or a group of humans. In such a system, these can have surprisingly non-deterministic roles and be flexibly adapted to the circumstances of the complex and dynamic environment in which they are used. In EP DST approaches, recurring patterns, relevant to the original social environment may be revealed through dynamic, nonlinear models (Richardson et al., 2014). That there are underlying patterns in samples of weapon points is for example reflected in size clusters that indicate a relation between specimen clusters and a type of delivery system (e.g., Christenson, 1986; Hughes, 1998; Riede, 2009; Lombard, 2021). Preferably, what is revealed by such an approach is the original intrinsic measurement system, i.e., a physically proper match between delivery system and point that was perceived as appropriate by the original society. The property variation of a sample of archaeological weapon points can be mathematically modelled to suggest the behavioural organisation of the hunting and combat guided system the weapon points were parts of (cf. Richardson et al., 2014:258ff.). To reveal such properties in a dataset of points would involve testing the object's properties in relation to many different variables. Here, archaeological knowledge could be combined with available anatomical and environmental data, such as skin density and temperature, to replicate or simulate how variables covary or vary. Given that the environment is perceived directly, the perceptual variables archaeological replicas reveal in relation to simulated data would also have been like the ones perceived by the original wielders (cf. Gibson, 1979:126). EP DST studies can already demonstrate which intrinsic measurement systems are relevant in particular human–object relations, for example, how a combination of mass and form, rather than mass in isolation is what humans detect (Gibson, 1966:127ff; Amazeen & Turvey, 1996; Wagman et al., 2016) and how the suitability of certain archaeological objects can be evaluated from an EP DST perspective (Wilson et al., 2016b).

Figure 1: a) The properties of the isolated point are unknown to both researcher and original wielder *a priori* "measurement". b) properties are manifested to researcher and original wielders through different types of "measurements". c) the information the original wielder "measured" is approached by the researcher. AI images generated by Microsoft Designer.

A consequence of adopting the ecological scale, is that the researcher is put on equal footing with the warrior/hunter/maker, in relation to the isolated artefact (Figure 1). Like us, the original wielder of the weapon point did not *know* the properties of the isolated point. Rather, the wielder was aware of, could predict or identify point properties that manifested through interactions with environmental phenomena when accomplishing specific goals (cf. Gibson, 1966:273ff.). In a general sense, the original wielder "measured" impredicative weapon point properties that emerged in complex and dynamic environments and could develop them accordingly (cf. Barad, 2003). Consequently, EP DST approaches, offer ways through which the information the original wielder detected can begin to be revealed to the researcher.

EP DST Approaches as Principles for Experimental Archaeology

The most important benefit of approaching weapon points and violence from an EP DST perspective is that it includes the organism, the human body, as a frame of reference (Gibson, 1979:68; cf. Warren, 1984; Fajen et al., 2011). The anatomy and physiology of the humans who originally interacted with the weapon points, shared basic qualities with us. Thus, the human body has often been used as a point of departure for interpretation in archaeology (e.g., Hamilakis et al., 2002; Malafouris, 2004; Van Dyke, 2015; Jones, 2020). From, the perspective of modern military technology, for example, the CWA case above, the Stone Age world also fundamentally differed in such an embodied respect. Disregarding mere morphological dissimilarities, traditional hunting technology is produced in proximity to usage (e.g., Wiessner, 1983; González-Ruibal et al., 2011) and its handling requires biomechanical proficiency. Even though there are societies with stone and organic technology that rely on specialist or semi-specialists for the creation of objects (e.g., Apel, 2000), most societies with this kind of egalitarian access to raw materials, especially hunter-gatherer societies, do not. Hence, the form of most archaeological stone and organic weapon points are much more directly related to usage and the capacities of those who used them, there is a craft-activity (cf. Elliott, 2019) and body performance-weapon proximity, i.e., the relation entails a very different ontogenetic process. These issues can be addressed by experimental archaeology adopting principles that guide EP DST experiments.

By implementing EP DST methods, approaches and principles, experimental archaeology could introduce a new type of quantitative information: emergent patterns in human-(object)-environment-(task) relations. Here, teleology (task goals) constrains the experimental process rather than variable control, a design that should be understood against the background of how Gibsonian ideas have developed into an experimental program. As an adherent of what has been defined as American naturalism (Chemero, 2009:21), Gibson rejected the key premise of cognitivism, the idea of environmental objects being mediated, mentally represented and processed by sensory organs, the brain or other parts of the nervous system before being perceived. Instead, Gibson conceived perception as unmediated and direct. Hence, it is the structure of the environment, in relation to the properties, goals and needs of the organism that is at the core of perception, the revelation of possible avenues of action, i.e., affordances (Gibson, 1966:285, 1979:119–135). That re-orientation of natural meaning/*affordance*, from a secondary quality to an ontological entity has had consequences for which other entities can be considered objects of inquiry and has impacted studies both within and without of the ecological psychological tradition (cf Chong & Proctor, 2020). The ways in which the affordance concept can be operationalized (e.g., Cutting, 1982; Chemero & Turvey 2007; cf. Shaw et al., 2018) and practically applied (e.g., Chow et al., 2021) alludes to the new perspectives and methods this conceptual re-orientation brings about. This includes perspectives and methods that pertain to object studies as well. Due to perception being direct, they only way things can be perceived as they are is if information or energy patterns are *specific* (Gibson, 1966:186–286; 1979:39–135; Shaw, 1979; Michaels and Carello, 1981; Turvey et al., 1981; Turvey, 2018) to the source and as a consequence grounded in lawful relations (Turvey, 2013, 2018:30; cf. Millikan, 2000:217–237). By combining that perspective with physics, especially thermodynamics and dynamics systems theory, works by EP DST researchers have demonstrated that information in the physical form of lawful energy patterns can be used to explain organismal adjustment (Haken et al., 1985; Kugler & Turvey, 1987:64–105; Kelso, 1994). Hence, EP DST researchers have developed experimental principles that quantitatively reveal how organisms as humans are affected by environmental properties such as objects. These quantitative studies have already been applied to experiments that are analogous to projectile/weapon point archaeology. In fact, emergent patterns in organism-object relationships are studied, constitutes an entire research program within EP DST. Experimental objects include pendulums (Kugler and Turvey, 1987), rods (Turvey & Carello, 2011), balls (e.g., Wilson et al., 2016a; Nordbeck et al., 2019) bows and archery targets (Lee et al., 2012). Furthermore, not only is physical behavioural organisation studied in ecological psychology, phenomena that may be described as psychophysiological – such as the effect of physiological reinforcements (e.g., Turvey, 2018:21ff.) – functional goals affecting behaviour and perception (Turvey et al., 1999; Lee et al, 2012; Zhu et al., 2013) and physiological states (Lee et al., 2017) are explored by examining lawful organism-(object)-environment-(task) relations.

In relation to an archaeological artefact, the EP DST approaches therefore entails a theoretical possibility that emergent patterns in a weapon point interaction has a quantitative relationship to ontogenetic processes, abilities, low-energy effects and psychophysiological states. The logical outcome of the EP DST approaches is an experimental archaeology where projectile experiments include not only the weapons and targets as independent variables, but also the experimental human subjects (cf. Apel, 2006; Silva-Gago et al., 2022) and other non-conventional variables, for example, weather, sleep, dreams, physical status, time constraints and size relations between experimental subjects and physical objects. Furthermore, not only do EP DST inspired experiments offer a quantitative, embodied alternative to cognitive archaeological experiments, the EP DST principles could be reversed in the archaeological experiments. By varying organism-weapon point-environment configurations and directing the human subject with task constraints or towards a "desired future" (Bernstein, 1966, 1961; cf. Latash, 2015), experiments could reveal how objects are affected by the participants psychophysical properties, social relations and relation to other environmental parameters. Even though such a program is difficult to realise, it demonstrates the potential of the ecological scale. It is an approach that potentially can generate material that pertains to both physical and "less-physical", subtler weapon point properties. Through a program, where natural and cultural meaning is viewed as a continuum (cf. archaeological theory inspired by American pragmatism, see Baron, 2021, for a review, and Tsoraki et al., 2020, for a case relevant to this study), weapon point studies could contribute to an understanding of what constitutes the underlying social relations behind conflict and hunting practices in a chosen context.

Case: The Northern Eurasian Inset Point

An example where an EP DST approach may be adopted concerns the Northern Eurasian inset point, remains of which were found in both the Barum and the Stora Bjers burials discussed in the introduction. Inset points, for example, slotted bone points (Figure 2), were composite weapon points used from the late Paleolithic (c. 11000 cal BP) until the Late Mesolithic (c. 7400 cal BP) (Manninen et al., 2021).

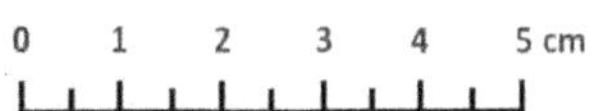

Figure 2: A stray find of a slotted bone point from Vellinge (Scania, Sweden) with some flint micro blades still attached. Swedish History Museum find 362392. Source: Eriksson, Thomas, Historiska museet/SHM (CC-BY 4.0). Edited by the author for the publication.

A brief overview of inset point literature reveals that to understand these as violent phenomena their other social roles cannot be ingnored and that the ecological scale is already an implicit way of addressing multiple roles of the points. An illustrative example is a study by Elston and Brantingham (2008) who have utilized Knecht's organic point experiments (1993, 1997) and Ellis' meta-ethnographical weapon point study (1997) to compare inset points with organic and stone points. In Elston and Brantingham's comparison, organic and stone point performance characteristics and situational use are listed. The lists contain descriptions that relate to impredicative properties since performance characteristics are "self-referenced", i.e., related to, for instance, weather, temperature, targets, other equipment, as well as specific multifactorial arrangements. Elston and Brantingham suggest that inset points were made to combine the best properties of organic and stone points in exchange for a time-consuming and skill demanding crafting process. According to them, inset points were preferred for tasks in specific situations where the costs of failure were high, for example, "when the prey is a key resource" or "when… a dangerous animal or human enemy [is] to be engaged at close quarters" (Elston and Brantingham, 2008:105). From that perspective, the ability of the inset points to penetrate and endure organic material and to damage tissue would have been suitable against dangerous and important animals, as well as the Stora Bjers man and Barum woman, if they were perceived as dangerous enemies or part of such a group. However, such a conclusion is obviously an oversimplification, a consequence of not considering other situational variables. In fact, it prematurely makes impredicative qualities predicates, i.e., situational results become universals. In this example, relatively high tissue penetration depth and more severe tissue displacement effects become "lethal" and better material strength becomes "durable". It also reflects the limitations of a weapon point analysis based on a binary classification, organic stone. Here, more detailed analyses could enable studies that look at minute property variation without making assumptions. Even with little prior knowledge of artefact usage, different object structures can be analysed and modelled with separate data analysis procedures and classification schemes. Distribution patterns revealed by these analyses could reflect parameters that originally were perceived as important. For the shape of a weapon point, that could, for example, be shaft size or shape, raw material structure or the conventions of a craft tradition (Lundström et al., 2023).

A few studies explore the implications of property variation in composite/inset points. One is Pétillon et al.'s (2011) pilot experiments with Magdalenian antler tips. These experiments indicate how several parameters affect functional variation, for example, cutting-edge length/bladelet numbers effect penetration depth, head bladelet shape affects penetrative ability and point-shaft form compatibility affects durability. In Pétillon et al. (2011) antler composite tips were mounted on dart shafts with a specific diameter and thrown with a spear-thrower at a deer carcass. Changing, for example, point raw materials from antler to bone, flint to quartz, shaft wood species, delivery system and targets to accommodate a Mesolithic setting, where properties would work equally effective, would require point shape and size adjustment. For example, if the wielder used a bow (as likely in the Mesolithic case) and if humans such as the Stora Bjers man and the Barum woman were common targets, points would have been either specifically adjusted or epiphenomenally suitable to support actions in such environments. The suitability of a weapon system for such actions can be assessed through static attributes such as size, shape, or performance characteristics within a dataset of representative weapon points. However, the form of a weapon point would also have been shaped by various external factors, including raw materials, craftsmanship, and contextual circumstances beyond the specific environment under study. For instance, while an arrowhead may have been designed for warfare, the experience of bow hunting certain types of prey could influence the conceptualization of a "war type." Conversely, features of a hunting point might reflect adaptations to specific types of armour used in a particular region.

A perspective on slotted bone point variation, where adaption, in combination with historical specificity and path-dependence is presented in Manninen et al. (2021). In the study, 17 new ^{14}C-dates slotted bone points are presented, and their wide spatiotemporal distribution is discussed. The authors conclude that because the history of the slotted bone points in Northern Eurasia encompassed varied environments, raw materials, technological organisations and cultural traditions, the sample indicates both situational solutions and path dependence. Adopting such an approach to the Stora Bjers and the Barum individuals, the "inter-human violence technology" therein could thus be analysed as both situational and dependent on historical processes. Hence, from a historical perspective, the impredicative properties at the ecological scale could be considered related to both the specific violent events and a wider set of social interactions outside of the specific environment of the buried individuals. These include both an extensive range of hunting episodes and craft processes accommodated to locally available raw materials and traditions. Simulations can reveal actual functional properties that relate to the original intrinsic measurement system at the ecological scale, for instance how well a specific weapon point, in a specific delivery system, at a specific velocity would penetrate a specific target. With modern digital techniques, it is possible to approach such properties in accurate proxies of original weapon points, for example by simulating 3D-modelled specimens in mechanical programs (Lundström, 2019a). If these points are simulated in collisions with sufficiently varied variables (e.g., shafts, velocities and targets), parameters that are specific to a group of artefacts regardless of, for example, variation in size, shape and material could be revealed and modelled mathematically. Furthermore, complimentary data procedures could be used to identify properties that correlate with certain environmental variables, such as those that would replicate targets, including those within interpersonal violence, such as human tissue or armour.

Weapon points rarely indicate behavioural patterns that emerge from more complex social relations. Recently, however, Jonuks et al. (2023) analysed a mimicry of an Early Mesolithic slotted bone point from Pärnu river, Estonia. The point lacked lithic insets, instead, these were carved out directly from the long bone and the object was in part covered in a red ochre/coniferous resin. The point also had a tip fracture characteristic of projectile use. Therefore, the authors conclude that the mimicked slotted bone point was used practically, while simultaneously being a bearer of extra meaning.

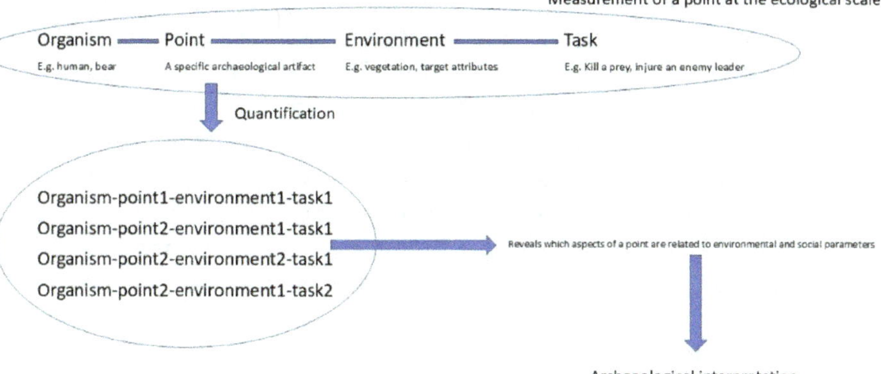

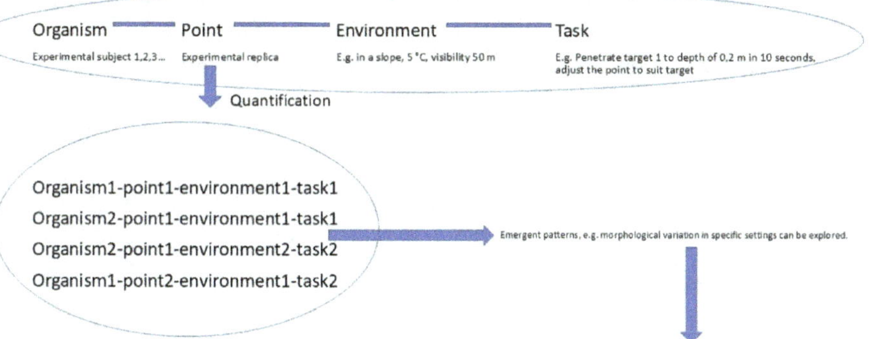

Figure 3: Archaeological models of weapon point measurements at the ecological scale. In these analyses, social relations are inserted through assigning environmental parameters and tasks, including those that may be related to conflict, for example, armour, palisades, non-lethal combat. The measurements can be done exclusively on archaeological data (a) or on data from archaeological experiments (b). The archaeological analyses can contribute information that relates to actual artefacts, while the experimental analyses can explore emergent patterns that relate to very specific organism-environment systems.

Without knowing the ontologies of these Early Mesolithic societies, it is difficult to appreciate how these mimicries and the slotted bone points from Stora Bjers and Barum were understood or appreciate all other social relationships that affected their form. Although a daunting task to explore, the ecological scale and EP DST offer a way to approach such objects through the "less-material", for example, psychophysiological patterns, via a theory that establishes a continuum to the physical, a continuum between the "cultural", "social" and "natural". By designing archaeological experiments in line with EP DST studies – specifically, by testing replicated weapon points with diverse human participants, environments, and task constraints – emergent behavioural patterns in human-weapon point-environment-task interactions can be explored. For example, researchers could examine whether a group of participants shows a tendency to craft points using a smaller or wider range of materials and colours when exposed to new environmental parameters or task constraints. Additionally, they could investigate how recorded sleep and dream patterns influence the execution of specific tasks involving particular objects. The behavioural patterns revealed through these analyses would open new interpretative possibilities for weapon point and conflict studies.

Conclusion

The functional role of a weapon point is important if warfare is to be viewed as a social or cultural phenomenon, given that it is through the practical role of the weapon point that it relates to both violence and other types of interaction. However, categorizing archaeological artefacts – and here specifically Mesolithic weapon points as warfare-related – is difficult since these could also have been used in other types of activities, especially violent activities that cannot be classified as war. Even with the advent of multiple precise measuring techniques and analytical protocols, there are no methods to relate the form and material of a particular point to a specific activity.

The study outlines the way Ecological Psychology and Dynamic Systems Theory has the potential to re-invigorate or re-socialize these long since silent weapon points (Figure 3). The approach quantitatively exploits that properties of a weapon point in both hunting and conflict depend on environmental and organismal relations, i.e., properties and emergent behavioural patterns can be related to specific human-weapon point-environment-task configurations. By extension, experimental archaeology can be designed with these principles. Such experiments would reveal what societal influences, psychophysiological states, experiences and anatomies and other environmental parameters could be related to a small hard-assembled component. The importance of such functional relations can be illuminated by the inset point remains that are associated with two Mesolithic persons who were possible victims of conflict, the Stora Bjers man and the Barum woman. Inset point research already reveal the importance of functional properties and environmental factors for such studies, but the role(s) of weapon points – and cases like Barum and Stora Bjers – could also be addressed by extending that work with EP DST approaches.

In general, Stone Age societies are also uniquely suitable objects of study for such an approach. In such societies, the locus between organism, environment, weapon and craft is particularly direct and dynamic since craft-usage and body performance-object proximity transcends generations and societal boundaries. Hence, studying and replicating the conditions of these kinds of societies could provide information about the ways in which humans relate to weapon technology that other studies cannot. Therein lies the well of information, the deep exploration space that Stone Age technology could bestow students of war.

Acknowledgements

I sincerely appreciate the reviewers for their insightful and valuable comments. Additionally, I would like to extend special thanks to Rolf Warming and Andrew Jones for their support of this study and the path it has led me on, both of which have become increasingly significant to my broader research.

References

Allen, M. W. & Jones, T. L. (Eds.), (2014). *Violence and Warfare among Hunter-Gatherers*. Walnut Creek.

Amazeen, E. L. & Turvey, M. T. (1996). Weight perception and the haptic size-weight illusion are functions of the inertia tensor. *J Exp Psychol Hum Percept Perform, 22*, 213–232. https://doi.org/10.1037//0096-1523.22.1.213

Apel, J. (2006). Skill and Experimental Archaeology. In J. Apel & K. Knutsson, (Eds.), *Skilled Production and Social Reproduction: Aspects of Traditional Stone-Tool Technologies* (pp. 207–218). Societas Archaeologica Upsaliensis, Uppsala.

Apel, J. (2000). From Marginalisation to Specialisation: Scandinavian Flint-Dagger Production During the Second Wave of Neolithisation. In K. Knutsson (Ed.), *Coast to Coast – Arrival.* Coast-to-Coast books 10. Uppsala.

Armit, I. Knüsel, C., Robb, J. & Schulting, R. (2006). Warfare and Violence in Prehistoric Europe: an Introduction. *Journal of Conflict Archaeology, 2*, 1–11. https://doi.org/10.1163/157407706778942349

Baggs, E. & Chemero, A. (2021). Radical embodiment in two directions. *Synthese, 198*, 2175–2190. https://doi.org/10.1007/s11229-018-02020-9

Barad, K. (2007). *Meeting the Universe Halfway: Quantum Physics and the Entanglement of Matter and Meaning.* Duke University Press, Durham, NC.

Barad, K. (2003). Posthumanist Performativity: Toward an Understanding of How Matter Comes to Matter. *Signs, 28*, 801–831. https://doi.org/10.1086/345321

Baron, J. P. (2021). Peirce and Archaeology: Recent Approaches. *Annual Review of Anthropology, 50*, 187–202. https://doi.org/10.1146/annurev-anthro-101819-110112

Bechelany, F. C. (2019). Hunting paths in the Amazon: technics and onto-genesis among the Panará. *Vibrant, Virtual Braz. Anthr., 16*, e16500. https://doi.org/10.1590/1809-43412019v16d500

Bernstein, N. A. (1966). *Essays on the Physiology of Movements and Physiology of Activity.* Moscow.

Bernstein, N. A. (1961). Urgent problems of the physiology of activity. *Problems of Cybernetics, 6*, 101–160.

Bornfalk Back, A. (2017). Gotland f.Kr. – en konfliktarkeologisk odyssé. In P. Wallin & H. Martinsson-Wallin (eds.), *Arkeologi på Gotland 2. Tillbakablickar och nya rön* (pp. 33–42). Department of Archaeology, Ancient History and Conservation: Uppsala University.

Brill, J. M. (2014). The Technology of Violence and Cultural Evolution in the Santa Barbara Channel Region. In *Violence and Warfare among Hunter-Gatherers* (1st ed.). Routledge.

Chapman, J. (1999). The origins of warfare in the prehistory of Central and Eastern Europe. In J. Carman & A. Harding, (Eds.), *Ancient Warfare: Archaeological Perspectives* (pp. 101–142). Stroud: Sutton.

Chemero, A. (2009). *Radical Embodied Cognitive Science.* The MIT Press.

Chong, I. & Proctor, R. W. (2020). On the Evolution of a Radical Concept: Affordances According to Gibson and Their Subsequent Use and Development. *Perspect Psychol Sci, 15*, 117–132. https://doi.org/10.1177/1745691619868207

Chow, J. Y., Davids, K., Button, C. & Renshaw, I. (2021). *Nonlinear Pedagogy in Skill Acquisition: An Introduction* (2nd ed.). Routledge, New York.

Choyke, A. & Bartosiewicz, L. (2004). Osseous Projectile Points from the Swiss Neolithic: Taphonomy, Typology and Function. In M. Roksandic (Ed.), *Violent Interactions in the Mesolithic, Evidence and Meaning* (pp. 75–88). Archaeopress: Oxford.

Christenson, A. L. (1986). Projectile Point Size and Projectile Aerodynamics: An Exploratory Study. *Plains Anthropologist, 31*, 109–128. https://doi.org/10.1080/2052546.1986.11909324

Cutting, J. E. (1982). Two Ecological Perspectives: Gibson vs. Shaw and Turvey. *The American Journal of Psychology, 95*, 199–222. https://doi.org/10.23 07/1422466

Darmangeat, C. (2019). Vanished Wars of Australia: the Archeological Invisibility of Aboriginal Collective Conflicts. *J Archaeol Method Theory, 26*, 1556–1590. https://doi.org/10.1007/s10816-019-09418-w

DeLanda, M. (2016). *Assemblage Theory*. Edinburgh University Press.

Elliott, B. (2019). Craft Theory in Prehistory: Case Studies from the Mesolithic of Britain and Ireland. *Proceedings of the Prehistoric Society, 85*, 161–176. https://doi.org/10.1017/ppr.2019.9

Ellis, C. J. (1997). Factors Influencing the Use of Stone Projectile Tips. In H. Knecht (Ed.), *Projectile Technology, Interdisciplinary Contributions to Archaeology* (pp. 37–74). Springer US, Boston, MA.

Elston, R. G. & Brantingham, P. J. (2008). Microlithic Technology in Northern Asia: A Risk-Minimizing Strategy of the Late Paleolithic and Early Holocene. In *Archaeological Papers of the American Anthropological Association* (pp. 103–116). https://doi.org/10.1525/ap3a.2002.12.1.103

Fajen, B. R., Diaz, G. & Cramer, C. (2011). Reconsidering the role of movement in perceiving action-scaled affordances. *Hum Mov Sci, 30*, 504–533. https://doi.org/10.1016/j.humov.2010.07.016

Fausto, C. (2007). Feasting on People: Eating Animals and Humans in Amazonia. *Current Anthropology, 48*, 497–530. https://doi.org/10.1086/518298

Fedato, A., Silva-Gago, M., Terradillos-Bernal, M., Alonso-Alcalde, R., Martín-Guerra, E. & Bruner, E. (2020). Hand morphometrics, electrodermal activity, and stone tools haptic perception. *Am J Hum Biol, 32*, e23370. https://doi.org/10.1002/ajhb.23370

Ferguson, B. R. & Whitehead, N. L. (2000). Preface of the second printing. In *War in the Tribal Zone. Expanding States and Indigenous Warfare*. School of American Research Press, Santa Fe.

Ferguson, B. R. & Whitehead, N. L. (Eds.) (1992). *War in the Tribal Zone. Expanding States and Indigenous Warfare*. School of American Research Press, Santa Fe.

Garofoli, D. (2019). Embodied Cognition and the Archaeology of Mind: A Radical Reassessment. In A. M. Prentiss (Ed.), *Handbook of Evolutionary Research in Archaeology* (pp. 379–405). Springer International Publishing, Cham.

Gejvall, N. (1979). *Sammandrag av den anatomisk-osteologiska undersökningen av skelettet från Stora Bjärsi Stenkyrka.* Arkeologi på Gotland. Gotlandica 14.

Gibson, J. (1966). *The Senses Considered as Perceptual Systems* (Revised ed.). Praeger, Westport, Conn.

Gibson, J. J. (1979). *The Ecological Approach to Visual Perception* (Classic ed.). New York.

Gomatam, R. V. (1999). Quantum Theory and the Observation Problem. *Journal of Consciousness Studies, 6,* 11–12.

González-Ruibal, A., Hernando, A. & Politis, G. (2011). Ontology of the self and material culture: Arrow-making among the Awá hunter-gatherers (Brazil). *Journal of Anthropological Archaeology – J ANTHROPOL ARCHAEOL, 30,* 1–16. https://doi.org/10.1016/j.jaa.2010.10.001

Greaves, R. D. (1997). Hunting and Multifunctional Use of Bows and Arrows. In H. Knecht (Ed.), *Projectile Technology* (pp. 287–320). Springer US, Boston, MA. https://doi.org/10.1007/978-1-4899-1851-2_12

Guilaine, J. & Zammit, J. (2008). *The Origins of War: Violence in Prehistory* (pp. 1–282). Wiley-Blackwell.

Günther, T., Malmström, H., Svensson, E. M., Omrak, A., Sánchez-Quinto, F., Kılınç, G. M., Krzewińska, M., Eriksson, G., Fraser, M., Edlund, H., Munters, A .R., Coutinho, A., Simões, L. G., Vicente, M., Sjölander, A., Sellevold, B. J., Jørgensen, R., Claes, P., Shriver, M. D., Valdiosera, C., Netea, M. G., Apel, J., Lidén, K., Skar, B., Storå, J., Götherström, A. & Jakobsson, M. (2018). Population genomics of Mesolithic Scandinavia: Investigating early postglacial migration routes and high-latitude adaptation. *PLOS Biology, 16.* https://doi.org/10.1371/journal.pbio.2003703

Haken, H., Kelso, J. A. & Bunz, H. (1985). A theoretical model of phase transitions in human hand movements. *Biol Cybern, 51,* 347–356. https://doi.org/10.1007/BF00336922

Hamilakis, Y., Pluciennik, M., Tarlow, S. (Eds.) (2002). *Thinking through the Body.* Springer US, Boston, MA.

Hanlon, C. Nilsson, B. (2004). The ever-changing Barum grave. *Fornvännen, 99,* 225–230.

Heath, J. M. (2017). *Warfare in Neolithic Europe: An Archaeological and Anthropological Analysis.* Pen and Sword Archaeology, Barnsley.

Hughes, S. S. (1998). Getting to the point: Evolutionary change in prehistoric weaponry. *J Archaeol Method Theory, 5,* 345–408. https://doi.org/10.1007/BF02428421

Hutton Estrabrook, V. (2014). Violence and Warfare in the European Mesolithic and Paleolithic. In M. W. Allen, & T. L. Jones, (Eds.), *Violence and Warfare among Hunter-Gatherers*. Routledge: New York.

Ingold, T. (2007). Materials against materiality. *Archaeological Dialogues, 14*, 1–16. https://doi.org/10.1017/S1380203807002127

Ingold, T. (2000). *The Perception of the Environment: Essays on Livelihood, Dwelling and Skill*. Routledge, London.

Iovita, R. & Sano, K. (Eds.) (2016). *Multidisciplinary Approaches to the Study of Stone Age Weaponry, Vertebrate Paleobiology and Paleoanthropology*. Springer Netherlands, Dordrecht.

Iovita, R., Schönekeß, H., Gaudzinski-Windheuser, S. & Jäger, F. (2016). Identifying Weapon Delivery Systems Using Macrofracture Analysis and Fracture Propagation Velocity: A Controlled Experiment. In R. Iovita & K. Sano (Eds.), *Multidisciplinary Approaches to the Study of Stone Age Weaponry, Vertebrate Paleobiology and Paleoanthropology* (pp. 13–27). Springer Netherlands, Dordrecht,.

Iversen, R. (2016). Arrowheads as indicators of interpersonal violence and group identity among the Neolithic Pitted Ware hunters of southwestern Scandinavia. *Journal of Anthropological Archaeology, 44*, 69–86. https://doi.org/10.1016/j.jaa.2016.09.004

Jones, A. (2020). An archaeology of affect: art, ontology and the carved stone balls of Neolithic Britain. *Journal of Archaeological Method and Theory, 27*, 545–560. https://doi.org/10.1007/s10816-020-09473-8

Jonuks, T., Chen, S., Kriiska, A., Oras, E., Presslee, S., Ueni, A. (2023). Stone Age imitation of a slotted bone point from Pärnu River (south-western Estonia). *Estonian Journal of Archaeology, 27*, 54–79.

Jung, M. (2020). Klassifikation, Typologie, Affordanzbestimmung und Funktionalitätsrekonstruktion. Verfahren zur Ordnung von Objekten am Beispiel bronzezeitlicher Waffen. *Praehistorische Zeitschrift, 95*, 606–628. https://doi.org/10.1515/pz-2020-0026

Keeley, L. H. (1997). *War Before Civilization: The Myth of the Peaceful Savage* (Illustrated ed.). Oxford University Press, New York.

Kelso, J. A. S. (1994). The informational character of self-organized coordination dynamics. *Human Movement Science, 13*, 393–413. https://doi.org/10.1016/0167-9457(94)90047-7

Knappett, C. (2004). The affordances of things: a post-Gibsonian perspective on the …. In E. DeMarrais, E. Gosden & C. Renfrew (Eds.), *Rethinking Materiality: The Engagement of Mind with the Material World* (pp. 43–51). McDonald institute for archaeological research: Oxford.

Knecht, H. (Ed.) (1997). *Projectile Technology, Interdisciplinary Contributions to Archaeology*. Springer US, Boston, MA. https://doi.org/10.1007/978-1-4899-1851-2

Knecht, H. (1993). Early Upper Paleolithic Approaches to Bone and Antler Projectile Technology. In G. L. Peterkin, H. M. Bricker & P. Mellars (Eds.), *Hunting and Animal Exploitation in the Later Paleolithic and Mesolithic of Eurasia* (pp. 33–47). American Anthropological Association. Arlington.

Kugler, P. N., Scott Kelso, J. A. & Turvey, M. T. (1980). On the Concept of Coordinative Structures as Dissipative Structures: I. Theoretical Lines of Convergence. In G. E. Stelmach & J. Requin (Eds.), *Advances in Psychology, Tutorials in Motor Behavior* (pp. 3–47). North-Holland.

Kugler, P. N. & Turvey, M. T. (1987). *Information, natural law, and the self-assembly of rhythmic movement.* Lawrence Erlbaum Associates, Inc, Hillsdale, NJ, US.

Kwon, H. (1998). The Saddle and the Sledge: Hunting as Comparative Narrative in Siberia and Beyond. *The Journal of the Royal Anthropological Institute, 4*, 115–127. https://doi.org/10.2307/3034431

Latash, M. L., (2015). Bernstein's 'Desired Future' and Physics of Human Movement. In M. Nadin (Ed.), *Cognitive Systems Monographs* (pp. 287–299). Springer International Publishing, Cham. https://doi.org/10.1007/978-3-319-19446-2_16

Latash, M. L. & Turvey, M. T. (Eds.) (1996). *Dexterity and Its Development* (1st ed.) Psychology Press.

Lee, Y., Lee, S., Carello, C. & Turvey, M. (2012). An Archer's Perceived Form Scales the "Hitableness" of Archery Targets. *Journal of experimental psychology. Human perception and performance, 38*, 1125–1131. https://doi.org/10.1037/a0029036

Lee, Y., Shaw, R. E. & Jin, Z. (2017). Gih (Qi): Beyond Affordance. *Frontiers in Psychology, 8.* https://doi.org/10.3389/fpsyg.2017.00556

Lobo, L., Heras-Escribano, M. & Travieso, D. (2018). The History and Philosophy of Ecological Psychology. *Frontiers in Psychology, 9.*

Loendorf, C., Simon, L., Dybowski, D., Woodson, M. K., Plumlee, R. S., Tiedens, S. & Withrow, M. (2015). Warfare and big game hunting: flaked-stone projectile points along the middle Gila River in Arizona. *Antiquity, 89*, 940–953. https://doi.org/10.15184/aqy.2015.28

Lombard, M. (2021). Variation in hunting weaponry for more than 300,000 years: A tip cross-sectional area study of Middle Stone Age points from southern Africa. *Quaternary Science Reviews, 264*, 107021. https://doi.org/10.1016/j.quascirev.2021.107021

Lowrey, N. S. (1999). An Ethnoarchaeological Inquiry into the Functional Relationship between Projectile Point and Armor Technologies of the Northwest Coast. *North American Archaeologist, 20*, 47–73. https://doi.org/10.2190/YG4T-2YG1-0NWP-HTCA

Lundström, F. (2019a). Secrets of the Spearhead: Developing Continuum Mechanical Simulations and Organic Residue Analysis for the Study of Scandinavian Flint Spearhead Functionality (Master thesis). Department of Archaeology and Classical Studies: Stockholm University

Lundström, F. (2019b). Mellan strid och jakt: Stenspetsar som utgångspunkt för analyser av effekt och handlingsmönster. *Forntid längs Ostkusten 5: Blankaholmsseminariet.*

Lundström, F., MacLeod, N., Isaksson, S., Glykou, A. (2023). The harpoon stands yonder: Shape variation and functional constraints in Mesolithic complex weapon points from the circum-Baltic Sea area. *Journal of Archaeological Science: Reports, 51,* 104148. https://doi.org/10.1016/j.jasrep.2023.104148

MacLeod, N. (2018). The quantitative assessment of archaeological artifact groups: Beyond geometric morphometrics. *Quaternary Science Reviews, 201,* 319–348. https://doi.org/10.1016/j.quascirev.2018.08.024

Malafouris, L. (2004). The Cognitive Basis of Material Engagement: Where Brain, Body and Culture Conflate. In *Rethinking Materiality: The Engagement of Mind with the Material World* (pp. 53–62). McDonald institute for archaeological research: Oxford.

Manninen, M. A., Asheichyk, V., Jonuks, T., Kriiska, A., Osipowicz, G., Sorokin, A. N., Vashanau, A., Riede, F. & Persson, P. (2021). Using Radiocarbon Dates and Tool Design Principles to Assess the Role of Composite Slotted Bone Tool Technology at the Intersection of Adaptation and Culture-History. *J Archaeol Method Theory, 28,* 845–870. https://doi.org/10.1007/s10816-021-09517-7

Michaels, C. F., Carello, C. (1981). *An Essay about Substance Concepts, Cambridge Studies in Philosophy.* Cambridge University Press, Cambridge. https://doi.org/10.1017/CBO9780511613296

Nelson, M. C. (1997). Projectile Points. In H. Knecht (Ed.), *Projectile Technology, Interdisciplinary Contributions to Archaeology* (pp. 371–384). Springer US, Boston, MA.

Nielsen, A. E. & Walker, W. H. (2009). Introduction: The Archaeology of War in Practice. In A. E. Nielsen & W. H. Walker (Eds.), *Warfare in Cultural Context: Practice, Agency, and the Archaeology of Violence* (pp. 1–14). The University of Arizona Press.

Nordbeck, P. C., Soter, L. K., Viklund, J. S., Beckmann, E. A., Kallen, R. W., Chemero, A. P. & Richardson, M. J. (2019). Effects of task constraint on action dynamics. *Cognitive Systems Research, 55,* 192–204. https://doi.org/10.1016/j.cogsys.2019.02.003

Olsen, B., (2010). *In Defense of Things: Archaeology and the Ontology of Objects.* AltaMira Press.

Orschiedt, J. (2020). Violence in Palaeolithic and Mesolithic Hunter-Gatherer Communities. In G. G. Fagan, L. Fibiger, M. Hudson & M. Trundle (Eds.), *The Cambridge World History of Violence: Volume 1: The Prehistoric and Ancient Worlds, The Cambridge World History of Violence* (pp. 58–78). Cambridge University Press, Cambridge.

Peterkin, G. L., Bricker, H. M. & Mellars, P. (1993). Hunting and Animal Exploitation in the Later Palaeolithic and Mesolithic of Eurasia. American Anthropological Association.

Pétillon, J.-M., Bignon, O., Bodu, P., Cattelain, P., Debout, G., Langlais, M., Laroulandie, V., Plisson, H. & Valentin, B. (2011). Hard core and cutting edge: experimental manufacture and use of Magdalenian composite projectile tips. *Journal of Archaeological Science, 38,* 1266–1283. https://doi.org/10.1016/j.jas.2011.01.002

Pétillon, J.-M., Cattelain, P., 2022. An Introduction to the Experimental Study of Prehistoric Projectile Points. In M. Mărgărit & A. Boroneanț (Eds.), *Recreating Artefacts and Ancient Skills: From Experiment to Interpretation* (pp. 143–162). Cetatea de scaun.

Richardson, M. J., Dale, R. & Marsh, K. L. (2014). Complex dynamical systems in social and personality psychology: Theory, modeling, and analysis. In H. T. Reis & C. M. Judd, *Handbook of Research Methods in Social and Personality Psychology* (2nd ed., pp. 253–282). Cambridge University Press, New York, NY, US.

Richardson, M. J., Shockley, K., Fajen, B. R., Riley, M. A. & Turvey, M. T. (2008). Ecological Psychology: Six Principles for an Embodied–Embedded Approach to Behavior. In P. Calvo & A. Gomila (Eds.), *Handbook of Cognitive Science, Perspectives on Cognitive Science* (pp. 159–187). Elsevier, San Diego. https://doi.org/10.1016/B978-0-08-046616-3.00009-8

Riede, F. (2009). The Loss and Re-Introduction of Bow-and-Arrow Technology: A Case Study from the Northern European Late Paleolithic. *Lithic Technology, 34,* 27–45. https://doi.org/10.1080/01977261.2009.11721072.

Rival, L. (2012). The materiality of life: Revisiting the anthropology of nature in Amazonia. *Indiana, 29,* 127–143.

Rival, L. (1996). Blowpipes and spears: the social significance of Huaorani technological choices. In P. Descola & G. Pálsson (Eds.), *Nature and Society: Anthropological Perspectives* (pp. 145–164). London: Routledge. DOI: 10.4324/9780203451069-16.

Roksandic, M. (2004). Introduction: how violent was the Mesolithic, or is there a common pattern of violent interactions specific to sedentary hunter-gatherers? In M. Roksandic (Ed.), *Violent Interactions in the Mesolithic: Evidence and Meaning* (pp. 1–7). Archaeopress, BAR International Series Volume 1237, Oxford. https://doi.org/10.30861/9781841715964.

Rosen, R. (2012). *Anticipatory Systems, IFSR International Series on Systems Science and Engineering.* Springer, New York, NY.

Russell, E. (2001). *War and Nature: Fighting Humans and Insects with Chemicals from World War I to Silent Spring.* Cambridge University Press.

Salili-James, A., Mackay, A., Rodriguez-Alvarez, E., Rodriguez-Perez, D., Mannack, T., Rawlings, T.A., Palmer, A. R., Todd, J., Riutta, T. E., Macinnis-Ng, C., Han, Z., Davies, M., Thorpe, Z., Marsland, S. & Leroi, A. M. (2022). Classifying organisms and artefacts by their outline shapes. *Journal of The Royal Society Interface, 19.* https://doi.org/10.1098/rsif.2022.0493

Schulting, R. J. & Fibiger, L. (Eds.) (2012). *Sticks, Stones, and Broken Bones: Neolithic Violence in a European Perspective.* Oxford University Press.

Shaw, M. T. & Robert, T. (1979). The Primacy of Perceiving: An Ecological Reformulation of Perception for Understanding Memory. In L.-G. Nilsson (Ed.), *Perspectives on Memory Research* (PLE:Memory). Psychology Press.

Sholts, S. B., Gingerich, J. A. M., Schlager, S., Stanford, D. J. & Wärmländer, S. K. T. S. (2017). Tracing social interactions in Pleistocene North America via 3D model analysis of stone tool asymmetry. *PLOS One, 12,* e0179933. https://doi.org/10.1371/journal.pone.0179933

Shott, M. J. (2020). Toward a Theory of the Point. In Groucutt, H. S. (Ed.), *Culture History and Convergent Evolution: Can We Detect Populations in Prehistory? Vertebrate Paleobiology and Paleoanthropology* (pp. 245–259). Springer International Publishing, Cham. https://doi.org/10.1007/978-3-030-46126-3_12

Silva-Gago, M., Fedato, A., Terradillos-Bernal, M., Alonso-Alcalde, R., Martín-Guerra, E. & Bruner, E. (2022). Not a matter of shape: The influence of tool characteristics on electrodermal activity in response to haptic exploration of Lower Palaeolithic tools. *American Journal of Human Biology, 34,* e23612. https://doi.org/10.1002/ajhb.23612

Smith, B. C. (1996). *On the Origin of Objects.* The MIT Press.

Spiers, E. M. (2010). *A History of Chemical and Biological Weapons* (1st ed.) Reaktion Books, London.

Sten, S., Ahlström, T., Alexandersen, V., Borrman, H., Christensen, E., Ekenman, I., Kloboucek, J., Königsson, L.-K., Possnert, G. & Ragnesten, U. (2000). Barumkvinnan: nya forskningsrön. *Fornvännen, 95,* 73–87.

Thorpe, I. J. N. (2005). The ancient origins of warfare and violence. In M. Parker Pearson & I. J. N. Thorpe (Eds.), *Warfare, Violence and Slavery in Prehistory: Proceedings of a Prehistoric Society Conference at Sheffield University* (pp. 1–18). BAR Publishing, Oxford.

Thorpe, I. J. N. (2003). Anthropology, Archaeology, and the Origin of Warfare. *World Archaeology, 35,* 145–165.

Tsoraki, C., Barton, H., Crellin, R. J. & Harris, O. J. T. (2020). Making marks meaningful: new materialism and the microwear assemblage. *World Archaeology, 52,* 484–502. https://doi.org/10.1080/00438243.2021.1898462

Turney-High, H. H. (1949). *Primitive war, its practice and concepts*. University of South Caroline Press, Columbia.

Turvey, M. (2013). Ecological Perspective on Perception-Action: What Kind of Science Does It Entail? Action Science: Foundations of An Emerging Discipline. In W. Prinz, M. Beisert & A. Herwig (Eds.), *Action Science: Foundations of an Emerging Discipline* (pp. 139–170). https://doi.org/10.7551/mitpress/9780262018555.003.0006

Turvey, M. T. (2018). *Lectures on Perception: An Ecological Perspective* (1st ed.) Routledge, New York London.

Turvey, M. T. (1996). Dynamic touch. *American Psychologist, 51*, 1134–1152. https://doi.org/10.1037/0003-066X.51.11.1134

Turvey, M. T. & Carello, C. (2011). Obtaining information by dynamic (effortful) touching. *Philos Trans R Soc Lond B Biol Sci, 366*, 3123–3132. https://doi.org/10.1098/rstb.2011.0159

Turvey, M. T., Shaw, R., Reed, E. S. & Mace, W. (1981). Ecological laws of perceiving and acting: In reply to Fodor and Pylyshyn (1981). *Cognition, 9*, 237–304. https://doi.org/10.1016/0010-0277(81)90002-0

Turvey, M. T., Shockley, K. & Carello, C. (1999). Affordance, proper function, and the physical basis of perceived heaviness. *Cognition, 73*, B17–B26. https://doi.org/10.1016/S0010-0277(99)00050-5

Van Dyke, R. M. (Ed.) (2015). *Practicing Materiality*. University of Arizona Press, Tuscon.

Wagman, J. B., Caputo, S. E. & Stoffregen, T. A. (2016). Hierarchical nesting of affordances in a tool use task. *Journal of Experimental Psychology: Human Perception and Performance, 42*, 1627–1642. https://doi.org/10.1037/xhp0000251

Waller, A. (2017). Violence and group cohesion in the European Mesolithic. *The Post Hole, 49*.

Warren, W. H. (2006). The dynamics of perception and action. *Psychol Rev, 113*, 358–389. https://doi.org/10.1037/0033-295X.113.2.358

Warren, W. H. (1984). Perceiving affordances: Visual guidance of stair climbing. *Journal of Experimental Psychology: Human Perception and Performance, 10*, 683–703. https://doi.org/10.1037/0096-1523.10.5.683

Whitehead, N. L. (2002). *Dark Shamans: Kanaimà and the Poetics of Violent Death*. Duke University Press, Durham, NC.

Whitehead, N. L. (2000). A History of Research on Warfare in Anthropology – Reply to Keith Otterbein. *American Anthropologist, 102*, 834–837.

Wiessner, P. (1983). Style and Social Information in Kalahari San Projectile Points. *American Antiquity, 48*, 253–276. https://doi.org/10.2307/280450

Wilson, A. D., Weightman, A., Bingham, G. P. & Zhu, Q. (2016a). Using task dynamics to quantify the affordances of throwing for long distance and accuracy. *Journal of Experimental Psychology: Human Perception and Performance, 42*, 965–981. https://doi.org/10.1037/xhp0000199

Wilson, A. D., Zhu, Q., Barham, L., Stanistreet, I. & Bingham, G. P. (2016b). A Dynamical Analysis of the Suitability of Prehistoric Spheroids from the Cave of Hearths as Thrown Projectiles. *Sci Rep*, *6*, 30614. https://doi.org/10.1038/srep30614

Young-Wolfe, H. (2015). Phenomenology and Monumentality in the Late Archaic of Peru. In R. M. Van Dyke (Ed.), *Practising Materiality*. University of Arizona Press, Tuscon.

Zhu, Q., Shockley, K., Riley, M. A., Tolston, M. T. & Bingham, G. P. (2013). Felt heaviness is used to perceive the affordance for throwing but rotational inertia does not affect either. *Exp Brain Res*, *224*, 221–231. https://doi.org/10.1007/s00221-012-3301-7

On Conflict and Cooperation: Dimensions of Warfare during the Nordic Bronze Age

Christian Horn & Barry Molloy

In the tension between opposing philosophical beliefs about the ancient world – whether it was inhabited by Hobbesian archetypes ensuring primitive life was nasty, brutish, and short or Rousseauian visions of noble savages – anthropology increasingly lands firmly in between these extremes (Vandkilde, 2003). Interpersonal violence, often extreme forms wiping out entire communities, was a recurring feature but this took place within often sophisticated cultural systems. Violent individuals – often warriors – were commonly well-equipped, highly skilled and a recurring feature of societies for millennia, such that their activities need to be read as falling within the parameters of how society was expected to function. That is, activities ranging across homicide, mass-killings and war were recurring phenomena that rendered the avoidance, mitigation, or de-escalation of them part of the very fabric of societies. For this reason, we may predict that the more complex the organisation of violence itself became, the more complex the social frameworks within which it was organised, morally and politically legitimised, and ultimately resolved.

The existence of armed conflict during the Nordic Bronze Age (1800–1700 BC) is now accepted as a facet of prehistoric life by most researchers, and different scales of conflict having been discussed in recent years ranging from interpersonal violence to open field battles with perhaps thousands of participants (Terberger et al., 2018; Jantzen et al., 2011). However, violent conflict is still marginalised in archaeological discourses on how Bronze Age societies functioned routinely, being relegated to a disruption that rarely exceeds a "blip" on the perceived timeline of social relationships or in other words it is seen as an irrational pathology (see Warming, this volume). It is viewed primarily as a destructive social force that killed anonymous persons or families and perhaps destroyed intercommunal ties. But these deaths and loss of connections would have had major real-time consequences in the past and so we must take the leap and presume that groups sought to manage violence for personal as much as political purposes.

While the destructive nature of raiding and other forms of warfare cannot be denied, this contribution seeks to explore how such practices could also foster local and even regional cooperation. The data includes bronze weaponry and depictions of warriors in rock art. Incorporating this wealth of data, we can additionally suggest that previous models have underappreciated the prevalence of small-scale warfare practices such as raiding. Such practices may have led to a permanently shifting and changing network of conflict and cooperation which was a major contributing factor to the outward cultural homogeneity of the Nordic Bronze Age that we perceive today.

Background

The Nordic Bronze Age (NordicBA) is known for its rich material culture including roughly 20,000 sites at which metalwork has been discovered. This includes c. 4,000 swords, 1,500 spears, 2,000 daggers, and 4,000 axes, or c. 11,500 objects that we see in use in on warriors in rock art. The images engraved into bedrock panels that inform us about these weapons are another defining feature of the time. Revealing their relative importance in society, more than 20,000 boats and more than 5,000 human depictions are known.

Based on these material and pictorial data, a dominant model for the Nordic Bronze Age identifies complex, decentralised social formations which have often been likened to chiefdoms (Earle, 2002; Ling et al., 2018b; Kristiansen, 2010; Nordenborg Myhre, 2004). Alternative models that embrace the patchy nature of archaeological data for reconstructing power networks in the hands of specific people envisage that power was distributed throughout different networks in society. An influential paper by Bruck and Fontijn (2013) argued that power was situational and distributed, so even if we cannot ultimately attribute political power to individuals, we can identify the myriad contexts in which it was articulated. This includes the cross-referencing of different forms of power, which in our case might include the use of weapons during violent events but also the regulation, de-escalation, place making or rehabilitative acts surrounding the deposition of those weapons thereafter (Fontijn, 2005; Horn, 2011). In either (non-exclusive) scenario, the person of the warrior remains a fulcrum for any model that views weapons as being socially empowered and empowering. In anthropology the polar positions of those that marginalise the importance of war and those that valorise it – respectively the doves and hawks in Otterbein's parlance (2004; 2009) – are increasingly being bridged by exploration of the social management of violence alongside and as part of studies on combat and warfare as arenas of action. In Bronze Age studies, by shifting our focus towards the venues where power was enacted or portrayed through the medium of weapons, we begin to follow suit and close the gap between archaeological positions that arguably mirror Hobbes' and Rousseau's ostensibly irreconcilable visions of violence in pre-state societies (Vandkilde, 2003). Roberts (2013) explores this in further detail in a Bronze Age context by emphasising an epistemological gap between archaeologists specialised in the study of material objects, metalwork in particular, who frequently engage with the theme of warfare and those that specialise in landscapes and settlements who more rarely consider it a force shaping the material record. The chaos and unpredictability of war was corralled and managed through sophisticated social controls and conventions, and so the capacity for conflict to boil over into random (reactive/anger), managed (premeditated/planned) or mandated (punitive/judicial) violence remained a constant.

Conflict

There is a rich array of sources that demonstrate that war-related violence took place in the Nordic Bronze Age, fulfilling most of the evidentiary criteria set out by Wileman (2009). We can now begin to better evaluate the different scales of conflict and warfare, its social organisation, and the impact on local societies' organisation, ideology, and networks of contact. Nonetheless, important avenues of research remain underdeveloped, for example how war related psychological development of individuals, cognitive development of people collectively, or the formation of conflict-related identities from individuals through to whole societies. In this short review, we focus on the richness of the available evidence.

Art

While Scandinavian rock art went through many social and ideological filters and depicts some otherworldly aspects, like human figures with two heads and wings, it is by now commonly agreed that the material culture and the depicted processes are based on real-life experiences by those who carved and their societies (Horn, 2018; Ling & Cornell, 2010; Skoglund et al., 2022). Thus, we can assume some reflections of reality in the depictions of weaponry and its uses. A limited number of scenes appear to depict swords being used in acts of fighting and killing (Figure 1), for example, on panels at Fossum and Brastad (Toreld, 2012; Ling & Bertilsson, 2017). The interpretation of these scenes is not straightforward, engendering debate about how they should be read, ranging from the depicting of the moment of killing (Horn, 2019) to portraying symbolic or ritual postures mimicking acts of killing (Harding, 2007:116–117; Nordbladh, 1989). The latter perspectives are in tension with recent readings that demonstrate how rock art can be read as supporting narratives and elements of heroic tales (Ranta, 2016; Skoglund et al., 2022; Ranta et al., 2019; Horn, 2022). A parallel for this interpretation is found in the reading of violent scenes on near-contemporary glyptic art in the Aegean as being extracts from oral tales or replicating specific known actions/events. This is most clearly demonstrated through the identical scenes rendered on the Battle in the Glen ring from Mycenae and the Combat Agate from Pylos (Kramer-Hadjos, 2023). In these Aegean scenes, the acts of killing are depicted as are individuals apparently slain through the combat actions depicted (Molloy 2008, 2024) In both the Aegean and NordicBA conventions, to capture the imagination of an audience, images appear to deliberately depict the moment just before something definitive, like the killing of a hero or a villain.

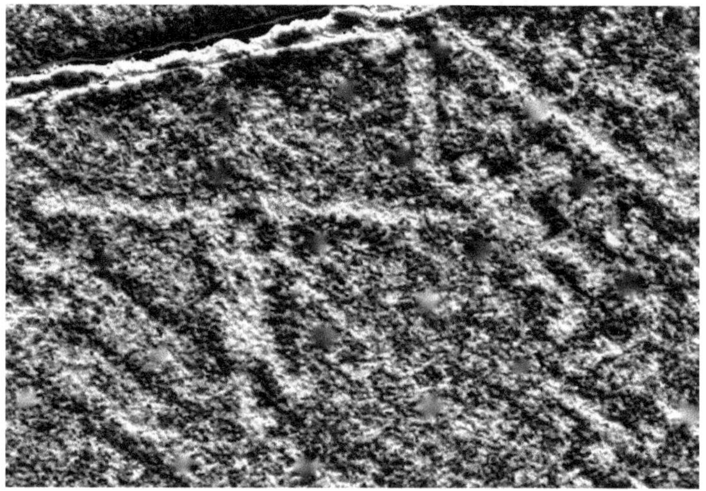

Figure 1: A spear fighter killing a warrior with a sword, club or axe in Brastad (617), Bohuslän, Sweden. Visualisation of a laser scan by Ellen Meijer using Topography Visualisation Toolbox (https://tvt.dh.gu.se/) with increased contrast (Original: https://shfa.dh.gu.se/image/133561).

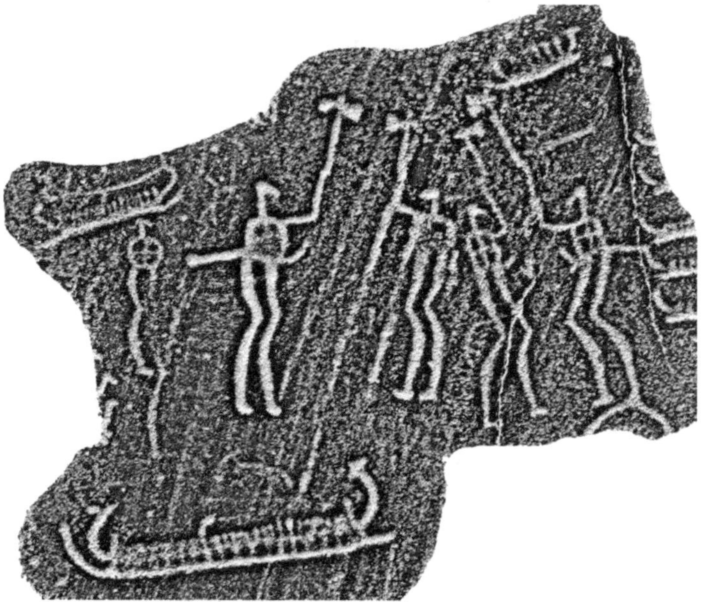

Figure 2: Four warriors with sheathed swords engaged in combat using axes in Aspeberget, Tanum (12:1), Bohuslän, Sweden. Visualisation of a laser scan by Ellen Meijer using Topography Visualisation Toolbox (https://tvt.dh.gu.se/) with increased contrast (Original: https://shfa.dh.gu.se/image/131841).

This maintains the suspense because the image does not give away the conclusion, but preserves a moment of uncertainty, a cliffhanger, in which the possibilities are still endless (Horn, 2022). This effectively means that rock art fighting scenes testify to the existence of real combat regardless of whether the killing itself was depicted.

Weaponry

While we will focus primarily on the bronze weapons, we begin by drawing attention to the high quantities of flint weapons including daggers, arrowheads and spears used in the Early BA (Apel, 2001; Sarauw, 2007; Goldhammer, 2015). These weapons were widely distributed in the Nordic world, as were the 11,500 metal weapons introduced above. As a signifier of rank and status, swords soon displaced all other items as the primary feature of material and symbolic value in high-status burials (Felding et al., 2020). They are also the weapon type most associated with human figures in rock art (Horn, 2019). Notably, swords are commonly depicted in their sheaths in rock art scenes, with spears and axes depicted being wielded or fought with (Nordbladh, 1989), such as on the famous panels in Vitlycke and Aspeberget (Figure 2).

The potential large-scale nature of violence during the Early NordicBA is supported by use-wear studies on bronze weaponry. Kristiansen (1984) was an early advocate of this method in the study of metalwork, followed by Bridgford (1997) on Irish BA swords, Molloy on Irish and Aegean swords, shields and spears (Molloy, 2006; 2017), Hermann and colleagues on British weapons (Hermann et al., 2020), and a renewed focus on Nordic weapons in the 21st century (Kristiansen, 2002; Horn, 2013; Horn & Karck, 2019). These data demonstrate unequivocally that swords were used in combat and that maintenance (removal of edge damage, resharpening) substantially reduced the size of many Nordic blades recorded in detail. Kristiansen's (1984; 2002) original argument that organic-hilted swords dated 1700–1500 BC were used for combat and metal-hilted swords were symbols of upper echelons of society, and less exposed to combat wear, was important for drawing attention to potentially variable biographies of ostensibly similar objects, though later studies do not support a strict division as metal-hilted swords also exhibited severe combat marks (Horn, 2013; Horn & Karck, 2019). It is difficult to translate wear damage to frequency or intensity of use on specific occasions, but taken on average, it suggests that blade-on-blade combat was employed regularly in combat styles and that such combat was particularly intense while the use of defensive weapons, such as shields, may not have been common. This latter point would be consistent with the rock art evidence.

The Period I evidence demonstrates that gaining status may have been closely linked to combat skills that related to violent and potentially lethal (as opposed to sports-like or symbolic) bloodshed. Interestingly, emerging evidence, like the development of specialised weaponry (halberds, battle axes, etc.) and their potential association with specific individuals even in collective burials, high frequency of lethal and other traumata, fortifications, etc., strongly suggests that this relationship between excelling in violence and social status was not a development of the Bronze Age but may be a continuation of earlier Neolithic traditions (4000–1700 BC). While in the Neolithic the emergent warrior ideal and image was less explicitly visually formulated than in the Bronze Age, it is increasingly likely that immense violence was a feature of this period that continued into the Bronze Age (Christensen, 2004; Fibiger et al., 2023; Horn, 2021; Sarauw, 2007; Schulting, 2013; Schultrich, 2021; Tornberg, 2022).

Bioarchaeology

Evidence of trauma on human bones is one of the clearest and indisputable markers of interpersonal violence, particularly when it can be attributed to weapons (Downing & Fibiger, 2017; Strong & Fibiger, 2023). The context of that violence, however, is not always clear and the issue can be compounded when the dead include non-combatants. The evidence for large combat forces taking the field in the Bronze Age has been demonstrated through the discovery of a battlefield at Tollense dated 1300–1250 BC. Over 100 individuals have been identified with a demographic overwhelmingly biased towards young to middle-aged adult males (Brinker et al., 2014; Uhlig et al., 2019). Based on contextual data and other evidence, the research team leading this investigation project maintain that more than 2,000 individuals were involved in the battle (Lidke et al., 2019). The large-scale violence that people during the Bronze Age were capable left undeniable proof with the discovery of the battlefield in the Tollense valley (Jantzen et al., 2011). These are astounding numbers considering demographic reconstruction, for example, from Denmark that estimate the total living population in Period II–III to be 220,000–330,000 people. That means 0.61–0.91 % of the entire population living over a span of 400 years would have participated in the battle.

Traces of smaller-scale conflicts are also well documented. The mass grave in Sund (Norway) contained the bones of at least 22 individuals of both sexes and spanning a wide age-range, including children, that had been brutally killed. The bioarchaeological study suggested that the deceased likely belonged to a lower stratum of society and were perhaps slaves that had suffered illness and starvation during their lives. The location of injuries suggests they were killed while fleeing their attackers (Fyllingen, 2003; Fyllingen, 2006).

Individual burials with evidence of perimortem trauma have been made throughout the Nordic area. An approximately 50-year-old man buried c. 1600–1500 BC in a stone cist in Over-Vindinge, Denmark had a spear tip stuck in his pelvis (Kjær, 1912; Vandkilde, 2011). A 30-year-old man discovered in Wiligard, NW Germany had been killed by a sword blow to the head in c.1500–1400 BC (Lidke & Piek, 1999). At the end of the Early Bronze Age a malnourished man was beheaded with a sharp blade and buried in Kråkerøy, Norway (Fyllingen, 2003; Holck, 1987). One male individual from Søborg, Denmark, dated to the Middle Bronze Age, is assumed to have been killed by a shot in the throat with an arrow (Bergerbrant, 2008). There are fewer bioarchaeological instances of perimortem violence during the Late Bronze Age (1100–550 BC) due to the practice of cremating the dead. One exception is the individual from Granhammar, Sweden, which had been killed c. 800 BC, perhaps aboard a boat, by several blows from a bladed implement, an axe, for example, to the head before being dumped into a shallow body of seawater (Lindström, 2009).

Scales of Conflict

Though the dataset is small, the bioarchaeological record provides some insights into attitudes to violence and scales of violence in the Bronze Age. The finds from Sund inform us about a pattern of group violence that led to the killing of many people in a single act, whether they be slaves, households or communities, was known in Scandinavia; mirroring a phenomenon detected widely across Europe during the Neolithic and Bronze Age (Novak et al., 2021; Schroeder et al., 2019; Szeverényi & Kiss, 2018; Meyer et al., 2014). Deaths of individuals ranged from respectful treatment, presumably by their own social group, to apparently unceremonious disposal into the water. The Granhammer individual has been interpreted as a murder victim (Lindström, 2009) whereas the Kråkerøy man may have been executed (Holck, 1987). In societies preceding the rule of law, it is plausible that such killings could mitigate or avoid wider-spread violence to avoid blood-feuds, for example. It remains plausible that the Granhammer individual was a combatant, because the "tools" used to infer a craftsperson identity, i.e., axes, could equally well have been used as weapons (see Figure 2).

These individuals exhibiting trauma may represent acts ranging from homicide to war, something the bioarchaeological data alone cannot address. The Tollense battlefield data has been a major advance, as it demonstrates large armies could be mustered in set circumstances. Extrapolating from this evidence for large armed forces in the Bronze Age demands reconsideration of other archaeological data. The most significant case is fortifications because they had regularly been considered too large for small forces to defend, but with larger forces now probable, their design can be seen as a general reflection of the size of armed forces planned to defend them, inferring that forces well into the hundreds, if not thousands when violence escalated to a multi-community or polity scale, would not have been unusual. In the end, as in other periods, a purpose of violent acts may not have been to excessively harm the enemy but to subdue them for the purpose of imposing hegemonic relations between communities or for the enslavement of defeated groups. This latter practice would, if successful, leave few if any archaeological traces but it may be hinted at in the evidence from both settlement structure and rock art, as set out in recent studies (Mikkelsen, 2020; Ling et al., 2018b; Horn et al., 2024).

We know what we do not know

While our evidence for the frequency, intensity, duration, and extent (spatially, demographically at risk) remains negligible, our improved understanding in recent years of the scales and social venues for the conduct and commemoration of violence is significant. Revisiting Kristiansen's argument for stratification of combatants, it is plausible that we are only identifying the upper echelons of warriors who were in possession of elaborate metal weapons and that these were the same self-aggrandising 'heroes' depicted in rock art (Figures 1–2). Though it is spatially and socially distant, it is evident from Bronze Age Linear B tablets in Greece that there was a hierarchy amongst those expected to fight, from those we may broadly consider conscripts to those enfranchised with power and command through central political authorities (Shelmerdine, 2024). While stratification remains more elusive in the Nordic context, there are some hints. The battlefield site of Tollense revealed the use of wooden clubs and the frequent use of bows – objects that either do not survive with frequency or can be problematic to tie to interpersonal violence if found in other contexts. Indeed, they suggest there might be entire weapon categories that we miss or underestimate their relative abundance in prehistoric times because of issues of preservation and interpretation, as well as their low status in Bronze Age society (Jantzen et al., 2011).

As blade-on-blade contact was damaging and thus to be avoided (as evident from the nature of use-wear traces), it is reasonable that not all combat actions led to visible wear on weapons (Horn & Holstein, 2017; Hermann et al., 2020; Gentile & van Gijn, 2019; Molloy, 2017). Weapons could have been recycled rather than deposited, and in fact significantly more weapons may have been produced than survive archaeologically (Molloy & Mödlinger, 2020).

Linear B records from Knossos in Crete indicate that in the fourteenth century BC, tens of swords were being dispensed at once from the palatial administration there (Molloy, 2012; Georganas & Kvapil 2024; Shelmerdine 2024). The exceptional preservation at

Tollense was not a product of the exceptional nature of the event, but rather of the depositional, preservation and recovery conditions (systematic excavation). The find from Sund was preserved due to the care taken to bury the deceased. As informative as the two cases are, their exceptional preservation reminds us that if the dead lie where they fell, in most cases battlefields and massacres simply disappear. From ethnographic studies, we know that it was common practice for the defeated deceased to be left intentionally exposed or unburied (Redmond, 1994). Furthermore, not all injuries are deadly which does not mean that combat was not serious, and as Tollense demonstrates, even those seriously injured in previous fights re-engaged (Brinker et al., 2014). The number of individuals at Tollense that evidently died in the battle but reveal no traces of perimortem trauma is a reminder that soft tissue is commonly a preferential target in armed combat, such as the major arteries, tendons, muscles, or organs. Debilitating injuries, whether fatal or not, may leave no material traces (Walker, 2001; Möckli 2011; Nerlich et al., 2009).

Taken the discussed evidence together, we can confidently say that we miss much of prehistoric warfare and violence, not only because of the nature of the archaeological evidence, but also due to other factors. For example, not every deadly injury leaves a trace. This exacerbates the fragmentary nature of our record. Thus, we know that we miss much in terms of number of weapons in use which is even worse if we consider that there may have been plenty of weapons made from easily perishable materials. This is something to be mindful about going forward.

Beyond War: Intra- and Inter-Group Cooperation in the Bronze Age

The "checklist" approach to identifying evidence for past events of a violent nature and then the methodological and/or theoretical tools that extrapolate from these to model warfare have a chain of inference that is subject to critique at each stage. Simply put, proving there was warfare in prehistory and defining how it was impactful on societies is a major challenge. This challenge is increased because it usually begins from an intellectually defensive position, whereby it is pushing back against an argument of silence (Molloy, 2024). That "argument" takes the form of dominant social discussions about the nature of prehistoric society in which warfare is either ignored as being formative and influential, or relegated to instances of crises where things went wrong. A consequence of this marginalisation is that this limits how we understand the mechanisms through which power was performed and perceived in prehistory. Political economies, status or identity categorisation/hierarchies and ritual practices are all phenomena in which power is articulated. Each of these is present in the causes, practice, and outcomes of warfare. Conversely, bronze tools of war were integral to each of the above, from the distribution of bronze to the deposition of weapons at boundaries like rivers. The burden of proof placed on warfare studies is disproportionate and in no small part the argument of silence resulting from this emerges from a right-minded attitude whereby our abhorrence of, and aversion to, violence in our lives translates into a colonised prehistoric world in which those values are imposed. Should the same burden of proof be placed on the study of ritual and religion or economics as arenas of power and interaction, we would have a very different view of this period in many parts of Europe. However, from the very earliest written myths and histories of all parts of Europe, war was both commemorated and elevated to a powerful force shaping social worlds, for example, the writings of Homer and Herodotus or the poems Beowulf and the Tain Bo Cuailgne.

Concerning ethnographic evidence, while the archaeological evidence for peace and peace-making has yet to be collected and critically reviewed, we can assume that all human societies are placed on a spectrum between relatively non-violent and peaceful, and relatively aggressive and warring (Sponsel, 1996). We would posit, therefore, that if we switch the burden of proof to demonstrating the prevalence of non-violent conflict resolution mechanisms – or a perpetual peace – then we may find a harder case still to objectively present (See Fry, 2007:50–64; Sponsel, 1996; Otterbein, 2004; 2009). Sponsel is quite open in acknowledging that there are only *relatively* non-violent and peaceful" (Sponsel, 1996:95; emphasis in the original) societies. Our point is not to infer war was a routine occurrence, but rather the permanent threat of war required ongoing investment in resources such as metal for weapons, training for combatants, fortification of centres and patrolling of boundaries. The threat of war also required social means to avert it, for example, through diplomacy. Transgressions in turn must have been dealt with through myriad judicial tools at the disposal of pre-rule-of-law societies to defuse the threat of war. Power and potential force were important tools to maintain the relative peace and thereby avoid war, and these required cooperation within and between groups. Ironically, cooperation can be conducted with violence and warfare in mind, and even for the purpose of achieving war aims. Weapons avert war but reveal the potential for conflict as being ever present – it is important to retain this divide, because the latter may be ever present, but the former is a state of affairs at the far end of a spectrum that moves from peace to violence. We look then to some of the pieces of evidence that reveal insights from the Nordic Bronze Age.

Archaeological evidence for alliances

Apart from, for example, guest friendship (Kaul, 2017), alliances are a social institution in which two or more groups cooperate peacefully. This has been discussed in the light of archaeological evidence. Kristiansen and Suchowska-Ducke (2015), for example, trace a vast network of connectivity during the sixteenth and fourteenth centuries BC based on different forms of spacer plates, ox hide ingots, rock art, Late Helladic pottery, and octagonal hilted as well as straight flange hilted swords. They see two large networks, a Nordic/Tumulus Culture network and a Mycenaean/western Mediterranean network as being tightly interlinked through alliances which also caused the rapid spread of such types (see also Iacono, 2020). Cavazzuti et al. (2022) make a compelling case for the spread of Urnfield mortuary practices from the Carpathian Basin to surrounding areas as reflecting a network centred on shared ideologies and homophily spanning parts of Central Europe. Vandkilde's (2014; 2016) position that the Carpathian Basin was a trans-cultural crossroad connecting northern and southern Europe bridges both perspectives and is reinforced by recent research on metal networks and settlement systems during these centuries (Ling et al., 2014; Gavranović et al., 2022; Molloy et al., 2023a, 2023b).

The relevance of this for our discussion is that displaced material is commonly seen as the outcome of trade interaction. That is, people willingly cooperate to ensure resources move through myriad regions in this continental scale network. This model leaves little space for the appropriation of resources through force (e.g., raids) or aggressive diplomacy (e.g., hegemonic subjugation of neighbours) (Olausson, 1988; Horn, 2018). Recent discussions in Mediterranean archaeology have emphasised the potential importance of piracy and freebooting (Hitchcock & Maeir, 2014; Jung, 2009; Cline, 2021; Emanuel, 2018; Molloy, 2016; but see Knapp, 2018). Ling et al. (2018b) have extended this discussion to Nordic Europe, exploring what they define as a maritime mode of production whereby raiding was a staple activity, commonly involving ship crews. Hitchcock and Maeir (2014) emphasise how piracy provided an alternative mechanism for community building and inter-group relations outside of the acts of raiding and violence.

A paradigm of co-operative economic interaction in this region is the Uluburun shipwreck (1400–1300 BC) with its vast cargo of copper, tin and countless other commodities from different parts of the Mediterranean (Pulak, 1998). However, so vast and diverse is the cargo on this single boat that it finds no parallels in the documented gift exchange inventories of the Egyptian and Hittite courts – some come close, but this is the single largest mention or discovery of copper. The unusual situation is intensified by the choice to place such great wealth in a single boat – placing all of the eggs in one basket. We propose an alternative reading of this cargo: it represents wealth gathered in a single location, whether for redistribution either by one of the major empires or the wealth of a single city state. A comparatively small raiding party may have been ill-prepared to have come across such large a bounty, having therefore to concentrate their voluminous plunder in one boat. Returning to our focus on cooperation and the argument for conflict relating to cooperation and community building, the weapons on board come from the Balkans, Italy, Greece, and the Levantine coast. That may fit the bill for Hitchcock and Maeir's vision of multi-ethnic groups assembling for short term raids. In the established view, that network would extend into the East Mediterranean ports visited on the Uluburun's route. Whether we view these weapons as markers for guards or raiders, they reveal that vast networks existed in which warriors from disparate areas would meet, engage, and cooperate in mutual endeavours.

Cooperation and alliances in the NordicBA

The Uluburun wreck – both scenarios – is an indication that alliances and co-operation can be identified ranging across the local and regional scale; something we can now consider in light of the Nordic data. Ling et al.'s (2018b) "maritime mode of production" model is predicated on small bands or confederacies of bands working together both aboard ship and in fighting. The model requires conceptual differences between home and affiliated groups (not to be attacked) and target groups. Targets in turn needed to be measured in terms of their vulnerability in the short-term (the attack) and long-term (potential for reprisal attacks). With this, we can turn towards Nordic evidence. We begin building our case based on hoards of metal weapons recovered.

Many large hoards of weaponry have been discovered in Scandinavia. This includes the hoards from Torsted (40 spears, 7 axes; Figure 3a), Smørumøvre (60+ spears, 94+ axes), Ostenfeld (33 axes), Glasin (24 spears), Svenes (20 spears), and Dystrup (8 swords; Figure 3b). The average crew on rock art boats indicated by simple lines is six to seven during the Early Bronze Age (Ling, 2014). However, from engravings like in Valeby (Bottna 43:1) where the strokes visualising the crew were accompanied by a double row of cup marks, we can understand that we are looking at a simplified side-on view requiring us to double the numbers for each side of the boat, resulting in crews of 12 to 14 (Figure 4). Meller (2017) has argued that certain hoards comprising weapons alone may be indicative, to an extent, of the size of warbands.

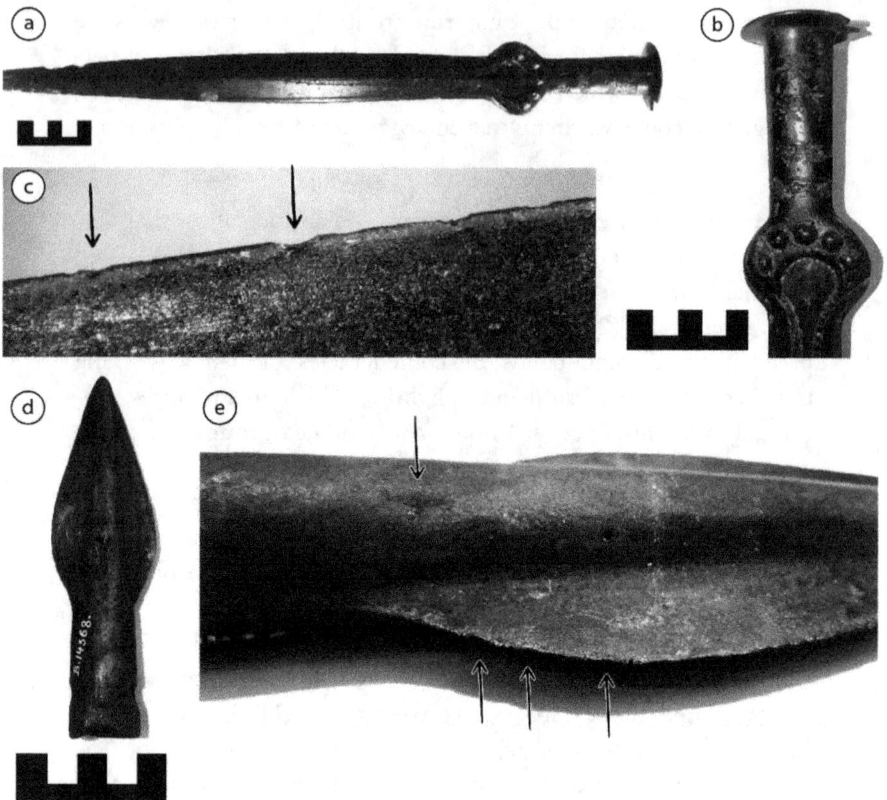

Figure 3: One of the swords from Dystrup (Museum Grenaa B17619): a. overview, b. hilt, c. combat damage (indentations) along the cutting edge (magnification x60); one spearhead from Torsted (National Museum of Denmark B14368): d. overview; e. combat damage (indentations) along the cutting edge and on the socket (blowmark).

Taking this concept loosely, Torsted represents around three ship crews, Smørumøvre represents 7–11 ship crews (individuals may have possessed both a spear and axe), Ostenfeld represents 2–3 crews, Glasin and Svenes 1–2 crews and Dystrup 1 to 8 crews. In the latter case, the estimate is based on an argument (Kristiansen, 2014) that leaders only wielded – perhaps full-hilted – swords in these crews, others used axes and spears.

Figure 4: Boat carving with a double row of cupmarks above the strokes indicating crew members located in Bottna, Bohuslän, Sweden. In total 28 crew are indicated in this case which is higher than the average number depicted (Ling, 2014). Photo: Vitlycke Museum (original: https://shfa.dh.gu.se/image/121850).

Looking to the weights, using the limited metric data from these hoards (Wincentz Rasmussen & Boas, 2006; Aner & Kersten, 1973–2017), but cognisant of the fact that many were deposited in an already diminished state (resharpened) or subsequently lost weight (taphonomic degradation/corrosion), allows for some further insights. It is possible to estimate the pattern of bronze consumption revealed by the weapons from these hoards broadly as follows: a typical axe-head weighed c. 200–250 g, a typical spearhead weighed c. 150–200 g, and a sword of the type deposited in Dystrup weighed c. 400 g. Each therefore represents many kilos of tin-copper alloy.

To produce the swords from Dystrup c. 3,200 g of bronze would have been needed, and for the objects in Torsted between 7,400 and 9,750 grams. According to the most recent estimates of about three tons of bronze entering the Nordic sphere annually, it has been calculated a typical farm had perhaps 100–150 g of new stock available each year on average (Earle et al., 2015; Rassmann, 2010). We may assume that wealthier farms had as much as 1 kg of new bronze per annum if we follow that model. In purely logistical terms, this means that to produce the swords of the Dystrup hoard an individual farm would have to dedicate over three years' worth of their newly acquired metal (working with the annual average model), or between seven to ten years' worth of metal to make the spears and axes deposited together in the Torsted hoard. This draw on resources could leave farms vulnerable to shortages and without the means to replace lost tools or weapons. While this is only a model, it gives a sense of the local-scale economic trade-offs for dedicating metal that would ulti- mately be "stored" for longer durations in the form of weapons. Thus, it can be assumed that several farms co-operated in the production of these objects. The findings in Dystrup perhaps support this because it is generally assumed that swords were the status signifiers of local chiefs or free farmers (Kristiansen, 2002; Bunnefeld, 2018). Thus, it is unlikely that a single farm possessed or required eight swords, instead we would argue they were produced for the leaders of several farms or communities. The risk of losing weapons through the death or capture of their wielders during wars conducted away from home meant that investing metal in weapons was risky. New weaponry would have to be produced, should conflict escalate, forcing farmsteads to compro- mise on other potential uses of their metal stock.

Perhaps three to four farms collaborated to produce the eight Dystrup swords, which would have been an investment of about one year's worth of metal. The same is true if seven to ten farms collabo- rated to produce the weapons of the Torsted hoard. If we conclude that each of the swords in Dystrup belonged to an individual leader of a farmstead then they would have to invest their supply of just under half a year. For the Torsted spears and axes, 14 to 20 communities would have to back the production with half a year's metal supply.

The similarities in the weapons from the Torsted and the Dystrup hoards suggest that the objects could conceivably have been made using the same template or mould, which means that all were pro- duced in the same community following limited design conventions and within a short time. The limited use-wear evident on these blades also indicates that, while they had been used in combat, they were removed from circulation prior to any repair. This pattern and some damage suggestive of ritualised killing or decommissioning of the objects themselves supports the interpretation that these weapons were sacrificed after perhaps only one engagement in combat (Horn, 2013). If hostilities did not cease in the region permanently after this sacrifice, we should include into our calculations that the weapons would need to be replaced increasing the necessary metal supply and perpetuating the need to co-operate.

Looking to the balance between what was once in use and what survives today, it is important that the discovery of the Torsted hoard tripled the number of spears of this type known (Becker, 1964). The Dystrup hoard equally increased considerably the number of Apa-like swords in the Nordic sphere (Wincentz Rasmussen & Boas, 2006). This suggests that the pattern of these swords, axes, and spears being recovered as isolated single finds renders an inaccurate image of what once was; a pattern that has been used to suggest that only few people possessed them during the Bronze Age. This in turn led to the argument that between 1700 and 1600 BC few people had the necessary resources to obtain them. However, it is evident by a lack of settlement finds that we are highly dependent on ritual practices that mandated the sacrifice of metal weaponry (Horn, 2018). While it is not within the scope of this paper to model the total number of axes and spears that existed during the Nordic Bronze Age, it can perhaps be suggested that similar production capacities demonstrated by the Torsted and later hoards were not isolated instances but represented a norm throughout the Nordic sphere. Thus, collaborations likely persisted in varying configurations.

Boats and cooperation

Non-violent co-operation and warfare could essentially co-exist in the same space. This can be seen in the potential connection linking weapons, boat crews and rock art. The use-wear traces on the weapons from hoards discussed above indicate their use in combat, potentially by a single warband in each case. There appears to be a hierarchy of weapons, with spears and axes used by lower status fighters, while the use of swords (exclusively) in high status burials has been argued to indicate a higher rank in society related to sword ownership (Felding, et al. 2020; Kristiansen, 1984; 2014). However, even lower ranks may have used weapons made of more mundane materials like the clubs in Tollense or bows in archery, which may have been seen as a lower-profile form of combat. Accepting that burial as a warrior need not define the deceased as a warrior in life (Georganas, 2018), the construction of the archetype in death whether idealised or reflecting reality demonstrates it held meaning to the participants in the funerary rite and the status was being imbued on or revealed about the deceased. Kristiansen's (2014) argument is that swords were reserved for the leaders of warbands, and their relative abundance and use in mortuary practice supports their discriminatory role in varied social practices, including warfare, status symbols, ritual acts, and burial. From rock art, we know combat aboard ships employed a variety of weapons, with scenes variably depicting combatants wielding axes, spears, and swords (Horn, 2022; Ling et al., 2018a). Both Torsted and Dystrup hoards were deposited within less than a day's march to the coast, supporting a maritime connection. We cannot unequivocally prove whether these weapons outfitted boat crews, but making that leap for heuristic reasons allows us to explore a potential scenario.

Considering that the number of crew in NordicBA boats is on average 12–14, then it may be no coincidence that in the early medieval poem Beowulf, the protagonist selects 14 warriors to accompany him to kill Grendel (Heaney, 2001). However, larger crews are indicated by archaeological boat finds dating to the Iron Age in Scandinavia, for example, in Hjortspring (Vinner, 2003). When biological sex is indicated on warriors and boat crews in Scandinavian rock art, this is overwhelmingly male, although notable exceptions occur where females are rendered with weapons or as crew members (Horn 2017; Bergerbrant & Wessman, 2018). This bias is in line with burial evidence for male social roles (Felding et al., 2020).

Based on structural layouts of buildings, it has been argued that 10–15 people lived on a typical Nordic Bronze Age farmstead (Rassmann, 2010; Holst et al., 2013). Farms are assumed to be inhabited and maintained by extended families (Mikkelsen & Kristiansen, 2018; Fokkens,

2003). However, if that was the case then the number estimates given appear rather low, because three generations would have lived on a farm, presumably cutting across various age ranges. Fokkens (2003) concluded that the number of people on any given farmstead might be upwards of twenty. If we add to this the potential number of unfree labourers or slaves (Mikkelsen, 2020), then a single farm might have been inhabited by 25–30 people. Discounting the elderly and small children, we may hypothesise that about half of a farm's population might be capable of going on boat journeys. Of these, roughly half (a quarter of the total house-group) were perhaps female and – if we follow the rock art – only rarely joined boat trips, especially those aimed at violence. Although it seems counter-intuitive, ethnography suggests that some of the unfree may have joined boat crews even those intended for raiding (Cameron, 2016).

Following this, we may estimate that perhaps 5–10 people per farm could potentially join a boat crew. Thus, even sending an average crewed expedition may have required several farmsteads to co-operate. On a rock art panel in Aspeberget is a row of fifteen contemporary boat carvings. Their position and dating suggest that they were made relatively close in time, and in fact they could have been the outcome of a single carving event depicting a fleet of boats. If we take this example, then this scene depicts c. 104 crew members if we double the depicted crew lines. That means 10–20 farms could have collaborated in outfitting this fleet. Calculating on the higher estimates for the farmsteads including unfree labour, outfitting and crewing the boats could have involved upwards of 300–600 people. The labour force could also have contributed in indirect ways such as providing nutrition, cutting wood, providing tools, etc. (Ling et al., 2018b; Horn, et al. 2024).

Conclusion

The large number of weapons with frequent traces of combat use and repair indicates that combat at any given scale was probably a quite common occurrence during the NordicBA (Horn, 2013; Horn & Karck, 2019). Such violence may have been carried out between a limited number of participants, because victims were mostly discovered as individuals with Tollense being an exception. However, this may be a preservation issue. Taken together with previous work indicating that Early Bronze Age weaponry was located close to crucial landing sites and passages for travel with boats (Horn, 2016) the evidence may indicate that small groups engaged in violence moving throughout Scandinavia and beyond in boats (Horn, 2016). This is supported by the Granhammar man, because he presumably fought and died close to water, perhaps on a boat, and further supported by rock art which shows warriors, combat, and boats as closely related, and the number of boats and boat crews involved in such violence (Ling & Toreld, 2018; Ling & Cornell, 2017; Lindström, 2009). While Cliffs End farm in Kent, UK indicates that raiding parties from Scandinavia may have covered great distances, rock art exclusively depicts violence carried out within the NordicBA sphere (Horn, 2023; McKinley et al., 2014).

Boat journeys for whatever purpose bore risks of violence because of misunderstanding, the risk of theft, and more. For that reason, even boat crews intended on non-violent interaction were probably outfitted with arms. If we accept the current paleo-demographic, metal supply, and metal consumption models for the NordicBA sphere, then it might be so that even to outfit and crew a single boat several farmsteads had to collaborate. Several boats may have been launched with the intention of raiding other communities in Scandinavia or elsewhere in Europe, or they intended to trade and protect their valuable cargo. We may speculate that the acquired goods or spoils were shared in accordance with each farmstead's contribution to the expedition, because the investment of valuables like metal surely was only done when a surplus of the respective material could reasonably be expected in return to keep the economic operations on these farmsteads running (Ling et al., 2018; Horn et al., 2024). Contributions could also be other raw materials such as wood for the boat or an investment in social capital, for example, of the farmstead from which the leader of the expedition is recruited who makes decisions such as where to navigate, when to fight, or the negotiations of exchange quantities.

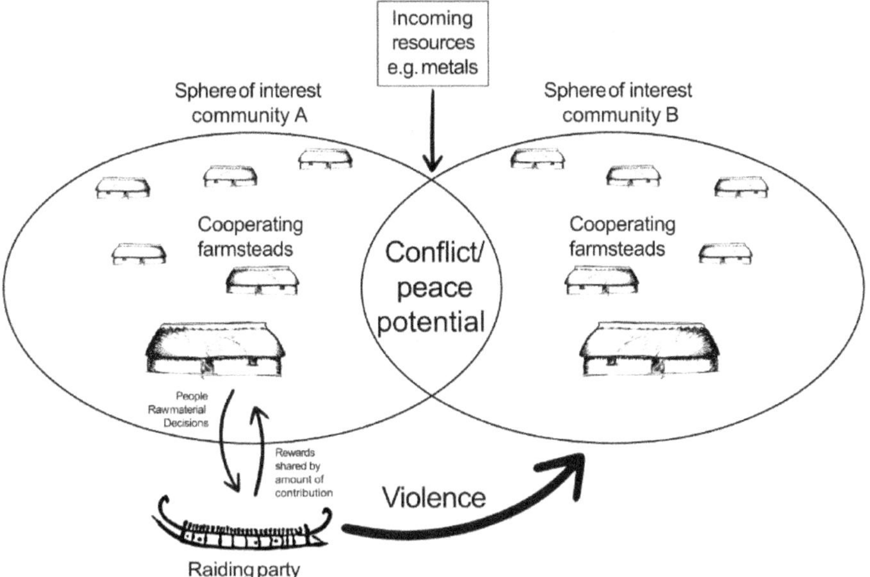

Figure 5: Social model attempting to visualise the coexistence of violent conflict and peaceful cooperation during the NordicBA.

Raids in themselves indicate clusters of in-group farms (not to be raided) and more numerous, perhaps distant, out-groups for which raids were not a transgression of local power management or dynamics (Figure 5). Longer term co-operation over generations in outfitting expeditions by boat and the externalisation of conflict may have established zones of relative internal peace which perhaps formed the kernel of the chiefdom-like social structures of the Nordic Bronze Age (Earle, 1997). Groups may have tried to extend this and include more groups along maritime routes, for example, through guest friendship and other customary rules (Kaul, 2017) or bring distant groups in to secure, for instance, access to appropriate timber in regions where such resources were rare like Limfjord, Denmark (Ling et al., 2018). This could have established alliances, like political confederacies between micro-regional polities to enable co-operation in long-distance exchange taking on geographically linear form, because they tended to follow major trade routes (Earle, 2017; Ling et al., 2018). Since not every group could participate, or have equal opportunities in such a system, conflicts of interest would arise that could easily violently disrupt this system to redress imbalances (Hirshleifer, 1995; Horn, 2023). The destabilisation of local, regional, and transregional alliances perhaps led to fracturing and reformation that may have given rise to the ever changing and shifting decentralised complexity observed in the Nordic sphere (Kristiansen, 2010; Horn et al., 2024).

The model developed here suggests that we need to avoid the trap of inadvertently casting society as being fundamentally warlike or peaceful as the background against which we aim to make sense of particular datasets, for example, weapons or settlement networks. Any such gap is of course artificial and a consequence of the topic in focus for a given study. Our argument has been that when we step away from dichotomies of peace versus warfare, and view society as existing on a spectrum between, we can pose more specific questions to the archaeological record. Conflict would have routinely been managed through violent and non-violent mechanisms and this that the impacts of onset, escalation, de-escalation or resolution would have been experienced across multiple facets of society at any given time. We have the means to explore the management of prehistoric conflict through archaeology by combining approaches – for example, evaluating how specific weapons were used during acts of place-making in the landscape in a way that conceptually brought together phenomena of violence, resolution, commemoration and political legacy. Depositing weapons in ritual contexts required the objects to have been empowered through recognition of their generic purpose or use in specific events, and the act of ritually depositing them in turn reflected a cessation of need and, by extension, a termination of hostility. In this, ritual and martial power were co-dependent and mutually constructed symbolically and practically. We hope that we demonstrated the need to develop an archaeological approach including theory and method to recognise peaceful episodes in prehistoric societies that is based on material remains and not on the perceived absence of certain features.

References

Aner, E. & Kersten, K. (1973–2017). *Funde der älteren Bronzezeit des nordischen Kreises in Dänemark, Schleswig-Holstein und Niedersachsen*. Neumünster: Wachholtz.

Apel, J. (2001). *Daggers, knowledge & power*. Uppsala: Uppsala University.

Becker, C. J. (1964). Neue Hortfunde aus Dänemark mit frühbronzezeitlichen Lanzenspitzen. *Acta Archaeologica, 35*, 115–152.

Bergerbrant, S. & Wessman, A. (2018). Women on the move in the Nordic Bronze Age: A case study based on rock art and costume. In J. Dodd & E. Meijer (Eds.), *Giving the past a future: Essays in archaeology and rock art studies in honour of Dr. Phil. h.c. Gherhard Milstreu* (pp. 121–135). Oxford: Archaeopress.

Bridgford, S. D. (1997). Mightier than the Pen?: An edgewise look at Irish Bronze Age swords. In J. Carman (Ed.), *Material harm: Archaeological studies of war and violence* (pp. 95–115). Glasgow: Cruithne Press.

Brinker, U., Flohr, S., Hauenstein, K., Piek, J., Mittlmeier, T. & Orschiedt, J., (2014). Die menschlichen Skelettreste aus dem Tollensetal: Ein Vorbericht. In D. Jantzen, J. Orschiedt, J. Piek, & T. Terberger (Eds.), *Tod im Tollensetal: Forschungen zu den Hinterlassenschaften eines bronzezeitlichen Gewaltkonfliktes in Mecklenburg-Vorpommern* (pp. 191–208). Schwerin: Landesamt für Kultur und Denkmalpflege Mecklenburg-Vorpommern.

Bunnefeld, J.-H. (2018). The Chief and His Sword?: Some Thoughts on the Swordbearer's Rank in the Early Nordic Bronze Age. In C. Horn & K. Kristiansen (Eds.), *Warfare in Bronze Age society* (pp. 198–212). Cambridge: Cambridge University Press.

Cameron, C. M. (2016). *Captives: How Stolen People Changed the World*. Lincoln: University of Nebraska Press.

Cavazzuti, C., Arena, A., Cardarelli, A., Fritzl, M., Gavranović, M., Hajdu, T., Kiss, V., Köhler, K., Kulcsár, G., Melis, E., Rebay-Salisbury, K., Szabó, G. & Szeverényi, V. (2022). The First 'Urnfields' in the Plains of the Danube and the Po. *Journal of World Prehistory, 35*(1), 45–86. DOI: 10.1007/s10963-022-09164-0.

Christensen, J. (2004). Warfare in the European Neolithic. *Acta Archaeologica, 75*(2), 129–156.

Cline, E. H. (2021). *1177 B.C.: The year civilization collapsed* (2nd ed.). Princeton: Princeton University Press.

Downing, M. & Fibiger, L. (2017). An experimental investigation of sharp force skeletal trauma with replica Bronze Age weapons. *Journal of Archaeological Science: Reports 11*, 546–554. DOI: 10.1016/j.jasrep.2016.12.034.

Earle, T., Ling, J., Uhnér, C., Stos-Gale, Z. & Melheim, L. (2015). The Political Economy and Metal Trade in Bronze Age Europe: Understanding Regional Variability in Terms of Comparative Advantages and Articulations. *European Journal of Archaeology, 18*(4), 633–657. DOI: 10.1179/1461957115Y.0000000008.

Earle, T. K. (2002). *Bronze Age economics: The beginnings of political economies.* Boulder: Westview Press.

Emanuel, J. P. (2018). *Black Ships and Sea Raiders: The Late Bronze and Early Iron Age context of Odysseus' second Cretan lie.* Lanham: Lexington Books.

Felding, L., Reiter, S. S., Frei, K. M. & Vandkilde, H. (2020). Male Social Roles and Mobility in the Early Nordic Bronze Age. A Perspective from SE Jutland: A Perspective from SE Jutland. *Danish Journal of Archaeology, 9,* 1–16. DOI: 10.7146/dja.v9i0.117955.

Fibiger, L., Ahlström, T., Meyer, C. & Smith, M. (2023). Conflict, violence, and warfare among early farmers in Northwestern Europe. *Proceedings of the National Academy of Sciences of the United States of America, 120*(4), e2209481119. DOI: 10.1073/pnas.2209481119.

Fokkens, H. (2003). The longhouse as a central element in Bronze Age daily life'. In J. Bourgeois, I. Bourgeois & C. Bart (Eds.), *Bronze Age and Iron Age communities in North-Western Europe* (pp. 9–38). Brussels: Paleis der Academiën.

Fontijn, D. (2005). Giving up weapons. In M. Parker Pearson & I. J. N. Thorpe (Eds.), *Warfare, Violence and Slavery in Prehistory* (pp. 145–154). Oxford: Archaeopress.

Fry, D. P. (2007). *Beyond war: The human potential for peace.* Oxford: Oxford University Press.

Fyllingen, H. (2003). Society and Violence in the Early Bronze Age: An Analysis of Human Skeletons from Nord-Trøndelag, Norway. *Norwegian Archaeological Review, 36*(1), 27–43. DOI: 10.1080/00293650307297.

Fyllingen, H. (2006). Society and the structure of violence: A story told by Middle Bronze Age human remains from central Norway. In T. Otto, H. Thrane & H. Vandkilde (Eds.), *Warfare and Society: Archaeological and Social Anthropological Perspectives* (pp. 319–329). Aarhus: Aarhus University Press.

Gavranović, M., Mehofer, M., Kapuran, A., Koledin, J., Mitrović, J., Papazovska, A., Pravidur, A., Đorđević, A. & Jacanović, D. (2022). Emergence of monopoly-Copper exchange networks during the Late Bronze Age in the western and central Balkans. *PLOS One, 17*(3), e0263823. DOI: 10.1371/journal.pone.0263823.

Gentile, V. & van Gijn, A. (2019). Anatomy of a notch. An in-depth experimental investigation and interpretation of combat traces on Bronze Age swords. *Journal of Archaeological Science, Vol. 105,* 130–143. DOI: 10.1016/j.jas.2019.02.004.

Georganas, I. & Kvapil, L. A., 2024. Weaponry. In L. Kvapil & K. Shelton (Eds.), *Brill's Companion to Warfare in the Bronze Age Aegean* (pp. 89–115). Leiden: Brill.

Goldhammer, J. (2015). *Studien zu Steinartefakten der Bronzezeit: Siedlungsinventare aus Nord- und Südschleswig im Vergleich*. Neumünster: Wachholtz.

Harding, A. F. (2007). *Warriors and Weapons in Bronze Age Europe*. Budapest: Archaeolingua alapítvány.

Heaney, S. (2001). *Beowulf: A new verse translation*. New York: Norton & Company.

Hermann, R., Dolfini, A., Crellin, R. J., Wang, Q. & Uckelmann, M. (2020). Bronze Age Swordsmanship: New Insights from Experiments and Wear Analysis. *Journal of Archaeological Method and Theory*, 27(4), 1040–1083. DOI: 10.1007/s10816-020-09451-0.

Hitchcock, L. A. & Maeir, A. M. (2014). Yo-ho, yo-ho, a seren's life for me!. *World Archaeology*, 46(4), 624–640. DOI: 10.1080/00438243.2014.928602.

Holck, P. (1987). Kråkerøy: Et gammelt kriminalmysterium?. *Borgarsyssel Museums Årbok* (pp. 31–42).

Holst, M. K., Rasmussen, M., Kristiansen, K. & Bech, J.-H. (2013). Bronze Age 'Herostrats': Ritual, Political, and Domestic Economies in Early Bronze Age Denmark. *Proceedings of the Prehistoric Society*, 79, 265–296. DOI: 10.1017/ppr.2013.14.

Horn, C. (2011). Deliberate destruction of halberds. In M. Uckelmann & M. Mödlinger (Eds.), *Bronze Age Warfare: Manufacture and Use of Weaponry* (pp. 53–65). Oxford: Archaeopress.

Horn, C. (2013). Weapons, fighters and combat: Spears and swords in Early Bronze Age Scandinavia. *Danish Journal of Archaeology*, 2(1), 20–44. DOI: 10.1080/21662282.2013.838832.

Horn, C. (2016). Nothing to lose: Waterborne raiding in southern Scandinavia'. In H. Glørstad, A. Zanette T. Glørstad & L. Melheim (Eds.), *Comparative Perspectives on Past Colonisation, Maritime Interaction and Cultural Integration* (pp. 109–127). Sheffield: Equinox.

Horn, C. (2017). 'It's a man's world'?: Sex and gender in Scandinavian Bronze Age rock art. In S. Bergerbrant & A. Wessman (Eds.), *New perspectives on the Bronze Age: Proceedings of the 13th Nordic Bronze Age Symposium held in Gothenburg 9th to 13th June 2015* (pp. 237–252). Oxford: Archaeopress.

Horn, C. (2018). Warfare vs. Exchange?: Thoughts on an Integrative Approach. In C. Horn & K. Kristiansen (Eds.), *Warfare in Bronze Age society* (pp. 47–60). Cambridge: Cambridge University Press.

Horn, C. (2019). Showmen and Fighters: Bronze Age Rock Art and Weaponry in Scandinavia. In S. Hansen & R. Krause (Eds.), *Materialisierung von Konflikten/Materialisation of Conflicts: Beiträge der Dritten Internationalen LOEWE-Konferenz vom 24. bis 27. September 2018 in Fulda/ Proceedings of the Third International LOEWE Conference, 24–27 September 2018 in Fulda* (pp. 45–65). Bonn: Habelt.

Horn, C. (2021). Trouble in paradise?: Violent Conflict in Funnel-Beaker Societies. *Oxford Journal of Archaeology, 40*(1), 43–64. DOI: 10.1111/ojoa. 12212.

Horn, C. (2022). Most Deserve to Be Forgotten: Could the Southern Scandinavian Rock Art Memorialize Heroes?. In L. F. Zubieta (Ed.), *Rock Art and Memory in the Transmission of Cultural Knowledge* (pp. 125–146). Cham: Springer International Publishing.

Horn, C. (2023). Warriors as a Challenge: Violence, Rock Art, and the Preservation of Social Cohesion During the Nordic Bronze Age. *European Journal of Archaeology, 26*(1), 57–80. DOI: 10.1017/eaa.2022.26.

Horn, C., Austvoll, K. I., Ling, J. & Artursson, M. (2024). *Nordic Bronze Age economies.* Cambridge: Cambridge University Press.

Horn, C. & von Holstein, I. (2017). Dents in our confidence: The interaction of damage and material properties in interpreting use-wear on copper-alloy weaponry. *Journal of Archaeological Science, 81*, 90–100. DOI: 10. 1016/j.jas.2017.04.002.

Horn, C. & Karck, T. (2019). Weapon and tool use during the Nordic Bronze Age. *Danish Journal of Archaeology, 8*, 1–20. DOI: 10.7146/dja.v8i0. 111834.

Iacono, F. (2020). *The archaeology of Late Bronze Age Interaction and Mobility at the Gates of Europe: People, Things and Networks Around the Southern Adriatic Sea.* London: Bloomsbury Academic.

Jantzen, D., Brinker, U., Orschiedt, J., Heinemeier, J., Piek, J., Hauenstein, K., Krüger, J., Lidke, G., Lübke, H., Lampe, R., Lorenz, S. & Terberger, T., (2011). A Bronze Age battlefield?: Weapons and trauma in the Tollense Valley, north-eastern Germany. *Antiquity, 85*(328), 417–433. DOI: 10. 1017/S0003598X00067843.

Jung, R. (2009). Pirates of the Aegean: Italy – the East Aegean – Cyprus at the end of the Second Millennium BC. In V. Karagiōrgēs & O. Kouka (Eds.), *Cyprus and the East Aegean: Intercultural contacts from 3000 to 500 B.C* (pp. 72–93). Nicosia: A.G. Leventis Foundation.

Kaul, F. (2017). The Xenia Concept of Guest-friendship: Providing an Elucidatory Model for Bronze Age Communication. In P. Skoglund, J. Ling & U. Bertilsson (Eds.), *North Meets South: Theoretical Aspects on the Northern and Southern rock Art* (pp. 172–198). Oxford: Oxbow Books.

Kjær, H. (1912). Et mærkeligt arkæologisk-antropologisk Fund fra Stenalderen. *Aarbøger for Nordisk Oldkyndighed og Historie, 2*, 58–72.

Knapp, A. B. (2018). *Seafaring and Seafarers: In the Bronze Age Eastern Mediterranean*. Leiden: Sidestone.

Kristiansen, K. (1984). Krieger und Häuptlinge in der Bronzezeit Dänemarks. Ein Beitrag zur Geschichte des bronzezeitlichen Schwertes. *Jahrbuch des Römisch-Germanischen Zentralmuseums Mainz, 31*, 187–208.

Kristiansen, K. (2002). The Tale of the Sword: Swords and Swordfighters in Bronze Age Europe. *Oxford Journal of Archeology, 21*(4), 319–332. DOI: 10.1111/1468-0092.00166.

Kristiansen, K. (2010). Decentralized Complexity: The Case of Bronze Age Northern Europe. In T. Douglas Price & G. M. Feinman (Eds.), *Pathways to Power: New Perspectives on the Emergence of Social Inequality* (pp. 169–192). New York, NY: Springer New York.

Kristiansen, K. (2014). The dialectics of gender: Ritualizing gender relations in Late Bronze Age Southern Scandinavia. In H. Alexandersson, A. Andreeff & A. Bünz (Eds.), *Med hjärta och hjärna: En vänbok till professor Elisabeth Arwill-Nordbladh* (pp. 339–354). Gothenburg: University of Gothenburg.

Kristiansen, K. & Suchowska-Ducke, P. (2015). Connected Histories: the Dynamics of Bronze Age Interaction and Trade 1500–1100 bc. *Proceedings of the Prehistoric Society, 81*, 361–392. DOI: 10.1017/ppr.2015.17.

Lidke, G., Brinker, U., Schramm, A., Jantzen, D. & Terberger, T. (2019). Warriors' lives: The skeletal sample from The Bronze Age battlefield site in the Tollense Valley, north-eastern Germany. In M. Dal Corso, W. Kirleis, J. Kneisel, N. Taylor, M. Wieckowska-Lüth & M. Zanon (Eds.), *How's Life? Living Conditions in the 2nd and 1st Millennia BCE* (pp. 35–55). Leiden: Sidestone Press.

Lidke, G. & Piek, J. (1999). Manipulationsspuren an menschlichen Schädelresten des Neolithikums in Mecklenburg-Vorpommern. *Jahrbuch der Bodendenkmalpflege in Mecklenburg-Vorpommern, 46*, 45–91.

Lindström, J. (2009). *Bronsåldersmordet: Om arkeologi och ond bråd död*. Stockholm: Norstedts.

Ling, J. (2014). *Elevated rock art: Towards a maritime understanding of Bronze Age rock art in northern Bohuslan, Sweden*. Oxford: Oxbow Books.

Ling, J. & Bertilsson, U. (2017). Biography of the Fossum Panel. *Adoranten, 2016*, 58–72.

Ling, J., Chacon, R. J. & Chacon, Y. (2018a). Rock Art, Secret Societies, Long-distance Exchange, and Warfare in Bronze Age Scandinavia. In A. Dolfini, R. J. Crellin, C. Horn & M. Uckelmann (Eds.), *Prehistoric Warfare and Violence: Quantitative and Qualitative Approaches* (pp. 149–174). Cham: Springer.

Ling, J. & Cornell, P. (2017). Violence, Warriors, and Rock Art in Bronze Age Scandinavia. In R. J. Chacon & R. G. Mendoza (Eds.), *Feast, Famine or Fighting?* (pp. 15–33). Cham: Springer International Publishing.

Ling, J., Earle, T. & Kristiansen, K. (2018b). Maritime Mode of Production: Raiding and Trading in Seafaring Chiefdoms. *Current Anthropology*, *59*(5), 488–524. DOI: 10.1086/699613.

Ling, J., Stos-Gale, Z., Grandin, L., Billström, K., Hjärthner-Holdar & E., Persson, P.-O. (2014). Moving metals II: Provenancing Scandinavian Bronze Age artefacts by lead isotope and elemental analyses. *Journal of Archaeological Science, 41*, 106–132. DOI: 10.1016/j.jas.-2013.07.018.

Ling, J. & Toreld, A. (2018). Maritime warfare in Scandinavian rock art. In C. Horn & K. Kristiansen (Eds.), *Warfare in Bronze Age society* (pp. 61–80). Cambridge: Cambridge University Press.

McKinley, J. I., Leivers, M., Schuster, J., Marshall, P., Barclay, A. J. & Stoodley, N. (2014). *Cliffs End Farm, Isle of Thanet, Kent: A mortuary and ritual site of the Bronze Age, Iron Age and Anglo-Saxon period with evidence for long-distance maritime mobility.* Salisbury: Wessex Archaeology.

Meller, H. (2017). Armies in the Early Bronze Age? An alternative interpretation of Únětice Culture axe hoards. *Antiquity, 91*(360), 1529–1545. DOI: 10.15184/aqy.2017.180.

Meyer, C., Lohr, C., Kubris, B., Dresely, V., Haak, W., Gronenborn, D. & Alt, K. W. (2014). Mass Graves of the LBK.: Patterns and Peculiarities. In A. Whittle & P. Bickle (Eds.), *Early Farmers: The view from archaeology and science* (pp. 307–325). Oxford: British Academy.

Mikkelsen, M. (2020). Slaves in Bronze Age southern Scandinavia? *Acta Archaeologica, 91*(1), 147–190. DOI: 10.1111/j.1600-0390.2020.12225.x.

Mikkelsen, M. & Kristiansen, K. (2018). Legaard. In J.-H. Bech, B. V. Eriksen, & K. Kristiansen (Eds.), *Bronze age settlement and land-use in Thy, north-west Denmark* (pp. 505–538). Højbjerg & Thisted: Museum Thy & Jutland Archaeological Society.

Möckli, D. (2011). *Medizinische Untersuchungen und Ergebnisse an Ötzi.* MA. *University of Zürich.*

Molloy, B. P. C. (2006). *The role of combat weaponry in Bronze Age societies: The cases of the Aegean and Ireland in the Middle and Late Bronze Age.* PhD. University College Dublin.

Molloy, B. P. C. (2024). Warfare in the EBA to the Beginning of the LBA. In L. Kvapil & K. Shelton (Eds.), *Brill's Companion to Warfare in the Bronze Age Aegean* (pp. 201–244). Leiden: Brill.

Molloy, B. P. C., Jovanović, D., Bruyere, C., Estanqueiro, M., Birclin, M., Milašinović, L., Šalamon, A., Penezić, K., Bronk Ramsey, C. & Grosman, D. (2023a). Resilience, innovation and collapse of settlement networks in later Bronze Age Europe: New survey data from the southern Carpathian Basin. *PLOS One, 18*(11), e0288750. DOI: 10.1371/journal.pone.0288750.

Molloy, B. P. C. (2012). Martial Minoans? War as social process, practice and event in Bronze Age Crete. *The Annual of the British School at Athens, 107*, 87–142.

Molloy, B. P. C. (Ed.) (2016). *Of odysseys and oddities: Scales and modes of interaction between prehistoric Aegean societies and their neighbours.* Oxford: Oxbow Books.

Molloy, B. P. C. (2017). Hunting Warriors: The Transformation of Weapons, Combat Practices and Society during the Bronze Age in Ireland. *European Journal of Archaeology, 20*(2), 280–316. DOI: 10.1017/eaa.2016.8.

Molloy, B. P. C. & Mödlinger, M. (2020). The Organisation and Practice of Metal Smithing in Later Bronze Age Europe. *Journal of World Prehistory, 33*(2), 169–232. DOI: 10.1007/s10963-020-09141-5.

Molloy, B. P. C., Bruyère, C. & Jovanović, D. (2023b). Rethinking Material Culture Markers for Mobility and Migration in the Globalising European Later Bronze Age: A Comparative View from the Po Valley and Pannonian Plain. In M. Fernández-Götz (Ed.), *Rethinking migrations in Late Prehistoric Eurasia* (pp. 142–169). Oxford: Oxford University Press.

Nerlich, A. G., Peschel, O. & Egarter-Vigl, E. (2009). New evidence for Ötzi's final trauma. *Intensive care medicine, 35*(6), 1138–1139.

Nordbladh, J. (1989). Armour and fighting in the south Scandinavian Bronze Age, especially in view of rock art representations'. In T. B. Larsson & H. Lundmark (Eds.), *Approaches to Swedish Prehistory: A spectrum of problems and perspectives in contemporary research* (pp. 323–333). Oxford: Archaeopress.

Nordenborg Myhre, L. (2004). *Trialectic archaeology: Monuments and space in Southwest Norway 1700–500 BC.* Stavanger: Arkeologisk museum i Stavanger.

Novak, M., Olalde, I., Ringbauer, H., Rohland, N., Ahern, J., Balen, J., Janković, I., Potrebica, H., Pinhasi, R. & Reich, D. (2021). Genome-wide analysis of nearly all the victims of a 6200-year old massacre. *PLOS One, 16*(3), e0247332. DOI: 10.1371/journal.pone.0247332.

Olausson, D. (1988). Dots on a Map: Thoughts about the way archaeologists study prehistoric trade and exchange. In B. Hårdh, L. Larsson, D. Olausson, & R. Petré (Eds.), *Trade and Exchange in Prehistory: Studies in honour of Berta Stjernquist* (pp. 15–24). Acta archaeologica Lundensia. Series in 80, Vol. 16. Blom.

Otterbein, K. F., 2004. *How War Began.* College Station: Texas A & M University Press.

Otterbein, K. F. (2009). *The anthropology of war.* Long Grove, Ill.: Waveland Press.

Pulak, C. (1998). The Uluburun shipwreck: an overview. *International Journal of Nautical Archaeologyi, 27*(3), 188–224. DOI: 10.1111/j.1095-9270.1998. tb00803.x.

Ranta, M. (2016). Do Rock Carvings Tell Stories?: Aspects of Narrativity in Scandinavian Bronze Age Petroglyphs. In *Proceedings of ICA 2016: Aesthetics and mass culture: [20th international congress of aesthetics, Seoul National University, Seoul, Korea, 24–26 July, 2016]* (pp. 523–531). Seoul: The Korean Society of Aesthetics.

Ranta, M., Skoglund, P., Cabak Rédei, A. & Persson, T. (2019). Levels of Narrativity in Scandinavian Bronze Age Petroglyphs. *Cambridge Archaeological Journal, 29*(3), 497–516. DOI: 10.1017/S0959774319000118.

Rassmann, K. (2010). Metallverbrauch in der frühen Bronzezeit Mitteleuropas: Produktion, Zirkulation und Konsumption frühbronzezeitlicher Metallobjekte als Untersuchungsgegenstände einer archäologischen Wirtschaftsgeschichte. *Archäologie in Eurasien, 24*, 341–363.

Redmond, E. M. (1994). *Tribal and chiefly warfare in South America*. Ann Arbor.

Roberts, B. (2013). Farmers in the Landscape or Heroes on the High Seas: Britain and Ireland in the Bronze Age. In H. Fokkens & A. Harding (Eds.), *Oxford Handbook of Bronze Age Europe* (pp. 531–549). Oxford: Oxford University Press.

Sarauw, T. (2007). Male Symbols or Warrior Identities? The 'Archery Burials' of the Danish Bell Beaker Culture. *Journal of Anthropological Archaeology, 26*(1), 65–87. DOI: 10.1016/j.jaa.2006.05.001.

Schroeder, H., Margaryan, A., Szmyt, M., Theulot, B., Włodarczak, P., Rasmussen, S., Gopalakrishnan, S., Szczepanek, A., Konopka, T., Jensen, T. Z. T., Witkowska, B., Wilk, S., Przybyła, M. M., Pospieszny, Ł., Sjögren, Zdzislaw Belka, K-G., Olsen, J., Kristiansen, K., Willerslev, E., Frei, K. M., Sikora, M., Johannsen, N. N. & Allentoft, M. E. (2019). Unraveling ancestry, kinship, and violence in a Late Neolithic mass grave. *Proceedings of the National Academy of Sciences 116*(22) (pp. 10705–10710). DOI: 10.1073/pnas.1820210116.

Schulting, R. J. (2013). War Without Warriors? The Nature of Interpersonal Conflict Before the Emergence of Formalized Warrior Elites. In S. Ralph (Ed.), *The Archaeology of Violence: Interdisciplinary Approaches* (pp. 19–36). Albany: SUNY Press.

Schultrich, S. (2021). *Kriegerideal und Netzwerke. Die Doppeläxte West- und Mitteleuropas im Kontext der jung- bis endneolithischen Kulturentwicklung* (PhD thesis). University of Kiel.

Shelmerdine, C. W. (2024). Mycenaean Warfare: The Evidence of the Linear B Tablets. In L. Kvapil & K. Shelton (Eds.), *Brill's Companion to Warfare in the Bronze Age Aegean* (pp. 116–160). Leiden: Brill.

Skoglund, P., Ranta, M., Persson, T. & Cabak Rédei, A. (2022). Narrative Aspects of Images of Spear Use in Scandinavian Rock Carvings. *European Journal of Archaeology, 25*(2), 176–195. DOI: 10.1017/eaa.2021.52.

Sponsel, L. E. (1996). The Natural History of Peace: A Positive View of Human Nature and Its Potential. In T. Gregor (Ed.), *A natural history of peace* (1ˢᵗ ed., pp. 95–125). Nashville: Vanderbilt University Press.

Strong, R. L. J. & Fibiger, L. (2023). An experimental investigation of cutmark analysis of sharp force trauma in the Bronze Age. *Journal of Archaeological Science: Reports, 48*, 103843. DOI: 10.1016/j.jasrep.2023.103843.

Szeverényi, V. & Kiss, V. (2018). Material evidence for warfare in Early and Middle Bronze Age Hungary. In M. Fernández-Götz & N. Roymans (Eds.), *Conflict archaeology: Materials of collective violence from prehistory to late antiquity* (1ˢᵗ ed., pp. 37–49). London: Routledge.

Terberger, T., Jantzen, D., Krüger, J. & Lidke, G. (2018). Das bronzezeitliche Kampfgeschehen im Tollensetal: Ein Großereignis oder wiederholte Konflikte?. In S. Hansen & R. Krause (Eds.), *Bronzezeitliche Burgen zwischen Taunus und Karpaten: Beiträge der ersten Internationalen LOEWE-Konferenz vom 7. bis 9. Dezember 2016 in Frankfurt/M. = Bronze Age hillforts between Taunus and Carpathian mountains: proceedings of the first international LOEWE Conference, 7–9 December 2016 in Frankfurt/M./herausgegeben von Svend Hansen, Rüdiger Krause* (pp. 103–124). Bonn: Verlag Dr. Rudolf Habelt GmbH.

Toreld, A. (2012). Svärd och mord: Nyupptäckta hällristningsmotiv vid Medbo i Brastad socken, Bohuslän. *Fornvännen, 107*, 241–252.

Tornberg, A. (2022). A prehistory of violence: Evidence of violence-related skull trauma in southern Sweden, 2300–1100 BCE. In A. Tornberg, A. Svensson & J. Apel (Eds.), *Life and afterlife in the Nordic Bronze Age: Proceedings of the 15ᵗʰ Nordic Bronze Age symposium held in Lund, Sweden, June 11–15. 2019* (pp. 99–118). Lund: Lund University.

Uhlig, T., Krüger, J., Lidke, G., Jantzen, D., Lorenz, S., Ialongo, N. & Terberger, T. (2019). Lost in combat? A scrap metal find from the Bronze Age battlefield site at Tollense. *Antiquity, 93*(371), 1211–1230. DOI: 10.15184/aqy.2019.137.

Vandkilde, H. (2003). Commemorative tales: Archaeological responses to modern myth, politics, and war. *World Archaeology, 35*(1), 126–144.

Vandkilde, H. (2011). Bronze Age warfare in temperate Europe. *Archäologie in Eurasien, 24*, 365–380.

Vandkilde, H. (2014). Breakthrough of the Nordic Bronze Age: Transcultural warriorhood and a Carpathian crossroad in the sixteenth century BC. *European Journal of Archaeology, 17*(4) 602–633. DOI: 10.1179/1461957114Y.0000000064.

Vandkilde, H. (2016). Bronzization: The Bronze Age as Pre-Modern Globalization. *Praehistorische Zeitschrift, 91*(1), 103–123. DOI: 10.1515/pz-2016-0005.

Walker, P. L. (2001). A bioarchaeological perspective on the history of violence. *Annual Review of Anthropology, 30*(1), 573–596.

Wileman, J. (2009). *War and rumours of war: The evidential base for the recognition of warfare in prehistory*. Oxford: Archaeopress.

Wincentz R. & Lisbeth, N. A. B. (2006). The Dystrup swords: A hoard with eight short swords from the Early Bronze Age. *Journal of Danish Archaeology, 14*(1), 87–108.

Written Sources on Medieval Fighting Practices

Antti Ijäs

This chapter seeks to answer the question of what can be learnt of medieval fighting practices and the associated social practices based on written sources produced in the period in question. Written sources on historical fighting practices come in various forms in terms of both materiality and kinds of literature. The sources may be manuscript, printed, or even inscribed onto various materials, and are typically composed in historical languages according to the conventions of their respective literary genres (Jaquet, 2018). Traditionally, the study of texts in their historical context has been the domain of philology, which covers, on the one hand, the study of semantics, morphology, syntax, and style of individual works or authors and, on the other hand, textual criticism and interpretation of the content. Accordingly, a researcher identifying as a philologist may be considered an amalgamation of a historical linguist, literary historian, and a codicologist. Moreover, the study of texts on historical practices requires giving some methodological consideration to what can be said about the nature of the practice which the texts refer to.

The central concepts for the purposes of this chapter are *practice* and *technique,* both of which can reveal much about the social context in which they are embedded. In the context of this chapter, practice is something that exists as occurrences in a specific time and place through the acts of the practicing individual. Technique, on the other hand, is most conveniently defined as a kind of knowledge that governs practice (Spatz, 2015:26–44). (Both concepts, as defined here, would fall within *practice* as understood in the framework of practice theory: Nielsen & Walker, 2009:4–6; Topic & Topic, 2009:18–19.) Thus, technique, like other kinds of knowledge, may be transmitted from one individual to the other through teaching, imitation, or even through embodiment in material objects.

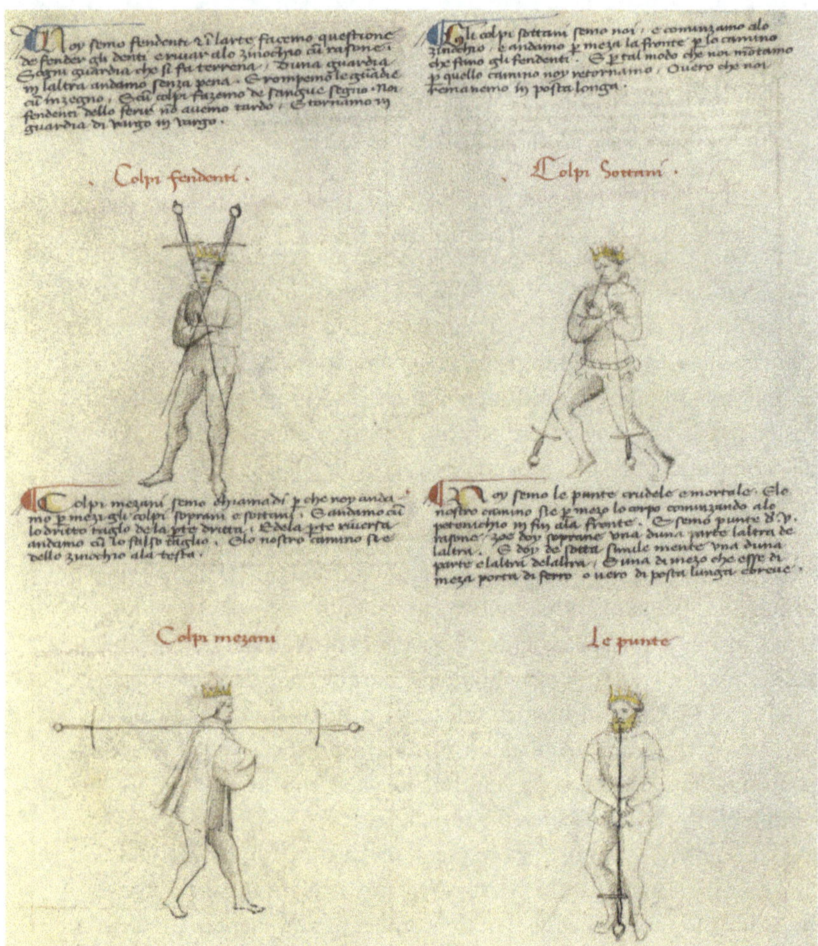

Figure 1: Conceptualising the six cuts and the thrust. Il Fiore di Battaglia, c. 1410. The J. Paul Getty Museum, Los Angeles, Ms. Ludwig XV 13, fol. 23r. (Public domain, https://creativecommons.org/publicdomain/zero/1.0/)

To avoid misunderstandings, it should be noted that technique as "knowledge" is not exclusively made up of propositions which can be appraised in terms of their truth value, though all technical knowledge does seem to carry the implication that it is the most convenient way of achieving a specific goal. For present purposes, the most important feature of technique as knowledge is that its explicit components can be referred to in writing. In the case of fighting, units of explicit technical knowledge comprise names of individual techniques (conceptualisation (Figure 1), combinations of techniques and their counters (an application of conceptualisation), and guidelines regarding individual actions or fighting in general (codified knowledge gained from practical experience). Knowledge regarding the rules and conventions for fighting belong here as well. Technique as knowledge is the central concept in approaching texts that refer to fighting practices, particularly if the text in question represents a "fight book", i.e., a work conveying or describing fighting technique, often authored by masters of arms as aides-mémoire for their noble clients in connection with a teaching appointment (or an attempt to acquire one) or for the community of bourgeois practitioners of the art of fencing (for a general introduction to this principally German literary phenomenon, see Forgeng, 2012; Boffa, 2014; Jaquet et al., 2016; Ijäs, 2022). As for other genres, explicit references to the details of fighting put in literary form have been filtered through the conceptions of the author, whether they are an expert on the subject or not. Accordingly, not only fight books, but other types of sources as well may be used as evidence of how fighting technique was conceptualised within a given literary culture.

Being the output of philological research, this chapter will present a series of examples of the various kinds of written sources available on fighting practices to illustrate what such sources can reveal about the actual activities they refer to, as well as the associated social practices. The sources range from medieval technical prose to a poetic rendition of an ancient novel. Due to practical limitations, no attempt at a general typology of sources is made, but the texts discussed are grouped according to their subject matter under "laws and conventions", "descriptions of practice", and "descriptions of technique". The examples have been chosen not only with the aim of representing a variety of genres but also with the hope that they will be of interest as far as their content is concerned as well. The content of the sources is discussed in terms of what it reveals of the conceptualisations of technique in different societies and how the different kinds of evidence can be used to reveal something not only of technique as a textual phenomenon of technical literature, but as pointing to actual fighting practices, complementing the study of material sources, the tools and what remains of the victims of interpersonal violence.

Laws and Conventions
Geoffroi de Charny's Questions

The first example comes from Geoffroi de Charny (c. 1306–19 September 1356), a French knight active around the first decades of the Hundred Years' War. Better known for his *Book of Chivalry* (Kaeuper & Kennedy, 1996), he also composed a set of questions pertaining to the laws of war, which were posed to the knights of the *Ordre de l'Étoile,* the Company of the Star, an order of chivalry founded in 1351. The particulars of the discussions and answers suggested for these questions by the knights have unfortunately not survived, but the questions are valuable, as they reveal many of the concerns men-at-arms had regarding their interactions in different kinds of conflicts. Translated below is one of Charny's questions, which pertains to what should constitute the legal act of surrendering to one's opponent:

> Men-at-arms ride out and encounter each other and fight. One of the men-at-arms in one party strikes his spurs to save himself, and three of the other side pursue him. The first stops him with the bridle, and he does not want to surrender to him. The second one takes him by the head and holds a knife at his throat, and again he does not wish to surrender to him. The third comes after and tells him to surrender to him, and that man-at-arms surrenders himself to the third. When in the evening each of the three uses all the good arguments he knows, and there are plenty, that this prisoner ought to belong to him, who will have him, and how will it be judged by the law of arms? (Muhlberger, 2014:97–98)

Obviously, the moral of the passage quoted above is not that if you simply ask nicely instead of using violence, people will be more inclined to surrender to you. Instead, this is a hypothetical example of a complicated situation that might come to pass during a battle or a tournament, requiring a resolution according to *ius belli,* a kind of international law regulating armed conflicts (see Keen, 1965).

The question discussed above pertains to the wider issue of regulating violence and warfare. In recent times, it has been pointed out that the difference between the states of war and peace has been blurred to some extent, with various forms of hybrid warfare taking place during peace time while remaining safely below the threshold of inciting a military escalation. The categorisation into times of peace and war is, of course, simply an attempt of the legislator to create order according to which the state is permitted to take various measures. Somewhat similar blurring of the lines occurred in Charny's time as well, during which war was endemic in Europe. Like in the present day, armed conflict as an international occurrence necessitated some kind of international conception of the rules that regulated violence. A specific battle standard such as the *Oriflamme* could be flown to signal that the battle would be fought with no quarter given; the white flag representing the opposite is the best-known example of regulation of violence, being valid in the modern battlefield as well. In Charny's time, the judging of individual cases could become very convoluted due to changing allegiances and the ambiguity of the signs used to indicate various legal acts. Even if the facts were seemingly unambiguous, there was potential for complexity in matters of law of arms, as exemplified by the case in the present passage.

Though Charny's main interest lies in the legal ramifications of the issue, the formulation of his question makes references to actual fighting practices as well. These are, in order of occurrence, taking the opponent's horse by the bridle, taking the opponent by the head and holding a knife at his throat, and simply ordering the opponent to surrender. The last manoeuvre is admittedly the least combative of the three and most likely did not create a particularly strong claim for its perpetrator, even though the opponent did decide to surrender to him. If the question is a reference to a case that occurred, this may have been due to the would-be-prisoner assuming this particular captor as the most likely to provide his prisoners with favourable treatment. In any case, the text does attest to two acts which may be interpreted as individual techniques of mounted combat, which will be discussed further below.

The context of Charny's questions is knightly combat, which occurred in different degrees of seriousness in jousts, tournaments, and war. These different environments would have determined what was acceptable conduct and what kind of repercussions and injuries the participants should expect. Before becoming an anachronistic sporting event, the joust was a component part of mounted combat technique. Mounted combat, in turn, occurred in both warfare and tournaments. In its earlier stages, the tournament was indeed a kind of regulated battle, but conventions ensuring the relative safety of the combatants were gradually developed, making tournament a way to practice combat. In other words, the tournament became more like a mock battle, something knights could take part in as preparation for a real one. In addition to mounted combat fought between two opposing groups, men-at-arms could also engage in single combat, either on horseback or on foot. Challenges to single combat could be given as part of warfare, but one of the most intriguing forms of single combat is the judicial duel, which will form the context of the next example.

Why Engage in Judicial Duelling

In societies where martial practices were embedded in civic life (see Tlustly, 2011), it might be expected that fighting would play a part in settling legal disputes. In its essence, judicial duelling is a method of coming to a verdict when other types of evidence are not available (for an overview, see Elema, 2019). Simply put, the theory was that when the two contestants fight on an equal footing with identical weapons and clothes, it is up to God to decide which of them will prevail, the victorious individual thus being the one whose case was just. This method of operationalising God for settling judicial disputes was, for obvious reasons, strongly opposed by the church, though it was practiced to some extent under the auspices of local lordships. The judicial duel is considered the precursor of the early modern duel fought for reasons of honour, the most important capital a gentleman would have had as a member of his class (for the concept of honour, see Peltonen, 2003:35–44). This connection brings us to an actual technical source on fighting technique, one of the fight books of Hans Talhoffer, a professional master of arms (Burkart, 2017; Welle, 2015; Hils, 1983). In his book dated 1459, the author discusses, among other things, the reasons men of his time would have engaged in duels. The relevant passages are provided here in both transcription and translation, as some of the readings recently published are not entirely accurate (cf. Jaquet, 2016:406, 2017:155; contrast the readings of Dreyer, 1754:165; cited in Hergsell, 1889:21):

> Item zu dem ersten maul daz Im nymant gern sin Eer laut abschniden mit wortten ainen der sin genoß ist; Er wolte Ee lieber mit im kempfen, wie wol er doch mit recht wol von Im kem, ob er wolte, und darumb so ist kämpfen ain můtwill. (Copenhagen, KB, Thott 290 2°, fol. 8r)

> *Item*, firstly, that nobody takes kindly having his honour taken from him by his equal, he would rather fight with him, even though he could still with reason leave him if he wanted to, which is why fighting is a choice.

The reference to one's equal is important since if one's honour is questioned by one's equal, it undermines their entire standing and the subsequent worth of their word of honour or oath. I have here rendered *můtwill* as 'choice', meaning 'an act of will', though an equivalent with more negative connotations could be used as well, such as '(act of) ill will'. In any case, the idea is that fighting would occur because one chooses to do so, not because they are legally obligated to. In addition to the above observation, Talhoffer lists several reasons to engage in combat:

> Item der sachen und Ardickelen sind siben Darumb man noch pfligt zu kempfen

> Item daz erst ist mortt
> Daz ander verräterniß
> Das dritt ketzerÿ
> Daz vierd wölher an sinem herrn truloß wirt
> Daz fünfft umb fanknuß in striten oder sunsst

Daz sechst um valsch

Daz sibent da ainer junckfrowen oder frowen benotzogt (Copenhagen, KB, Thott 290 2°, f. 8r)

Item, there are seven causes and articles for which one still tends to fight:

item, the first is murder,
the second treason,
the third heresy,
the fourth unfaithfulness to one's lord,
the fifth capture in combat or otherwise,
the sixth perjury,
and the seventh raping a virgin or a married woman.

As already pointed out, engaging in judicial duelling was not a matter of avenging a deed but of establishing guilt. The passages quoted above do not contain direct references to the technical aspects of fighting, but they do provide context for the following descriptions of duels, the first one being about the curious kind fought between a man and a woman.

Descriptions of Practice

A Fictional Description of a Duel between a Man and a Woman

Unlike the previous examples, the following one is not a technical source but an actual literary source in the narrower sense of the word: a fictional account of a duel fought between a man and a woman found in the version of the story of Apollonius of Tyre composed by Heinrich von Neustadt in the late thirteenth century. Though the setting is fictional, the passage is nevertheless relevant as a source for judicial history concerning gendered norms on sanctioned violence and has been published multiple times in German research (Fehr, 1931:219–226; U[kert], 1812:401–406; U[kert], 1836:123–128).

In the story, Flordelîse challenges Silvian of Nazareth to a duel, because he has unjustly accused her sister Claramie of adulterous conduct. The background of the matter is that Claramie's husband Lafet had prevailed against Silvian in a tournament, which had angered Silvian to the point of trying to get revenge by raping Claramie.

Figure 2: Illustration of Flordelîse's duel, c. 1456/1467. Forschungsbibliothek Gotha, Chart. A 689, fol. 156r. (CC BY–SA 4.0; https://creativecommons.org/licenses/by-sa/4.0/).

Silvian failed in his attempt, but this did not prevent him from claiming to Lafet that Claramie had offered herself to him. Lafet, unfortunately, believed in Silvian's report, and decided to punish his wife Claramie by imprisoning her in a dungeon, where she had to eat with the dogs and drink sewage water. Flordelîse presents her accusation against Silvian in front of the king, and because Silvian, of course, denies everything with his oath, she demands a judicial duel, believing that God will help her prevail. This presents another set of problems. In the king's words: *Si ist ain weib, er ist ain man* ('She is a woman, he is a man', 20155; (ed.) Singer, 1906). Luckily, they need not trouble themselves with this complex issue for long, as there is an old bishop present, who has read in a book (!) how such a duel should be arranged (Figure 2). The man should be waist deep in a pit, with his right hand bound behind his back, armed with a one-cubit-long stick. The woman should be armed with a piece of cloth with a three-pound stone in it. Flordelîse is fine with these arrangements, and despite Silvian's objections, they proceed with the duel.

At this point, Heinrich provides his readers with a detailed description of the fight. Silvian swings his stick around, but Flordelîse evades his blows by jumping around "like a goat" and hits him with her stone on the head. Unfortunately, the hit has little effect, and Silvian manages to hit her in turn, making her cry out in pain. Silvian proceeds to grab her by her clothes and pulls her towards him. At this point, the spectators think she is doomed (*Flordelise di ist tod*, 20281). Flordelîse, however, manages to hit Silvian in the hand, making him drop his stick; she proceeds to hit him on the top of his head and on his temple, making him cry like a sheep:

> Do slug sy im ains auff den schiel
> Und dar nach ains auff den slaf,
> Das er reret als ain schaff. (20286–8)

Having suffered a series of blows, Silvian is lying in his pit lifeless, and Flordelîse declares victory. The crowd wants to burn Silvian's corpse, but suddenly he starts moving and confesses to the king that he had lied and that Claramie was innocent.

Depictions of a duel between a man and a woman may be found in the fifteenth-century fight books by Hans Talhoffer (Copenhagen, KB, Thott 290 2º, fols. 80r–84r; Munich, BSB, cod. icon. 394a, fols. 122v–126v) and a seventeenth-century compilation based on Talhoffers' and other relevant manuscripts found at the time in the Ducal Library of Gotha (Wolfenbüttel, HAB, Cod. Guelf. 125.16. extrav., fols. 38v–42v), which have been cited in scholarly works on legal history since the early eighteenth century (e.g., Gerhardus, 1711:para. VII note c; Thomasius, 1711:22 note r; Heineccius, 1737:595–596; L[anger], 1799). The number of secondary references to this practice may have contributed to the conception that this was something of a common occurrence in medieval times. Even though the handicap described may be found in legal works as well, the only known occurrence of an actual duel between a man and a woman took place in Bern on 4 January 1288 (Pettengill, 1914:46–48; MGH, SS 17:215, 271). In this case, as in Heinrich's story, the woman was victorious, but no other details are directly recorded (except that the duel took place in Matten in the place where the churchyard wall was later built; Studer, 1871:29). It is tempting to speculate that Heinrich's description may have preserved some elements of how the actual duel took place, such as the woman disarming the man with a strike to his hand. Unfortunately, the sequences depicted in the Talhoffer's fight books do not match the description given by Heinrich von Neustadt, so there is no corroborating evidence available, even though some individual moves are arguably somewhat similar. Talhoffer shows various tricks, some of them explicitly labelled as "finishing moves", which could be performed by either combatant, possibly to showcase his exceptional range as a teacher. His professional rival, Paulus Kal (Hils, 1985:178–181), apparently preferred to produce a simpler version that explicitly depicts the man as the ultimate winner of the exchange, perhaps illustrating what the man could have done had he been taught by Kal (Munich, BSB, cgm 1507, fols. 49v–51v). Before the finishing move, Kal's book shows the woman striking the man in the head and disarming him, like in Heinrich's story.

A Non-fictional Description of Single Combat

The historical curiosity discussed above may be contrasted with the next example, an eye-witness description of a duel that took place in 1478. Unlike in Flordelîse's case, in which the law prescribed clothes and weapons peculiar to judicial duelling, here we may witness the full range of knightly arms and modes of fighting. A further difference is that the cause of the duel is not rape but capture, the fifth item on Talhoffer's list quoted above from the Copenhagen codex. Jorge von Rosinberg accused Symon von Stetin of capturing his friend or treating him in captivity in a way that offended his honour. As he reportedly said, *Er had mir myn frund gefangen vnbewart siner eren* ('he has captured my friend paying no heed to his honour'). Symon, of course, denied the allegation, claiming that they were fighting due to Jorge's *großen hoemut vnd stoltzigkeit* ('great wantonness and arrogance'), echoing the reservation mentioned in Talhoffer's codex.

The vivid account of the ensuing duel summarised below comes from a letter to Albert III the Bold, Duke of Saxony and his brother Ernest, Elector of Saxony, sent by their uncle William III the Brave, Landgrave of Thuringia, dated 14th January 1478 (printed in Langenn, 1838:538–541; the part concerning grappling is discussed in Welle, 1993:222–224). The original author is unknown, as William's preface indicates that it is a copy of a written account he had received.

Symon starts with his lance couched, whereas Jorge has it by his foot. When the horn blows, both combatants charge: Jorge hits Symon's shield, but Symon misses. In the second pass, Jorge loses his shield and holds his lance with both hands. Symon brandishes his sword and cuts at Jorge's lance making him drop it. Jorge then draws his sword, and both try to thrust each other in the face. Jorge hits Symon's horse in the eye, making the poor animal unwilling to continue the fight. Then, Jorge thrusts at Symon for the tenth time, but Symon parries the attack. Symon's horse starts rearing, almost throwing him from its back. Jorge grabs him by his helmet and pulls him to the ground, demanding that he surrenders to him as his captive. Symon, who is almost choking, is still holding his sword, which Jorge then takes from his hand. Suddenly Symon's horse runs past them, and Symon manages to take a hold of it, but falls again. Jorge tries to trample on him, but his horse refuses to do that and throws Jorge to the ground.

Both combatants end up on foot. Symon tries to pick up a lance, but Jorge steps on it and tells Symon to leave it be. Jorge then thrusts with his sword at Symon, but Symon parries the thrust, making Jorge drop his sword, and attacks him unarmed. Jorge manages to throw Symon to the ground and again tells him to surrender, threatening to stab him to death. Symon promptly surrenders, and the ring guards stop the fight and help Symon back to his residence. Jorge then thanks God and sends a messenger to Symon demanding him to pay 200 Guldens. Symon opines that since no due date was set, he can pay in four or six years. The margrave, who acted as the guardian of the duel, orders him to pay *uff Sanct peters tag* (by St Peter's Day) and invites both combatants to his house for dinner. What the two did not know was that the margrave had set a time limit of fifteen minutes for the fight; had it gone on longer, he would have stopped the fight.

The fact that such judicial duels were not particularly common in the fifteenth century may very well explain the attention given to it in the source. There is also another account of the duel, written by Ludwig von Eyb the Elder (1417–1502), which omits technical details, but does not contradict anything in the previous account, even though he gives the name of the plaintiff as Sigmund instead of Symon

(Höfler, 1849:139–140). According to Ludwig, the two combatants accomplish nothing in the joust, draw swords, and after a while both fall from their horses and run into each other to wrestle; Jorge throws Sigmund on his back and claims victory with his dagger, after which both are invited by their noble patron to dinner.

As descriptions of duels, the account summarised above can be compared with the previous passage by Heinrich von Neustadt. In Heinrich's case, the duel between a man and a woman takes place in the fictional setting of a retelling of a story set in antiquity. The work does, however, transmit some of the contemporary attitudes towards and conventions applied in this unusual kind of duel. The situation is something of an oddity that requires the arcane learning of an old bishop to resolve it. The special skills involved in this setting would not have been part of the martial training of men-at-arms or knights, even though Hans Talhoffer and Paulus Kal appear to make some attempts at conceptualising a few tricks that might be employed in such a situation in their respective fight books, though probably not for the benefit of their noble patrons. In the case of the duel between Jorge and Symon (Sigmund), however, the situation is somewhat different.

It seems safe to assume that the anonymous author was relying on his memory when he set out to describe the duel in writing. This brings up some important considerations regarding the reliability of the report insofar as the actual occurrence is concerned. One's perception is shaped by the knowledge one has, and the more one knows, the easier it is to recognise and remember meaningful details. For example, people with military backgrounds can probably memorise the details of a uniform immediately, whereas someone else might struggle with counting chevrons and memorising the exact shapes of the various insignia. In the account of the duel, the formal side of the proceedings recorded in the account (omitted in the summary above) may reflect knowledge of the relevant conventions, and the same holds true for the details. Without a cinematographic record it is obviously not possible to control the accuracy of the author's recollection, but the main points are corroborated by Ludwig von Eyb, and there is no reason to assume that the author would have deliberately invented any of the details. Therefore, what the author says regarding the details of the fight stems from their intellectual models for conceptualising mounted and armoured combat. Having such martial education makes it possible to pick up things a layman would not have recognised as anything but chaotic movement. Even if the description does not match the actual events, which we cannot know, it would still most likely match the ideas of martial practices of the time or at least the author's individual experience of the martial culture he was part of. To better understand this martial culture, we may then turn to other sources that refer to individual units of fighting technique, namely the technical works that describe fighting technique.

Descriptions of Technique (Fight Books)

Several details of the above description are corroborated by descriptions found in fifteenth-century fight books.

In them we may find examples of men-at-arms holding their lances either couched or low (e.g., Los Angeles, J. Paul Getty Museum, Ms. Ludwig XV 13, fol. 41r), using swords against the lance (e.g., Munich, BSB, cod. icon. 394a, fol. 263r), a horse getting stabbed in the eye (e.g., Los Angeles, J. Paul Getty Museum, Ms. Ludwig XV 13, fol. 43r, Figure 3), and fencing on horseback (e.g., Munich, BSB, cod. icon. 394a, f. 254r). There are also depictions fitting the final phase of the fight involving grappling in armour and stabbing the loser with a dagger (Munich, BSB, cgm 1507, f. 35v), illustrating the seriousness of the threat issued by Jorge to Symon.

As for the actions referred to in Charny's questions, even taking the opponent's horse by its bridle (Los Angeles, J. Paul Getty Museum, Ms. Ludwig XV 13, fol. 45v) and grabbing the opponent's head and putting a knife at his throat (Munich, BSB, cgm 582, fol. 111r) are found in fight books. Such actions are, of course, quite generic and should not be taken as evidence of any stream of influences between the sources. Nevertheless, their inclusion in sources separated by time, space, and genre can be taken as indicating that they did belong to the conceptual canon of medieval combat technique.

A more complex matter is how does the inclusion of techniques for the duel between a man and a woman in fight books relate to the description given by Heinrich von Neustadt.

Figure 3: Interspecies violence in Fiore's fight book. *Il Fior di Battaglia,* a. 1410. The J. Paul Getty Museum, Los Angeles, Ms. Ludwig XV 13, fol. 43r. (Public domain; https://creativecommons.org/publicdomain/zero/1.0/)

The actions described by Talhoffer are found in the Copenhagen (KB, Thott 290 2°, fols. 80r–84r) and Munich (BSB, cod. icon. 394a, fol. 122v–126v) codices from 1459 and 1467, respectively. A version of the first sequence is found in Paulus Kal's fight book (Munich, BSB, cgm 1507, fols. 49v–51v) from c. 1470 and its copies.

A depiction of the basic setup is also found in the Cluny fight book (Paris, Musée national du Moyen Âge, MS Cl. 23842, fol. 194v) dated to c. 1480–1500 and in a book of arts and wonders (Rome, Biblioteca Apostolica Vaticana, Cod. Pal. lat. 1888, fol. 91v), which, despite its relatively early dating of c. 1430, cannot be the ultimate inspiration of the later illustrations.

Though R. W. Pettengill noted a 'marked resemblance' between the tactics described by Talhoffer and those in Heinrich's poem (making the comparison based on a written description of a copy of Talhoffer's images; Pettengill, 1914, pp. 48–49), the only action that is found in both is the man pulling the woman towards him. In Talhoffer's illustration, the man has thrown the woman down and proceeds to strangle her (*da hatt er sie zu im gezogen vnd vndersich geworffen vnd wyl sie wurgen,* cod. icon. 394a, fol. 123v, a variation is shown on fol. 125r), whereas in Heinrich's poem, Silvian manages to pull her towards him (*Er zoch sy pey dem claide/zu im,* 20277–8) only to be promptly countered with a debilitating blow to his hand. In Paulus

Kal's depiction, pulling, throwing, and strangling (?) the woman secures victory for the man (cgm 1507, fol. 51rv). Based on the available sources, one may venture the tentative conclusion that the woman combatant managed to counter such a manoeuvre in Bern in 1288; a less tentative conclusion would be that such an attack was widely considered as something the man in the pit ought to attempt against his smaller and weaker female adversary.

Conclusions

Based on the cases discussed above, it may be safely concluded that studying historical fighting practices based on literary sources is not a simple process of accumulating references to technique and drawing conclusions based on quantitative observations. Instead, the sources must be appraised not only through the usual precepts of historical source criticism but also considering that writings about practices may very well be more revealing of the perceptions and attitudes of the authors and their respective societies than what happened in combat or in training. As such, historical fighting practices cannot be examined as isolated phenomena but necessitate an appreciation of their respective social contexts.

Together the sources discussed reveal the range of technical ideas the practitioners recognised as something that had at least potential to be used in violent encounters. Even if the actual practice of fighting was chaotic and unpredictable, the individual techniques described in the sources create order in that chaos by dividing it into parts of something of a technical canon learnt by men-at-arms or knights. In addition, an important theme that permeates all the passages discussed is the need to regulate violence. Regulating violence does not necessarily lead to dissecting the technique of violence into its component parts, but it is still worth noting how in Charny's account the very technique of interpersonal combat appears to be tightly tied to the legal questions pertinent to violent encounters. In addition, judicial duels could impose artificial winning conditions reminiscent of rules in combat sports, such as simply hitting the opponent or touching the ground with one's hand or arm (L[anger], 1799:322).

How the exact forms of fighting are discussed is revealing of their societal significance. In Charny's case, jousting, tourneying, and waging war was part of the everyday life of his social class and required scrutiny and control. For the knightly class, this also meant maintaining the ability to fight through the acquisition and maintenance of arms and the relevant skills in their use, some of this activity falling outside the actual acts of fighting. In other words, the ability to display martial prowess would have become an important part of identity. A similar preoccupation with fighting among the nobility in the following centuries, even if increasingly a historical relic, is exemplified by the depictions and explanations of individual fighting techniques in the fight books of Hans Talhoffer and Paulus Kal prepared for the benefit of their patrons. The disproportionate attention given to the special case of a duel between a man and a woman is indicative of its breach of what was considered usual. Even so, rules aiming to make such a fight fair and its conclusion a result of solely divine intervention existed as well.

As for disseminating technical knowledge, it is interesting to note that the narrative examples discussed do not perhaps differ much from the average medieval fight book in terms of how accurately technical knowledge is conveyed, as both tend to refer to technique that exists in the relevant culture and is therefore not entirely unfamiliar to the assumed reader (cf. also Burkart, 2016). This is indicative of the relatively broad reach of knowledge on fighting in society. This being the case, both types of texts, narrative and technical, are, to some extent at least, equally useful as sources for the actual technique that shaped historical fighting practices.

References

Boffa, S. (2014). *Les manuels de combat* (Fechtbücher *et* Ringbücher). Typologie des sources du moyen âge occidental, 87. Brepols.

Burkart, E. (2016). Limits of Understanding in the Study of Lost Martial Arts: Epistemological Reflections on the Mediality of Historical Records of Technique and the Status of Modern (Re-)Constructions. *Acta Periodica Duellatorum*, 4(2), 5–30. https://doi.org/10.36950/apd-2016-010

Burkart, E. (2017). Body Techniques of Combat: The Depiction of a Personal Fighting System in the Fight Books of Hans Talhofer (1443–1467 CE). In J. Rogge (Ed.), *Killing and Being Killed: Bodies in Battle Perspectives on Fighters in the Middle Ages* (pp. 109–130). Transcript Verlag. https://doi.org/10.1515/9783839437834-009

Dreyer, Joh. C. Henr. (1754). *Sammlung vermischter Abhandlungen zur Erläuterung der teutschen Rechte und Alterthümer, wie auch der Critic und Historie. Erster Theil.* Berger und Boedner.

Elema, A. (2019). Tradition, Innovation, Re-enactment: Hans Talhoffer's Unusual Weapons. *Acta Periodica Duellatorum, 7*(1), 3–25.

Fehr, H. (1931). *Das Recht in der Dichtung.* Francke.

Forgeng, J. L. (2012). Owning the Art: The German Fechtbuch Tradition. In T. Capwell (Ed.), *The Noble Art of the Sword: Fashion and Fencing in Renaissance Europe 1520–1630* (pp. 165–175). The Wallace Collection.

Gerhardus, E. (1711). *Tractatio juridica de judicio duellico vulgo, Vom Kampf- und Kolben-Gerichte.* Gedruckt bey Johann Adolph Müllern.

Heineccius, Io. Gottl. (1737). *Elementa iuris Germanici tum veteris, tum hodierni, tomus II.* Impensis Orphanotrophei.

Hergsell, G. (1889). *Talhoffers Fechtbuch (Ambraser Codex) aus dem Jahre 1459. Gerichtliche und andere Zweikämpfe darstellend.* Published by the author.

Hils, H.-P. (1983). Die Handschriften des oberdeutschen Fechtmeisters Hans Talhoffer. *Codices manuscripti: Zeitschrift für Handschriftenkunde, 9*(3), 97–121.

Hils, H.-P. (1985). *Meister Johann Liechtenauers Kunst des langen Schwertes.* Europäische Hochschulschriften (Reihe III) 257. Peter Lang.

Höfler, C. von (Ed.) (1849). *Ritter Ludwig's von Eyb Denkwürdigkeiten brandenburgischer (hohenzollerischer) Fürsten: Mit einem aus Archivalien des ehemal. Brandenburgischen geh. Haus- und Staatsarchive verfaßten historischen Commentare.* Buchner.

Ijäs, A. (2022). Medieval Fight Books. In H. Klemettilä, S. Niskanen, & J. Willoughby, (Eds.), *Routledge Resources Online – Medieval Studies.* Routledge. https://doi.org/10.4324/9780415791182-RMEO370-1

Jaquet, D. (2016). 'Personne ne laisse volontiers son honneur être tranché' Les combats singuliers 'judiciaires' d'après les livres de combat. In C. Girbea (Ed.), *Armes et jeux militaires dans l'imaginaire. XIIe–XVe siècles* (pp. 389–412). Classiques Garnier.

Jaquet, D. (2017). Six Weeks to Prepare for Combat: Instruction and Practices from the Fight Books at the End of the Middle Ages, a Note on Ritualised Single Combats. In J. Rogge (Ed.), *Killing and Being Killed: Bodies in Battle Perspectives on Fighters in the Middle Ages* (pp. 131–164). Transcript Verlag. https://doi.org/10.1515/9783839437834-009

Jaquet, D. (2018). Martial Arts by the Book: Late Medieval and Early Modern European Martial Arts. In P. Bowman (Ed.), *The Martial Arts Studies Reader* (pp. 41–56). Rowman & Littlefield International.

Jaquet, D., Verelst, K. & Dawson, T. (2016). *Late Medieval and Early Modern Fight Books: Transmission and Tradition of Martial Arts in Europe (14th–17th Centuries)*. Brill. https://doi.org/10.1163/9789004324725

Kaeuper, R. W. & Kennedy, E. (1996). The Book of Chivalry *of Geoffroi de Charny: Text, Context, and Translation* (4th ed.). University of Pennsylvania Press.

Keen, M. H. (1965). *The Laws of War in the Late Middle Ages*. Routledge: Kegan Paul. University of Toronto Press.

Langenn, F. A. von. (1838). *Herzog Albrecht der Beherzte, Stammvater des königlichen Hauses Sachsen: Eine Darstellung aus der sächsischen Regenten-, Staats- und Culturgeschichte des XV. Jahrhunderts, großentheils aus archivalischen Quellen*. Hinrichs.

L[anger], [Ernst Theodor]. (1799). Gerichtlicher Zweykampf zwischen Mann und Weib: Nach Thalhöfers ungedrucktem Fechtbuche und andern Handschriften. In P. J. Bruns, *Beyträge zu den deutschen Rechten des Mittelalters aus den Handschriften und alten Drucken der akademischen Bibliothek in Helmstädt* (pp. 313–332). C. G. Fleckeisen.

Muhlberger, S. (2014). *Charny's Men-at-Arms: Questions Concerning The Joust, Tournaments and War*. Freelance Academy Press.

Nielsen, A. E. & Walker, W. H. (Eds.). (2009). *Warfare in Cultural Context: Practice, Agency, and the Archaeology of Violence*. Amerind Studies in Archaeology 3. University of Arizona Press.

Peltonen, M. (2003). *The Duel in Early Modern England: Civility, Politeness and Honour*. Cambridge University Press.

Pettengill, R. W. (1914). The Source of an Episode in Heinrich's von Neustadt Apollonius. *The Journal of English and Germanic Philology, 13*(1), 45–50.

Singer, S. (Ed.). (1906). *Heinrichs von Neustadt 'Apollonius von Tyrland' nach der Gothaer Handschrift, 'Gottes Zukunft' und 'Visio Philiberti' nach der Heidelberger Handschrift*. Weidmannsche Buchhandlung.

Spatz, B. (2015). *What a Body Can Do: Technique as Knowledge, Practice as Research*. Routledge.

Studer, G. (Ed.). (1871). *Die Berner-Chronik des Conrad Justinger*. K. J. Wyss.

Thomasius, C. (1711). *Dissertatio inauguralis iuridica, de occasione, conceptione ac intentione constitutionis criminalis Carolinæ*. Typis Io. Chr. Henckelii.

Tlusty, B. A. (2011). *The Martial Ethic in Early Modern Germany: Civic Duty and the Right of Arms*. Early Modern History: Society and Culture. Palgrave Macmillan.

Topic, T. L. & Topic, J. R. (2009). Variation in the Practice of Prehispanic Warfare on the North Coast of Peru. In A. E. Nielsen & W. H. Walker (Eds.), *Warfare in Cultural Context: Practice, Agency, and the Archaeology of Violence* (pp. 17–55). https://doi.org/10.2307/j.ctv1jf2ctn.4

U[kert], [F. A.]. (1812). Ueber den Zweikampf zwischen Mann und Frau. (Nach handschriftlichen Quellen bearbeitet). *Curiositäten der physisch-literarisch-artistisch-historischen Vor- und Mitwelt, 1*(5), 395–406.

U[kert], F. A. (1836). "Fechtkunst". In Fr. Jacobs & F. A. Ukert (Eds.), *Beiträge zur ältern Litteratur oder Merkwürdigkeiten der Herzogl. Öffentlichen Bibliothek zu Gotha. Drittes Heft oder zweiten Bandes erstes Heft* (pp. 102–144). Dyk'sche Buchhandlung.

Welle, R. (1993). '…*Und wisse das alle höbischeit kompt von deme ringen*'. *Der Ringkampf als adelige Kunst im 15. Und 16. Jahrhundert.* Forum Sozialgeschichte 4. Centaurus.

Welle, R. (2015). Talhoffer, Hans. In W. Achnitz (Ed.), *Deutsches Literatur-Lexikon. Das Mittelalter. Bd. 7. Das wissensvermittelnde Schrifttum im 15. Jahrhundert* (col. 428–434). De Gruyter.

CHAPTER 7

Ships or People? On Material Agency and the New Early Modern Warships

Johan Rönnby

The Question: Who is the Actor?

"Guns don't kill people, people kill people" (and similar variants) is a slogan used in the American debate regarding gun ownership. It is applied as an argument against the demands for restrictions for sale of handguns which often occur in connection with mass shootings at schools and other public places. The wording has been used by gun advocates in the US since at least the early 1900s and is today strongly associated with the National Rifle Association (NRA). The subject concerning killing and access to weapons is also a relevant issue with reference to gang crime and use of handguns by youths in Sweden and other European countries during the 2020s.

It might be a little surprising that American gun lobbyists seem to prefer a sort of social explanation. However, there is reason to suspect that most of those who mobilize around the above expression do not attach any deeper theoretical meaning to it. They only see it as a useful slogan for justifying the ownership and sale of weapons. At first glance, the argument may seem difficult to counter. On closer reflection, however, one realizes that the sentence is an example of a logical fallacy. The two statements are not mutually exclusive and there is no reason to claim that it is either or. Furthermore, it is not obvious that the slogan necessarily supports gun ownership. Contrary to the argument of the NRA, the statement that "people kill" could in fact also be an argument that people's access to lethal weapons should be limited.

In any case, and more theoretically interesting is if we consider the slogan in light of a discussion about the "moral status of technological artefacts" (cf. Kroes & Verbeek, 2014) or how "technical mediation" works (specifically discussing guns and people, Latour, 1994:34ff.).

The subject also concerns an even larger discourse about the influence of the material world and people's relationship to objects, a topic that can be said to be one of the classic questions in social theory and historical research (see Liedman, 1991:28–30). The two extreme perspectives between which one then moves are a kind of material/technological determinism or a pure social/cultural explanation. The claim of the different killing capacity of guns and humans can also be seen in the light of these two opposite poles.

However, in the human sciences, and in society at large, it is usually not a question of choosing either/or, but rather of positioning oneself somewhere on a scale between them. This means advancing suggestions and theories about the nature of the interface between human agency and matter, how we interact with our things and what impact different contexts play in affecting the relations existing between us and things.

Within all humanistic and social research disciplines, discussions are ongoing about the role and importance of technology and material objects in affording human agency, not least in relation to conflicts. For example, the introduction of new stone tools for hunting has been discussed in connection to early killings of fellow humans and "the first wars" in history (Dawson, 1996:26ff). The Neolithic transformation with farming and increased residency has further been seen as a period where a new way of living led to an entanglement with things as well as a need to arm oneself for the protection of a stored surplus (Hodder, 2012:171, Hagberg & Wiman, 2016:203–213, Rönnby 2019: 258–259).

Against this background, this article extends the contemporary American debate on whether it is guns or people that kill by exploring the broader impact of material objects on conflicts, power dynamics, and societal change. From this starting point the focus in this article is on the role of heavily armed warships in the fifteenth and sixteenth centuries, analysing how these technological innovations contributed to the transformation from Medieval to Modern society. The study employs a contextual and historical analysis of archaeological and historical evidence from the Baltic Sea region and Scandinavian countries, seeking to explore the material and technological factors influencing societal transformations. New ships and weapons are prevalent phenomena throughout Europe during the period in question. The focus on the Nordic and Baltic Sea regions in this study is chosen to easily clarify details regarding the material conditions and the actions of various actors.

Approaching the issue theoretically through various forms of materialism and concepts like dialectic, entanglement, affordances and possibilism, the aim is to provide a nuanced understanding of how material objects, notably warships (together with human agents), have played a pivotal role in shaping historical and social developments. In so doing, the paper seeks to establish an archaeological interpretation of Early Modern ships that avoids the two extreme perspectives of a technological determinism or a pure social/cultural explanation. The warships during this period represent critical junctures where material innovations fundamentally altered human capacities for conflict and societal transformation. By analysing the entanglement of humans and technology from an archaeological perspective, this paper situates warships within a broader discussion of material agency, underscoring their comparability with other transformative technological artifacts.

Theory: Material Things and Humans

An important starting point in all studies is to first try to clarify the basic theoretical premises regarding the current issue. A classical materialist perspective holds that matter is the basic substance of the world, and that everything, including social conditions as well as mental state and consciousness, are the result of material things and circumstances. Materialism stands in contrast to idealism, according to which mind, ideas and thoughts are the starting points for defining the nature of reality. Materialism has its roots in Greek antiquity, and was widely discussed during the nineteenth century, unsurprising given the dramatic industrial and technological changes taking place at the time (see Lange, 1913).

Archaeology is often defined as the study of man based on a source material consisting of manmade things, what in the discipline is referred to as *material culture* (ex. Mortimer Wheeler, 1954; Moberg, 1969; Johnson, 2010). Thus defined, it is obvious that the relationship between people and things is a central question within the subject of archaeology. At different times during the development of this research field, the shaping of material culture has been interpreted as a product of ethnicity, race, culture, function and environment.

During the first half of the 1980s, within so called postprocessual archaeology, the meaning and symbolism of things was strongly emphasized. This is to say, things were seen as communication and should be "read" in their context, and "in action" (see Hodder, 1982, 1986). How loaded each thing was with "meaning" of course varied, not at least in accordance with the contexts within which different things were situated. But while either "manifest" or "latent" (cf. Andren, 1985:9–11) everything a human makes and uses, can be said to have some kind of cultural content created by their specific societal context. However, this does not mean that there must be a sharp contradiction between things as "culture" or "symbols", on the one hand, and their "functional" value, on the other. Things can of course be both, the level and extent of this co-dependence will depend on situation and circumstances. Weapons and war equipment are good examples of this, given their practical function but also their great "symbolic" importance. The same goes for castles, roads, churches and ships. While fulfilling different practical needs, they can also be seen as power demonstrations and ideological messages in a landscape, in a city or on the sea (cf. Johnson, 2003).

There has in the humanities for a period been an 'new materialist' trend, sometimes referred to as a "material turn" in understanding social and cultural phenomena. Since the mid-1990s, some scholars have argued for turning our analytical focus to the role of matter and things in relation to humans and society. In part this has meant moving beyond an anthropocentric view of the world and recognizing the agency of non-human actors. Nature, animals, technology and material artefacts are then said to be co-creators of social and political conditions. Humans and non-human things (and other living creatures) are defined as equal agents or "actants". "Group formations" or "assemblages" of different actants are said to form collaborative networks and can be linked together in "hybrid social entities" (cf. Latour 2005, Müller 2015). Discussions following this can be found within archaeology (see, e.g., Whitmore 2014, Alberti et al. 2013, 2014:1–44, Olsen et al. 2012, Hodder & Lucas 2017) but also within several other disciplines (see Knapet & Malafouris 2008, Harvey 2009, Karlholm 2017, Choat 2017:3).

However, understanding the material world as part of complex networks is a perspective that has been used by scholars for a long time, inspired by Marxist social theory (see for example, Wigfors 1970:7–93, Gunnarsson 1971:34–39, Cohn 1978, Nyström 1985:95–121). Within historical materialism, material agency is recognized by focusing on the role of material and economic conditions in shaping society and history. But the role of things and their part within possible "assemblages", their interplay with other "actants", are not seen independently; instead, they are contextualized within specific economic and social formations that are created by historically formed conditions. In classical orthodox Marxism, it is ultimately class struggle that is emphasized in the establishing of these different social formations in history. Even if the role of materiality often is related to processes of production and economic forces, there is also, in historical materialism, a broad discussion of how ideology, is linked to various interests and power relations within a given social formation. This then also includes approaches where things are described as a kind of "sociomateria" acting as ideological mediator between society's members (see Österberg 1977, 1989:81–125).

When discussing and studying the agency of material culture, it seems important not to confuse a recognition of the social importance of things with a simplified pure materialism, material determinism, or what Karl Marx already labelled as "objectification" and "commodity fetishism". Meaning that social structures and power relations are masked and mystified by things being animated and attributed to a false meaning that reduces human agency and the possibilities for subject-directed change (cf. Nussbaum 1995, Hornborg 2013, 2017:96). There are reasons not to overinterpret what new materialists have called a "symmetrical" relationship (see, e.g., Latour 1994, Witmore 2007, Shanks 2007). Such a perspective risks diminishing human influence and responsibility regarding how societies change and function. What "symmetry" could, however, plausibly refer to is the importance of materiality in affecting the extent to which humans' influence their surroundings. This is not the same as saying that things and people have the same role. Although humans and non-humans are jointly part of changing the world, they do not do so in the same way.

Human agency with intentions must be understood differently to that of a flintstone or a warship. The historically determined context, and not least embedded power relations, is an important part of the motives, liaisons, and the capacities of human actors. Human agents can also adjust, develop or totally change their strategy and goal. Artefacts are further material things intentionally made by human for particular uses, thereby tying material objects to human values and practices. Things and technology are therefore not independent or neutral (cf. Kroes & Verbeck 2014:1–9).

Regarding humans and things, a wider discussion surrounding their dialectical relation is also relevant (cf. Bhaskar, 2008). We shape things out of need and aspiration but once they exist, they change our individual and collective behaviour and impose constraints upon us. Which is to say, our relationship with material things changes us and the societies we live in. We can describe this relationship in terms of an "entanglement" (Hodder, 2012), "affordances" (Gibson, 1979:29) or simply say that things have "consequences" (Hornborg, 2017).

Within the discipline of geography, a long-established perspective regarding the role of the landscape is known as "possibilism" (Östman, 1985, Rubenstein, 2002:19). One also finds this concept within anthropological studies. The material world is seen as a framework of constraints as well as possibilities. On this "scene" people act and "perform" their roles. A possibilistic viewpoint, combined with a dialectical understanding of humans and their surroundings, resonates with a central insight in historical materialism, namely that people "make their own history but based on circumstances encountered and transmitted from the past". This claim then not only refers to the landscape and physical environment but also to social and economic conditions.

To conclude this discussion about different theoretical approaches concerning the relation between the material world and human agency, one should probably always keep in mind that theories are just working tools for trying to understand the tangle of events and history.

Even if some theories can be said to work better than others, they should not be confused with reality (cf. Nyström 1985:115, Rönnby 1995:25–27). The role of material culture in social change, and the dialectic between things and people, will now be exemplified and interpreted in relation to the building and use of the new warships during late the Medieval and the Early Modern period.

The Material Agents: Ships and Guns

Things and material culture do not suddenly arise at a certain time, they have both a societal and technological background that is important to try to understand. During the Middle Ages, the North German Hanseatic cities and their partners were leaders in ship-building in Northern Europe. The type of ship mainly associated with them is the load-bearing cog (see Ellmer, 1994). The medieval ship stock included other ship types than what we today define as cogs and there were also hybrid forms (see discussion in Rönnby & Björdal, 2023:37–46, cf. also Åkerlund, 1951).

The fifteenth century was a time of structural change for the construction and rigging of larger ships. A distinctive novelty was that in Northern Europe hulls were first built on the largest ships, with planks laid edge to edge using so-called carvel technique instead of overlapping clinker planks. This simplified the planning and construction of large ships (see Adams, 2013). A marked increase in the size of ships also characterized the first part of the sixteenth century.

The shipbuilding development and innovations at the end of the Middle Ages probably took place initially largely in connection with capital-strong Mediterranean cities with a long maritime tradition, such as Genoa and Venice. Here, there were both resources and the need to create safe and efficient ships for both trade, passenger transport and warfare. As important trading centres with long-distance contacts, conditions were available for combining different building traditions. In the Italian ports, the northern European cogs met the round-bellied, Latin-rigged and cravel-built Mediterranean ships (Ellmers, 1994; Friel, 1994). A common name for the large cargo-bearing sailing ships that resulted from the combining of northern European cogs and the Latin-rigged Mediterranean ships was "cochas", but soon some were also called "carakes", possibly referring to the larger ones among them (see Adams, 2013:69–70).

Through close economic contacts across Europe, the building technology innovations of the time spread north to the Atlantic coast and the existing commercial metropoles in today's Belgium and Holland. An unusually sensational example of such connections is the wrecking described by Pietro Quertina. In 1431, he sailed with a great Venetian carrack from Crete with a cargo of wine, spices, cotton and wax. The destination was Flanders and the city of Bruges. After a dramatic journey in the North Atlantic he and his crew ended up on the island of Röst in Northern Norway (see Wold, 2004).

In terms of adaptation for ocean shipping, the Iberian Peninsula was also an important area for the development of shipbuilding technology at the end of the Middle Ages. In connection with the voyages of discovery initiated by prince Henrik the Navigator during the fifteenth century, new well-sailed ships were built on the Atlantic. The planking on these ships was, as on all southern European ships, done with the planks laid edge to edge. The most common name for these Portuguese ships was caravels. The word "carvel", which became the term in Northern Europe for laying the table planks edge to edge" seems to derive from the name of this type of ship (see discussion in Adams, 2013:70–71). However, larger ships in Portugal and Spain were often called "nau" not caravels.

During the fifteenth century, the caravels were rigged with Latin sails, often on two masts. Early evidence of a ship rigged in a new way, combining square sails on the fore- and mainmast with a Latin sail on the mizzen mast, can be found in a Catalan document from 1406. A dish from Málaga dated to about 1400 is also usually considered to be the first depiction of a three-masted ship with such a modern rig (Adams, 2013:70, Landström, 1969:96).

The carvels, and maybe especially the large "Mediterranean carracks", can architecturally be seen as the starting point for the new warships and the continued development of European large ships that would soon take place in the new state-owned shipyards. The Hanseatic network also meant that the innovations in ship technology eventually also reached the Baltic Sea (see Zwick, 2016). Early repair and construction of carvel ships took place, for example, in Gdansk in the 1470s (Mozejka, 2019).

"Carack" was the most common name for the new modern large ships on the Atlantic coast and in the Mediterranean during early modern times. In the Nordic countries, however, that name was never used. Rather, the most common local name for the new type of ship seems to have been "kravel", referring to the construction of the planking (cf. Glete, 1977:29).

The change in shipbuilding is also linked to military-technical development and armament. The first large late medieval warships were intended for boarding combat. The shops were built big and high to accommodate many soldiers armed with melee weapons, crossbows and small firearms along the railing or up in the fighting tops. The small guns on board were meant to fire at soldiers rather than blast enemy ship hulls. The high fore and aft castles are reminiscent of the walls and towers of strongholds and castles on land. The ships were in this respect a kind of fortress under sail.

Cannons appeared sometimes on battlefields already during the fourteenth century and were also sometimes taken on board ships during this time (for development of power guns see Alm, 1933; Hedberg, 1975; Hall, 1997; Rosborn, 2007; Mortensen, 1999, 2022). However, in the Middle Ages they did not play an important tactical role in warfare. They were relatively rare, unreliable and difficult to handle. A turning point is usually said to have been the French Charles VIII's campaigns in northern Italy in the 1490s. The French king's heavy field guns easily destroyed the medieval Italian fortresses (Parker, 1996:9–16). Machiavelli, the contemporary portrayer of power and the art of governance by princes, described the new mobile siege artillery as impressively efficient. New star-shaped fortresses with bastions had to be erected to withstand the heavy guns. This, in turn, led to the possibility of it taking months to conquer fortified cities. Sieges became more numerous and more important in war than in battles (Sjöblom, forthcoming).

The new strategies for fortress building and sieges were transferred to warships, which could now also take on a more offensive role in attacks on harbours and coastal defences. With the development of gunports in the hull side around 1500, increasingly heavier siege guns could be taken on board. Compared to artillery on land, the potential firepower of a ship became very large. (Parker, 1996:82–91; Rodger, 1996; Hildred, 1984, 2011; Warming, 2019; Rönnby & Sjöblom, in print; Sjöblom, forthcoming).

Heavy infantry on land during the Early Modern period often fought with pikes and halberds arrayed in squares supported by bows and crossbows. Increasingly these began to be replaced by different types of handguns. This change regarding the use of handguns also occurred on board warships (Warming, 2019).

In terms of warfare in the Mediterranean, the galley had long dominated, and for the expansion of the Ottoman Empire, the large rowing ships were of great importance. The dominance of the galley was challenged during the sixteenth century with the new sailing gunships. The Battle of Lepanto in 1571 (outside present-day Greece) is usually said to be the end of the heyday of manned galleys (Parker 1996).

The Contextual Scene: A New Time

Part of understanding the significance of things is, of course, their general historical context. From the sixteenth century onwards, it is usually said that the Middle Ages ends and the Early Modern period begins. To support this, researchers often point to the fact that several political, economic, social, religious, and cultural changes took place in Europe at the time, and that much of what we associate with modernity – such as globalism, rationality and individualism – begins to emerge. At this time also Renaissance ideas manifested themselves in art, literature, architecture, and science, while the power of the once powerful Catholic Church was further weakened by the Reformation.

In terms of the basic structure of society, new economic activity and the emergence of early capitalism disrupted the old feudal order in Europe. A new political order emerged where the new economic interests formed an alliance with the most powerful "princes" (in the Machiavellian meaning) who now alone took control of larger territories and countries. Within the framework of newly formed states, new forms and ways of resource utilization, technological development and monopoly of violence emerged (see Andersson 1974; for complementing and different perspectives: Wallenstein, 1974; Tilly, 1975; Rogers, 1995; Gustafsson, 1998; Glete, 2002).

In contrast to the Middle Ages, when power was often dispersed and relatively changeable, the new states were led by a new type of ruler with dynastic ambitions. During the sixteenth century, typical representatives of this were, for example, Henry VIII in England, Frances I in France, Charles V in Austria/Spain. In the Nordic country's there was Christian I, John, Christian II and Frederick I in Denmark and in Sweden Gustav Vasa and his three sons, Erik XIV, Johan III and Karl IX. Despite differences in power and ability, alongside some chronological differences between the centre and the periphery, these new rulers were engaged in similar political projects. They strengthen the central bureaucracy, introduce new forms of taxation, and invest in military power (for war organization in the Nordic countries see Hallenberg & Holm, 2016; 27–38, Neuding Skoog, 2018:22ff.; Sjöblom, 2016). What also unites them is that they established new shipyards where they had ships built (see Glete, 1976, 1977, 1993, 2000, 2002; Barfod, 1995).

The contemporary ship-based geographical discoveries of new areas offered goods and resources through colonialism and exploitation. An activity that would change Europe but also have far-reaching and lasting effects for people on all other continents (see, e.g., Monie Nordin, 2020). Globalization meant a further mental expansion of the contemporary "space". Detailed maps and charts of the oceans and the world were made, the theoretical knowledge of navigation was developed, and new instruments were designed to measure star altitudes and latitudes (Law, 1986, 2002). Already in the middle of the fifteenth century, large parts of the west coast of Africa were mapped, and in the second half of the century, long-distance fishing around Iceland was well established. From the 1540s, there was a Basque whaling station at Red Bay in Labrador (Grenier et al., 1994, 2007). There was now the opportunity to ship home commodities and resources from a global world that had become much larger.

For countries such as England, Spain, the Netherlands and, to some extent, Denmark, the new "space ambitions" were about the world's oceans. For the new state of Sweden and the Vasa kings, it was mainly about control and mastery of the Baltic Sea. In the Stockholm archipelago, Gustav Vasa appointed Anders Båtelsson as pilot at Landsort in the 1530s. Remains of older lighthouse installations in the same area on Gunnarstenarna, as well as on Viksten, could also be ways of establishing a connection with Swedish state's desire to expand as well as control sea space and shipping (Landin et al., 2011:43–48; cf. Eriksson, 2022). Perhaps even more clear are the Danish royal power's ambition for spatial maritime control when, in the early 1560s, the first permanent lighthouses were created on Skagen, Kullen and Anholt.

In the Middle Ages, castles and fortified manors were part of the landscape of power. They functioned as a way for kings as well as regional rulers to both economically and strategically control their territories. During the period of state formation, the most important and largest castles become more firmly tied to the regents and their power network for the state. Bailiffs and close relatives to the rulers were stationed in castles around the landscape. The most important of these fortresses were rebuilt with the ambition of transforming them into more Renaissance-like palaces. Moreover, the majority of the king's castles had a location close to harbours or strategic straits, thereby illustrating how maritime connections became increasingly important during this time.

Similarities in construction and armament for warfare suggest that large new ships served as a kind of "floating castle" or "floating fortress" (cf. Bill, 2005; see discussion in Adams, 2013:95–97). Considering the new spatial ambitions, one should also talk about "movable castles". The ship was useful not only for strategic control but for long-distance representation of, and ideological purposes within the kingdom. Based on this, the superstructures of the large early modern ships often have architectural similarities with castles and Renaissance palaces, as is the case with the use of long colourful fabric banners, which were not only suspended on top of the towers of castles or the city walls but were also hung from the masts and the fighting tops of ships. In connection with spatial ambitions, it is also important to add that new large ships were initially a kind of combined ship used not just for warfare but also for shipping of goods and trade. The historical sources describing the great ship *Peter from Danzig's* travels during 1462–1475 clearly highlight this (see Mozejka, 2019).

The first big ships during the fifteenth and early sixteenth centuries were initially part of a late medieval Machiavellian power game. Apart from kings, local landowners, noblemen, bishops and rich trading cities, had fleets and some large new ships. However, big warships and modern cannons were resource intensive. Over time, the possession of big, well-armed ships therefore became something that set apart lesser power holders from the more powerful kings and state builders. This development becomes very clear during the sixteenth century once warships became increasingly specialized for carrying heavy cannons (see below).

Performance and Practice: Fighting at Sea

People's "things" are closely linked with how they are used, their practices. The great warships, like the new early modern state, needed to be organized and systematized. The careful, but still somewhat scattered, regulation of responsibility and order on board can be seen as part of the general process in society during the sixteenth century. The modern organized state was still at this time under construction (see Rönnby & Sjöblom, 2024; cf. Thorelli, 2023:9).

An aspect of the relation between humans and contemporary war technology that has gone unacknowledged concerns the behaviour of people aboard during naval battles. How did one convince soldiers to enter an enemy ship in the middle of the battle? How did one convince a cannon crew to stay at their post and continue to collectively cooperate when the air was full of fire, smoke, and wood splinters? What did the technical and tactical change mean for the dispositions of the crew, as duties and roles became increasingly important on board? (cf. Warming, 2014; Sjöblom, 2016:439–459; Sjöblom, 2016b:22–68; Warming, 2019; Warming, in prep.). Modern studies of soldiers in war tend to emphasize the differences in disposition between close combat and killing the enemy at a distance (Warming 2014, in prep.). However, all normal people seem to have had a hard time killing other people; using guns at a distance might make it more indirect but is still something very unpleasant. Prior experience of fighting in battlefields may make killing easier, but also systematic training, where certain battle exercises are repeated, or, in the present day, where soldiers become used to slaughter and killing by watching films or playing computer simulations. Such examples can reduce our normal inhibitions against taking human lives (Grossman, 2009; Bourke, 1999:57ff; Rönnby, 2019:260–263; Warming, in prep.).

During the first part of the sixteenth century, one can say that, regarding war strategy, the large ships were a kind of *hybrid*. The high fore and aft castles of the first generation of large warships, used for boarding combat, were still used, but now they were combined with an increasing number of guns on board placed on purpose made gundecks (Warming, 2014). Not allowing the ship's superstructure to detrimentally restrict its navigation and sailing abilities became an important issue, especially with the use of heavier guns. During the second half of the sixteenth century, one can see on pictures that while the fore castle became lower, its position on the ship was moved backwards. In front of the stem post, the images from the time show the beginnings of a protruding construction, a so-called galleon (Figure 1). In ship literature this is usually seen as a transition from *carrack* to *galleon* ships (Hough, 1969:69–104; Kirsch, 1990, Glete, 2000).

In Northern Europe the victory of the mobile English galleons over the large, "clumsy" carracks, which formed part of the Spanish Armada in 1588, is usually seen as a decisive blow to old practices, ushering in a tactical change from boarding to cannon warfare. It is of course a simplification and the fate of *Mars* and the events off Öland in 1564 is an example that shows that this was a process already underway earlier (see also Warming, 2014, 2019). The battle between the Swedish ships and a combined Danish and Lübeckian fleet lasted for two days, 30–31 May 1564.

It started well enough for Swedish Admiral Bagge's flagship *Mars*, which, with its many and heavy guns, seriously damaged the Danish Admiral Herluf Trolle's ship *Fortuna*, as well as sinking the Lübeckian ship *Alte Bark*. These events are early examples of a "modern" use of the cannons on a warship.

Figure 1: A Swedish and Danish ship in battle. Drawing from a manuscript by Rudolf van Deventer (Berich vom Pulver und Feuerwerken, c. 1585) in the Danish Royal Library in Copenhagen. (http://www5.kb.dk/manus/vmanus/2011/dec/ha/object 448306/da#kbOSD-0=page:8). Public Domain.

The next day, however, events turned decisively against the big Swedish ship. Due to strong winds, the Swedish fleet was scattered. The prevailing naval battle tactic during this time was for the large capital ship to fight together with two smaller ships in a unit of three ships. But because of the wind, *Mars* now had to fight alone. Two Lübeckian ships, *Der Engel* and *Peter und Paul*, managed to hook onto *Mars* with tugs and ropes. The Danish warship *Byens Löwe,* on the other hand, was effectively pushed away with long sticks held by the Swedish crew through the gun ports. A ferocious battle began aboard *Mars* as the Germans entered the ship, which at the same time began to burn. The fire was so violent that many of the loaded cannons exploded on deck. The Danish ship withdrew from the battle to avoid becoming entangled in the burning rig. The Swedish crew surrendered and the Lübeckian crewmen plundered the ship. After a while, however, the flames reached the gunpowder cloth, consisting of several tons of gunpowder. The entire front of the ship exploded, and she quickly sank (Figure 2; Sjöblom, 2003).

Human Agents: The Prince's Ship

To understand the significance of material culture the human actors and context must be identified.

Figure 2: One of the large bronze guns on the great warship *Mars Makalös*. The Swedish King Erik XIV's new and "matchless" ship sank in a naval battle in 1564. Photo: The Mars Project/Tomasz Stachura

The character of the late medieval princes and their role as historical actors during this period can be illustrated by considering the last Nordic Union Regents. The so-called Kalmar Union, which united Denmark, Norway and Sweden, was still in effect at the turn of the sixteenth century, even though domestic *riksföreståndare* ("state governors") ruled over the Swedish area for long periods of time.

Large Danish and Nordic royal capital ships are known already from the time of Valdemar Atterdag: Queen Margareta's, Eric of Pomerania's and Christopher of Bavaria's. Their largest ships were cogs or variants of medieval northern European clinker construction. The Oldenburg regents, Christian I, and his son John, had, during the second half of the fifteenth century, new and greater maritime ambitions. These included not only territorial control over the Baltic Sea, but also ocean shipping, privateering, fishing in the North Atlantic, and western naval crusades (Jensen 2007).

King Christian I and his influential queen Dorothea had good European contacts, including Edward IV (1442–1483) in England and Alfonso V (1432–1481) in Portugal (Barfod, 1990:47–48). The two Danish regents also had family ties around Europe, and in 1474 they visited both the Pope in Rome and Duke Galeazzo Sforza in Milan. From 1482 Leonardo da Vinci was working for the powerful Sforza ducal family. He was employed at the court as painter and sculptor but also as an army engineer inventing and constructing ingenious new weapons. Da Vinci remained with the Sforzas until 1499, when the French army occupied Milan. In 1502, however, the highly regarded polymath joined Machivelli's main character, Cesare Borgia, in the book *The Prince*, and accompanied him on his campaigns.

Since Christian and Dorothea belonged to the European power elite, they should have known about the most modern ships of the time, for instance where they were built and their capabilities (see Rönnby, 2021:83–84, Adams and Rönnby, 2022). The first mention of a carvel-built ship, built by the Danes, is from 1474. The privateer captain Hans Pothorst operated around the East Frisian coast with the help of two such ships (Barfod, 1990:50). When in 1476 King Christian sent Pothorst and his colleague Pinning, along with a Portuguese seafarer (assumedly João Vaz Corte Real) to Greenland – and probably further west to the "cod land" – they were certainly using modern carvels (see Landström, 1964:205; Möller Jensen, 2007:185; Ullidtz, 2017).

Domestically organized shipbuilding had of course been established for a long time in Denmark (see, e.g., Bill, 2009). When exactly new developments in shipbuilding were used in the Nordic countries is, however, uncertain. Perhaps there was a gradual adaptation, such as in the number of masts used and in the design of the castles in the bow and stern (cf. Jahnke, 2006:85–95). In 1488, however, there is information that the new king, John (1455–1513), commissioned a Dutch shipbuilder to build a new carvel on Holmen outside Copenhagen. At the beginning of the sixteenth century, King John also began the construction of two new very large ships, the *Engelen* and *Maria*, later taken over by his son Christian II. A new state shipyard was set up at Engelborg on Slotö, but royal ships were also built at Sønderborg and in Copenhagen.

From 1487 there is an early record of 12 ships having formed part of a fleet under King John. However, many of the ships mentioned were still privately owned by various noblemen and were summoned by the king, when necessary, in a kind of late medieval array known as *ledung* (see Sjöblom 2016). Regarding name and size, one can assume that several of these ships would have been relatively large carvel-built ships.

One of the larger ships mentioned in the list is the *Grifun* (or, as referred to in some sources, the *Gribshund*). In 1495 the king travels to Kalmar for an important meeting with the powerful Swedish nobleman Sten Sture the Elder. With negotiations imminent surrounding the royal power in Sweden, the two "princes" converged in the city with their ships and fleets. Halfway ahead of them, towards Copenhagen, a fire broke out on the *Grifun* and it sank. The remains of King John's cravel today lies ten meters under water (see Einarsson, 2008, 2008b; Rönnby, 2021; Adams & Rönnby, 2022).

Dendroanalysis shows that the wood from the *Grifun* comes from the upper course of the river Meuse on the west side of the Ardennes (Lindersson, 2020). Here in Flanders and Brabant, at the intersection of France, the Netherlands and the Burgundian Empire and close to England across the water, were some of the most powerful and financially dominant trading cities of the second half of the fifteenth century, places with strong historical and economic ties to the Mediterranean area. Early evidence for the construction of new modern warships can be found in this area. In 1439, Philip of Burgundy, as Count of Flanders, is said to have given orders to a Portuguese shipbuilder to build a nao and a carvel in Brussels (Sleesvig 1989:226).

In 1475, King Christian I visited Charles the Bald in Burgundy. Kristian stayed for several months and passed through the Netherlands on his way home. It is likely that the *Grifun* was a ship that in the early 1480s was obtained from this area by either Christian I himself or his son John. Buying or capturing a ship were two ways to acquire a new ship. Another possibility was to receive a ship as a gift. Ships as gifts was part of the social power play between the European princes of the time (see Adams & Rönnby, 2022). In 1468 Christian I was given a ship, named *Valentin*, by the English King Edward. In 1514 King John's son Christian II would give away his newly built ship

Engelen to Queen Elisabeth's brother, the future Holy Roman Emperor and King of Spain, Charles V (Barfod, 1990:119, 131, 190).

Gifts to socially "bind" other people to oneself were a common phenomenon in various societies at different times (cf. Mauss, 1972). Indeed, it has been suggested that the social value of any material gift given in Europe during the Middle Ages can be compared to the logic of commodity fetishism that Marx would analyse in capitalism, and analogous to the setting of economic price as the standardized measure for all things (Gurevitj, 1979). A striking example of this type of gift practice in the Middle Ages is found in the behaviour of the brave knight Willhelm Marshal (Duby, 1985).

On board their large ships, the kings naturally surrounded themselves with both important people and valuable things. The importance of exhibiting such "material" abundance is clearly underlined by the multifaceted and rich finds that have come to light through archaeological excavations on board King John's *Grifun*.

According to written sources, the king lost his "best fatabur" (his property and household) with the sinking of his ship after a fire on board (Sjöblom 2015; Warming 2020b). What remains of his royal possession from the wreck are among other things: clothing; barrels for beer; kitchen equipment; meat bones; spices; tin plates, and a wooden tankard engraved with a royal crown (see Jahrehorn, M., 2009, Rönnby, 2021, Macheridis et al., 2020, Ingvardson G., et al. 2022, Hansson et al., 2022, Foley, 2022, Björk, 2023).

In terms of the remains of armament on board, finds have included wooden carriages for guns, tools for ammunition making, and parts of a hauberk made in Nurnberg (see Warming, 2020, 2021; Warming & Rönnby, 2024). Several crossbow stocks have been found as well as parts of "hand cannons". This kind of firearm was held under the arm when used, and Leonardo da Vinci depicted a similar weapon in a sketch he made while working for the duke of Milano (Sjöblom, 2021:129ff.). The presence of both crossbows and handguns side-by-side clearly shows the transition period between the Middle Ages and the Modern period. One theory is that the arms may have belonged to groups of German mercenaries that seem to have been on board (Warming, 2020b).

Large ships were important both practically and symbolically for the new "princes". In many ways they functioned as an alter ego for the ruler. King John's *Grifun* was over 30 meters long ship, at around 600 tons; it had fore and aft castles and a grinning wooden monster in the bow. From the mast, colourful long pieces of cloth and flags hung. Attached along the railing were breech-loaded iron cannons, while many of the soldiers on board would have carried state-of-the-art handguns. It was an exceptionally looking ship for its time. Owning such a ship, signing letters on board and using it to travel to important meetings, showed that the Danish King John belonged to an exclusive elite of rulers in late medieval Europe. In the coming century, the power of these chosen late medieval "princes" would grow and their ships would become even larger and more heavily armed.

Power and Domination: Warships and State Building

It has here been suggested that studies into the workings of the state, especially the ways in which it concentrates power, can cast light on the relationship between humans and new technology. (McCarthy, 2017:13). The same can probably also be said about wars and conflicts, with their ability to mobilize resources and create innovations for destruction and combat. An illustrative example of this is the formation of the new Swedish state during the first half of the sixteenth century.

The Swedish nobleman Gustav Eriksson Vasa's rebellion against the Danish union king, King John's son Christian II, was initially successful. But the Swedish based fleet, which had earlier belonged to Sten Sture the Younger, no longer existed, and Gustav Vasa needed naval forces, above all to defend Stockholm along the coastline. The city of Lübeck, which was at war with Denmark and had financial interests in opposing the Danish king, was more than willing to help. They allowed Gustav Vasa to buy ships and hire crews and soldiers. In the summer of 1522, about ten ships from the German Hanseatic city arrived at Stegeborg in the mouth of the river Slätbaken near Söderköping.

It can be assumed that most of the new ships were clinker-built ships of varying sizes, which had earlier been used for trade. Some were probably more modern carvel-built ships. One differed markedly from the others. *Lybska Svanen* was more than twice as expensive as the other ships (Glete, 1977:37; Glete, 2010:349–350, 735; for possible other ships in the new "vasafleet", see also Adams & Rönnby, 2013b).

On midsummer 1523, Stockholm capitulates. Owning a large modern battleship with high castles that stood out compared to most other ships was, during this time, certainly very important, especially for the power-ambitious young Gustav Vasa. It is therefore hardly a coincidence that the Danes and those loyal to the Union were forced to sign the capitulation documents under the supervision of the newly elected Swedish king aboard *"paa wort skip SWANEN"*. A large ship was a fitting setting for a new Swedish ruler, the right attribute for an early modern prince (Daggfeldt, 1963:8, Adams & Rönnby, 1996, 2013).

Immediately after having come to power, Gustav Vasa began building a new fleet. Until the middle of the century, the royal shipyard in Stockholm was located directly below the royal castle. However, it would later move to Blaiseholmen. The master shipbuilder, mainly responsible in Stockholm during the first period 1527–1532, was called Hans Hake, who probably came from Gdansk.

The design of the Vasa King's new ships were a development of the Danish Union King's early carvels and ships, initially bought and captured from German cities. The shipbuilders in Stockholm during this period were aware of technical solutions and design ideas circulating around contemporary Europe with respect to the construction, architecture and decoration of a ship. Arcs, openings and decoration on the new European large carvels have similarities with the kind of style adopted for contemporary renaissance palaces in, for example, Venice.

Gustav Vasa, who like a large estate owner, tried to take command over both large and small issues within his new kingdom, obviously had a definite idea of how his fleet and large ships should be built and equipped. Master builder Adrian Hollender, like many others, experienced what it was like to work for autocratic and stingy masters. At one point, Gustav Vasa became upset, believing Adrian wasted expensive timber, ordering the governor in Stockholm, Anders Rålamb, to put Master Adrian in prison until further notice, unless he gives up his "shady business" (Börjeson, 1942:79, Ekman, 1942b:104).

After *Lybske Svan*, the king's new flagship became *Stora Kraveln*, built in Stockholm in the early 1530s (Glete, 2010:683). *Stora Kraveln* successfully participated in the Battle of Bornholm in 1535 and the siege of Copenhagen in 1536, during the so-called Count's Feud (1534–1536). She was nicknamed "the big cow" by the German enemy, possibly indicating her sailing qualities were somewhat lacking. In his description of the Nordic countries, Olaus Magnus writes that the king has a ship that can take 1,000 men on board, this must refer to *Stora Kraveln* (Figure 3; Sjöblom, 2016:99).

In 1554, a new main ship called *Elefanten* was built in Stockholm. After having been involved in a naval battle on the 14th and15[th] August 1564, north of Öland, *Elefanten* sailed in the direction of Kalmar for repair. However, she sank in the bay outside Björkenäs shipyard. An extensive salvage operation started soon after to raise her. Stone coffins were built, and divers ("men who could go under water") were used. Despite all efforts the salvage, attempts were fruitless, and she was left at the bottom of the sea (see Ekman, 1942; Rönnby & Adams 1994; Sjöblom, in prep.).

Master Holger Olsson, who initially participated in the construction of *Elefanten* in Stockholm, was responsible in the late 1550s for the construction of the carvel *Sankt Erik*. This ship was completed in 1559, and she participated in Erik XIV's courtship expedition to England, when he unsuccessfully tried to marry the "virgin queen" Elisabeth. The fact that he did not make the journey in person, but only sent his brother Johan with a portrait of himself to show the queen, hardly improved his odds. However, the tennis-playing Prince Johan is said to have been popular at the English court.

The next assignment for Master Holger Olsson at the shipyard in Björkenäs, after the construction of *Sankt Erik,* was to build a new ship, bigger than any before it, on behalf of the newly crowned King Erik XIV (for discussion regarding the size see Ekman, 1939; Glete, 2010:283; Eriksson, 2019). The new ship, which came to be called *Mars* (and sometimes *Makalös*), was quickly built. There was a war, and she was needed in the navy. She was keel stretched in 1561 and sometime during the summer of 1563 sailed to Stockholm, and was completed, fitted out and made ready for battle.

Figure 3: A Swedish warship in the middle of Olaus Magnus's (1490–1557) large map of the Nordic countries and the Baltic Sea. The *Carta Marina* was printed in Venice in 1539 after the priest went into exile in connection with King Gustav Vasa's implementation of the Reformation in the country. (Uppsala University library, Public Domain urn:nbn:se:alvin:portal:record-88495. http://www.alvin-portal.org/alvin/view.jsf?pid=alvin-record%3A88495&dswid=5781)

As his first flagship, *Mars* had been important for the young and ambitious new Vasa King. It was an impressive ship, a floating relative to the nearby Kalmar castles, which Erik XIV had been rebuilding around the same time.

At the end of May 1564, the great ship, named after the Roman war god, sailed with a fleet of 35 Swedish ships south towards the enemy. She was armed with over a hundred guns. A total of 60 large cannons were placed on the two battery decks, while the smaller guns ended up in the fore and aft castles, at the railing and in the different fighting tops (Sjöblom, 2003, 2016). However, as described above, *Mars'* service was short. Following an explosion during the battle, she sank northeast of Öland.

A new ship called *Neptunus* (later renamed *to Röda draken)* was, to replace *Mars*, built in the town of Västervik (Rönnby & Sjöblom, 2015). In the archives there is correspondence from the king to the master shipbuilder Master Adrian regarding how to build the new flagship: it should be "slightly larger than Mars was." Erik XIV also writes that he sent a "scampulun" to Västervik. This is probably some kind of model, which, in that case, is a very early example of this procedure in ship-building (cf. discussion in Lemée, 1995). Perhaps, here one can imagine a difference in "requirement specification" between the practically and functionally oriented "King Gösta" and his Renaissance-educated son? It is perhaps also indicated by the fact that the main ships' names allude to antiquity: Mars, Neptune and Julius Caesar. The obsession with anti-quity should be seen in light of the Renaissance's central concept of empire. The Roman Empire with its colonies and conquered resource-rich territories served as a kind of exemplar for new state builders (see Edman Ansell, 2021:131–).

There are also instructions from King Erik as to where resources and workers for the building of *Neptunus* should be taken. Shipbuilders from the archipelago between Västervik and Nyköping were recruited. Several cities along the east coast and the principality of Östergötland were ordered to provide resources, while the bailiffs were instructed to supply food, timber and workers from the annual tax. The people of Västervik had to provide mast wood and other timber.

The largest Swedish warship of all during the sixteenth century was built after Erik XIV's brother, Johan III, had replaced him on the throne. This ship was built at the small shipyard at Drakenäs in Mönsterås. Building began in the 1570s, but progress was slow, due to other priorities in the fleet. When *Julius Caesar* was finally finished, it was essentially never to be used; it was to be stationed at the quay in Stockholm until it was decommissioned (Glete, 1993b; see Rönnby & Sjöblom, 2024).

During the reign of the early Vasa kings, the most prominent master shipbuilders were in a variety of ways involved in the construc-tion of all major ships. The connections and the close contacts between these select few men during this intensive period of new shipbuilding show that they learned from each other and probably developed and discussed specific technical solutions together. This, together with the first Vasa kings' sense of pride in their own ships, probably led to a local building tradition in the construction of large Swedish warships.

Despite a late start, the first Vasa kings' construction of a modern navy with large ships for artillery combat remains early within a wider European perspective. It is also surprising that the relatively small, poor and new country of Sweden built a large number of warships during this period that, in both size and armament, compare if not even surpass, the warships of the largest contemporary European states (cf. Glete, 1993b). Competence and resources had to have been acquired and organized for large and complicated ships to be built.

That this was possible is in great part because of the absolute power of the new Vasa monarchs, and the fact that the country was in a relatively country unthreatened position. The various building sites, the royal shipyards, were spread out around suitable places with plenty of oak forests. An important resource that the Swedish kings could also control was iron mining and production. Through the kings' decisions and regulations, the country's resources could be used by the state. It has also been suggested that the ability of the early Swedish monarchy to come to agreements with the large class of independent Swedish farmers could also be seen as an important explanation for Sweden's extensive shipbuilding ability during the sixteenth century (Johansson 2023).

Conclusion: Ships with Consequences?

During the end of the Medieval period shipbuilding underwent major changes. New carvel-built ships became more tactically advantageous, as they began to be more systematically equipped with heavy gunpowder cannons. The result was a new kind of complex nautical artefact that gave possibilities for warfare and conquest that had never been seen before.

However, this new nautical technology does not arise out of nowhere. As mentioned above in terms of shipbuilding, the "new ship" has its roots in Northern European cogs as well as the Latin rigged carvel-built ships of the Mediterranean. Also, the gunpowder cannons had predecessors as early as during the fourteenth century. The appearance of a new type of warship can therefore be seen as a development and combination of existing material technology.

The changes in the shipyards and on the seas occur at the same time as other economic and political transformations happen in societies. Around Europe, more powerful states were created. Central protagonists in these changes are a new type of dynastic royal rulers, who strive to be regents over countries, rather than just hold on to their existing lot, as main medieval noblemen as done so before. The need for ships, cannons and fleets during the sixteenth century required resources and organization in the form of an arms race spiral, from which power becomes increasingly concentrated. The sharpest minds of the time are employed by the most powerful princes to develop both weapons and shipbuilding. How involved the new rulers were in military planning, strategic thinking and shipbuilding is evident not least from the Nordic regents acting during this time.

The warships were practical tools for blockades, sieges, conquests and dominance at sea, and gave economic advantages, since they facilitated trade. For the Nordic countries it was mainly about the control of the Baltic Sea, but through geographical discoveries, it became a global issue during this time. The ships provide the opportunity for the exploitation of new unknown areas. New commodities and the global possibilities affect Europe dramatically and change both the rulers and their countries (Wallerstein, 1974; Braudel, 1981; Nordin, 2010).

The ships were also a prestige object, a kind of alter ego and a powerful symbol for new European state builders. At a time when territorial space was growing, they were useful not just for their practical function but also as a material representative of the rulers and their ambitions. The ships could further be used politically and be given away as grand social binding gifts. By possessing modern warships, regents such as Christian I, John, Gustav Vasa, and Erik XIV, felt and became more powerful and successful. The great ships made them into different kings.

As discussed in the beginning of this text, the role and meaning of material culture is formed in and through the very times in which it is created. This means that the same changes and patterns can also be found in other contexts and entities, thereby allowing for opportunities for comparison (Rönnby, 1995:25–26). The early modern transformation can therefore also be studied by, for example, looking into society's contemporary informal and formal power structures (see Thorelli, 2023), in the organization of the army (Neuding, 2018) and in the attempt to find resources for new shipyards (Johansson, 2023).

An interesting material analogy here, which we have already mentioned above, is with castles and palaces. Just like ships, they can be seen as a kind of big scale architecture that manifests material culture (cf. Johnson, 2003). If one wants to deepen the analogy between ships and buildings on land, one could point to some similarities during the Early Modern changes to the society (cf. Adams, 2013:95–97; see further Rönnby & Sjöblom, 2024). A first period would be then during the fifteenth century, when land castles still were part of Medieval regional networks, as strategic locations but also fulfilled a function for goods distribution and trade. The same combination of military and economic use for trading is also typical for the first generation of large carvel ships.

The next period would then be characterized by the fact that both the most important castles and ships were more strongly tied to royal power. New forts were built and some of the old Medieval castles were given bastions and other new fortifications. At the same time, the ships started to combine the high wooden for- and aft castles with heavy artillery on gundecks. Regarding the specialization of some of the largest ships for warfare, this seemed to happen in Denmark, at the end of the fifteenth century, and in Sweden with the start of Gustav Vasa's own shipbuilding in the 1530s. At this point ships, like castles, became representatives of Renaissance state rulers. As such, they were designed, decorated and named accordingly (cf. Adams, 2013:97)

During the late sixteenth and seventeenth centuries, with the consolidation of the state, a new change occurs. The army becomes more organized while the fortifications improve. Meanwhile, ships have their own purpose-built gundecks, which become more standardized, both regarding armament and tactical use. At this time, though, ships could also be said to have the same symbolic and representative function as baroque palaces in the cities (cf. Soop, 1992; Cederlund, 1994;

Rönnby & Adams, 1994:68; Wallace, 2013; cf. also, regarding Dutch fluits, Eriksson, 2014).

Regarding the initial question about the role of technology and material things, it can be concluded that the "New Ship" changes society and the world at the end of the Middle Ages. But it was not the "New Ship" alone that accomplished these changes. There is instead a dialectical interplay where not only power holders at the time built and used the ships, but that the new ships themselves changed Late Medieval princes and princesses, giving them affordances and possibilities to develop and act in new ways. This interaction ultimately leads, together with other components, to changes in the entire society.

By way of a final comment, one can say that "things" can be very important for how humans act and for societal changes, but that the material impact must be understood within the framework of a specific historically determined situation. This context includes available technological know-how and resources but also historically determined human agency and the struggle for social and economic power.

If we finally also scale the question down to the contemporary issue regarding the connection between fatal shootings and access to weapons, one could conclude that it is not just "guns that kill" (as little as it is the ships themselves that change history). But this does not mean that the American gun advocates mentioned in the beginning of this text are right. The case of early modern warships demonstrates how material innovations become deeply intertwined with human agency, shaping and being shaped by historical conditions. Just as firearms redefined individual and collective capacities for violence, warships symbolized and enacted shifts in political power, economic systems, and military strategies. By framing these examples together, we see how material objects serve not only as tools but as active participants in broader societal transformations.

Notwithstanding this comparison, it should be highlighted that handguns have their own unique historical background and context. Since the time when the first handguns were drawn by Leonardo da Vinci in the fifteenth century, their efficiency and capabilities have evolved greatly. They have also through history been loaded with meaning in terms of power, domination and masculinity, not at least in our time by books, films and popular media. In certain contexts, and societal situations, it is certainly so that such powerful and dangerous artefacts have, in the hands of a human agent, the ability to cause fatal consequences.

Acknowledgements

The article's archaeological source material is based on field studies carried out together with many colleagues, all of whom are hereby thanked for their various efforts. Regarding the more theoretical reasoning about warfare and the importance of ships in that context, I would like to especially thank my colleagues Jon Adams, Ingvar Sjöblom and Rolf Warming for their views and our many exciting discussions. This article is also based on texts, material, reasoning and conclusions from several other publications (specifically Adams & Rönnby 2019, 2022 and Rönnby & Sjöblom 2015, 2025).

References

Adams, J. & Rönnby, J. (2002). Kuggmaren 1: the first cog find in the Stockholm archipelago, Sweden. *The International Journal of Nautical Archaeology, 31*(2).

Adams, J. & Rönnby, J. (Eds.) (2013). *Interpreting shipwrecks: maritime archaeological approaches.* Southampton: Highfield Press.

Adams, J. & Rönnby, J. (2013b). One of His Majesty's 'Beste Kraffwells': the wreck of an early carvel-built ship at Franska stenarna, Sweden. *The International Journal of Nautical Archaeology, 42*(1), 103–117.

Adams, J. & Rönnby, J. (2019). The consequences of new warships. Medieval to modern and our dialectical relation with things. In J. Rönnby (Ed.), *On War on Board. Archaeological and Historical perspectives on Early Modern Maritime Violence and Warfare.* Södertörn Academic Studies.

Adams, J. & Rönnby, J. (2022). The Danish Griffin: The Wreck of an Early Modern Royal Carvel from 1495. *International Journal of Nautical Archaeology, Vol. 51*(1), 46–72

Adams, J. (2013). *A Maritime Archaeology of Ships. Innovation and social change in medieval and early modern Europe.* Oxbow Books. Oxford.

Alberti, B., Jones, A. & Pollard, J. (Eds.) (2013). *Archaeology after interpretation: returning materials to archaeological theory.* Walnut Creek, Ca: Left Coast Press Inc.

Alm, J. (1933). *Eldhandvapen I. Från deras tidigaste tillkomst till slaglåsets allmänna införande.* Militärlitteraturföreningens förlag. Stockholm.

Anderson, P. (1974), *Lineages of the Absolutist State.* London: New Left Books.

Anderson, R. C. (1939). The Mars and the Adler. *Mariner's Mirror*, 25(3), 296–299 DOI: 10.1080/00253359.1939.10657346.

Andrén, A. (1985). *Den urbana scenen: städer och samhälle i det medeltida Danmark = [The urban scene]: [towns and society in mediaeval Denmark]* (Dissertation). Lund: University.

Ankarberg, C. H. (2015). Två svenska "nationalmonument" – Dekorerade med danske Kungens vapen, i *Tidskrift i Sjöväsende*, 3. Stockholm, Kungliga örlogsmannasällskapet.

Bhaskar, R. (2008) (1993). *Dialectic. The Pulse of Freedom*. Verso. London.

Barfod, J. H. (1990). Flådens fødsel – Den danske flådes historie – 1533. *Marinehistorisk Selbskabs Skrift*, 22. Copenhagen: Marinehistorisk Selskab.

Barfod, J. H. (1995). Christian 3.s flåde – Den danske flådes historie 1533–1588. *Marine historisk Selbskabs Skrift*, 25. Copenhagen: Marinehistorisk Selskab.

Batchvarov, K. (2011). The Black Sea Shipwreck from Kitten and Mediterranean Whole-Moulding. In A, Catsambis, B. Ford & D. L. Hamilton (Eds.) *Oxford Handbook of Nautical Archaeology*. Oxford: Oxford University Press.

Bill, J. (2002). Castles at sea – The warship of the High Middle Ages. In A. Nørgård Jørgensen (Ed.), *Maritime warfare in northern Europe: technology, organisation, logistics and administration 500 BC–1500 AD: papers from an international research seminar at the Danish National Museum, Copenhagen, 3–5 May 2000*. Copenhagen: National Museum.

Bill, J. (2009). From Nordic to North European – Application of Multiple Correspondence Analysis in the Study of Changes in Danish Shipbuilding A.D. 900–1600. In R. Bockius (Ed.), *Between the Seas. Transfer and Exchange in Nautical Archaeology. Proceedings of the Eleventh International Symposium on Boat and Ship Archaeology*. Mainz: ISBSA.

Björk, M. (2023). *Gribshunden marinarkeologisk forskningsundersökning av skeppsvrak vid Stora Ekön, L1978:2168/RAÄ Ronneby 728. Marinarkeologisk undersökning, 2022. Rapport 2023.4* (Unpublished Report). Karlskrona (Blekinge Museum).

Bourke, J. (1999). *An intimate story of killing face to face killing in twentieth-century warfare*. New York. Basic books.

Braudel, F. (1981). *Civilization and Capitalism 15th–18th Century, Vol. 1 The Structures of Everyday Life*. Berkley, Los Angeles: University of California Press.

Burwash, D. (1969). *English Merchant Shipping: 1460–1540*. Newton Abbot: David & Charles. Cambridge: Cambridge University Press.

Börjeson, H. (1942). Sjökrigsmateriel och skeppsbyggnad under äldre Vasatid. In O. Lybeck (Ed.), *Svenska Flottans historia, Vol. 1*. (pp. 45–88). Allhem, Malmö.

Cederlund, C. O. (1994). The Royal Ships and Divine Kingdom. *Current Swedish Archaeology*, 2, 47–85. DOI:10.37718/CSA.1994.03.

Cederlund, C. O. (1995). Svanen Som Blev en Anka. Vrakidentifiering och marknadsföring av nationella myter. Tvärnsitt, 1. Swedish Science Press. Uppsala.

Choat, S. (2017). Science, Agency and Ontology: A Historical-Materialist Response to New Materialism. *Political Studies*, 66(4), 1027–1042. https://doi.org/10.1177/ 0032321717731926.

Cohen, G. A. (1978). *Karl Marx's theory of history: a defence*. Princeton, N. J.: Princeton University Press. dagar. Bd 1, [1521–1679]. Malmö: Allhem.

Daggfeldt, B. (1963). Lybska Svan. *Tidskrift I Sjöväsendet*, 3–27.

Dawson, D. (1996). The Origin of War. Biological and Anthroplogical Theories. *History and Theory*, 35, 1–28. Wesleyan University.

Duby, G., 1985. *William Marshal eller Den bäste riddaren i världen*. Stockholm: Atlantis.

Edman Ansell, J. (2021). *Maktens tal och talets makt: Kunglig maktlegitimering i Erik XIV:s och Johan III:s tid* (Dissertation). Uppsala: Uppsala University.

Einarsson, L. (2008a). Ett skeppsvrak i Ronneby skärgård. In G. Jeppsson (Ed.) *Ale, Historisk tidskrift fr Skåne, Halland och Blekinge 2008. 2*, 1–15

Einarsson, L. (2008b). "In navi nosta GRIFFONE". Griffen i djupet. In *Blekingeboken Årg 86*, 22–49. Karlskrona: Blekinge hembyggdförbund förlag.

Ekman, C. & Unger, G. (1942). Svenska flottans sjötåg fram till Kalmarkriget. In O. Lybeck (Ed.), *Svenska flottans historia, band 1* (168–181). Malmö, Allhem.

Ekman, C. & Unger, G. (1942). Svenska flottans sjötåg fram till Kalmarkriget. In O. Lybeck (Ed.), *Svenska flottans historia: örlogsflottan i ord och bild från dess grundläggning under Gustav Vasa fram till våra dagar. Bd 1, [1521–1679]*. Malmö: Allhem.

Ekman, C. (1939). The Swedish Ship Mars or Makalös. *Mariners Mirror, Vol. 25*, 1–10.

Ekman, C. (1942a). Stora kraveln Elefanten. In O. Lybeck (Ed.), *Svenska flottans historia: örlogsflottan i ord och bild från dess grundläggning under Gustav Vasa fram till våra dagar. Bd 1, [1521–1679]*. Malmö: Allhem.

Ekman, C. (1942b). Skeppsgårdar och varv under äldre vasatid. In O. Lybeck (Ed.), *Svenska flottans historia: örlogsflottan i ord och bild från dess grundläggning under Gustav Vasa fram till våra dagar. Bd 1, [1521–1679]*. Malmö: Allhem.

Ekman, C. (1946). Skeppstyperna under Gustav Vasas och Erik XIV:s tid. *Sjöhistorisk årsbok*.

Ellmer, D. (1994). The Cog as a Cargo Carrier. In: R. J. Gardiner (Ed.), *Cogs, Caravels and Galleons: the sailing ship 1000–1650*. London: Conway Maritime Press.

Eriksson, N. & Rönnby, J. (2017). *Mars* (1564). The Initial Archaeological Investigations of a Great 16th Century Warship. *The International Journal of Nautical Archaeology*, 46(1), 92–107.

Eriksson, N. (2014). *Urbanism Under Sail: An Archaeology of Fluit Ships in Early Modern Everyday Life* (Dissertation). Huddinge: Södertörn University.

Eriksson, N. (2022). *Stormaktsskärgård: marin landskapshistoria utmed farlederna mot Stockholm*. Lund: Nordic Academic Press.

Eriksson, N. (2019). How Large Was Mars? An investigation of the dimensions of a legendary Swedish warship, 1563–1564. *The Mariner's Mirror, Vol. 105*(3), 260–274.

Friel, I. (1994). The Carrack: The Advent of the Full Rigged Ship. In R. Gardiner & R. Unger (Eds.), *Cogs, Caravels and Galleons: the sailing ship 1000–1650* (pp. 77–90). London: Conway Maritime Press.

Friel, I. (1995). *The Good Ship: Ships, Shipbuilding and Technology in England 1200–1520*. London.

Foley, B. (2022). Gribshunden: Marinarkeologisk forskningsundersökning av skeppsvrak vid Stora Ekön L1978:2168/ RAÄ Ronneby 728. *Marinarkeologisk forskningsundersökning, 2022* (Unpublished Report). Karlskrona. Blekinge Museum.

Gardiner, R. & Unger, R., (Eds.) (1994). *Cogs, caravels and galleons: the sailing ship 1000–1650*. London: Conway Maritime Press.

Garpenby, S. (1967). Skeppsbyggeriet i Västervik genom tiderna. In *Tjustbygden* (pp. 11–79). Meddelande nr 24. Tjustbygdens kulturhistoriska förening. Västervik.

Gibson, J. J. (1979). *The Ecological Approach to Visual Perception*. Boston: Houghton Mifflin.

Glete, J. (1976). Svenska örlogsfartyg 1521–1560: flottans uppbyggnad under ett tekniskt brytningsskede. [1]. *Forum navale, 30*, 7–74. Sjöhistoriska samfundet.

Glete, J. (1977). Svenska örlogsfartyg 1521–1560: flottans uppbyggnad under ett tekniskt brytningsskede. *Forum navale, 31*, 23–119. Sjöhistoriska samfundet.

Glete, J. (1993). *Navies and nations: warships, navies and state building in Europe and America, 1500–1860*. Acta Universitatis Stockholmiensis: Stockholm.

Glete, J. (1993b). Johan III:s Stora Skepp. Att finna ett skepp i 1500-talets skeppsgårdsräkenskaper. *Forum navale*. Skrifter utgivan av Sjöhistoriska samfundet nr 49.

Glete, J. (2000). *Warfare at Sea 1500–1650. Maritime Conflicts and the Transformation of Europe*. London: Routledge.

Glete, J. (2002). *War and the state in early modern Europe. Spain, the Dutch Republic and Sweden as Fiscal-Military States 1500–1660*. London. Routledge.

Glete, J. (2006). *Svenska örlogsfartyg 1561–1570*. Accessed online: http://www2.historia.su.se/personal/jan_glete/Glete-SvenskaOrlogsfartyg 1561-1570.pdf.

Glete, J. (2010). *Swedish naval administration, 1521–1721: resource flows and organisational capabilities*. Leiden: Brill.

Grenier, R., Loewen, B., and Prouix, J-P. (1994). Basque shipbuilding technology c. 1560–1580: The Red Bay Project. In C. Westerdahl, (Ed.) *Crossroads in Ancient Shipbuilding*, 137–141. IBSA 6.

Grenier, R., Stevens, W. & Bernier, M-A., 2007. *The Underwater Archaeology of Red Bay: Basque Shipbuilding and Whaling in the 16th Century*, Vol. III. Ottawa: Parks Canada.

Grossman, D. (2009). *On killing: the psychological cost of learning to kill in war and society*. New York: Little, Brown and Co.

Guérot, M. & Rieth, E. (1998). The wreck of the *Lomellina* at Villefranche sur Mer. In M. Bound (Ed.) *Excavating Ships of War* (pp. 38–50), International Maritime Archaeology Series 2. Oxford: University of Oxford.

Gunnarson, G. (1971). *Socialdemokratiskt idéarv: utopism, marxism, socialism*. Stockholm: Tiden.

Gustafsson, H. (1998). The Conglomerate State: A Perspective on State Formation in Early Modern Europe. *Scandinavian Journal of History*, *23*(3–4), 189–213. DOI:10.1080/03468759850115954.

Hagberg, B. & Widman, M. (2016). *Att döda en människa: på spaning efter det första kriget*. Stockholm: Norstedts.

Hall, B. S. (1997). *Weapons and warfare in Renaissance Europe: gunpowder, technology and tactics*. Baltimore: Johns Hopkins University Press.

Hallenberg, M. & Holm, J. (2016). *Man ur huse. Hur krig, upplopp och förhandlingar påverkade svensk statsbildning i tidigmodern tid*. Lund: Nordic Academic Press.

Harvey, K. (Ed.) (2009). *History and material culture: a student's guide to approaching alternative sources*. London: Routledge.

Hansson, A., Linderson, H. & Foley, B. (2022). Casks from Gribshunden (1495). Dendrochronology of Late Medieval Shipboard Victual Containers. *International Journal of Nautical Archaeology*, *51*(2). DOI: 10.1080/10572414.2022.213271

Hedberg, J. (1975). *Kungl. artilleriet Medeltid och äldre vasatid*. Stockholm: Militärhistoriska.

Helms, M. W. (1988). *Ulysses' sail: an ethnographic odyssey of power, knowledge, and geographical distance*. Princeton, NJ: Princeton University Press.

Hildred, A. & Rule, M. (1984). Armaments from the Mary Rose. *Antique Arms and Militaria*, *4*, 17–24.

Hildred, A. (Ed.) (2011). *Weapons of Warre: The Armaments of the Mary Rose*. Portsmouth, England: Mary Rose Trust.

Hodder, I. & Lucas, G. (2017). The symmetries and asymmetries of human – thing relations. *Archaeological dialogues, Vol. 24*(2). Cambridge: Cambridge University Press.

Hodder, I. (1982). *Symbols in action: ethnoarchaeological studies of material culture*. Cambridge: Cambridge University Press.

Hodder, I. (1986). *Reading the past: current approaches to interpretation in archaeology*. Cambridge: Cambridge University Press.

Hodder, I. (2012). *Entangled: an archaeology of the relationships between humans and things*. Malden, MA: Wiley-Blackwell.

Hornborg, A. (2013). Technology as Fetish: Marx, Latour, and the Cultural Foundations of Capitalism. *Theory, Culture & Society, 31*(4): 119–140. DOI: 10.1177/0263276413488960tcs.sagepub.com.

Hornborg, A., 2017. Artifacts have consequences, not agency: Toward a critical theory of global environmental history. *European Journal of Social Theory, Vol. 20*(1), 95–110. DOI: 10.1177/1368431016640536.

Ingvardson, G. T., Müter, D. & Foley, B. (2022). Purse of medieval coins from royal shipwreck revealed by X-ray microscale Computer Tomography scanning. *Journal of Archeological Science*. Reports 43.

Jahnke, C. (2006). Dronningens skibe for kongens flåde. Dronning Dorotheas af Brandeburgs skibsbyggning omkring 1486. In E. Göbel, & C. Lemée, (Eds.), *Skibsbygge og Sofart i Renaessance* (pp. 85–94). Maritim kontakt 28. Copenhagen.

Jahrehorn, M. (2009). *Föremål från ett medeltida skeppsvrak St. Ekö, Ronneby kommun*. Konserveringsrapport. Kalmar: Kalmar läns museum.

Johansson, D. (2023). *Makt och motstånd: bönderna, örlogsflottan och den svenska staten 1522–1640*. Diss, Stockholm: Stockholm University.

Johnson, M. (2003) *Behind the castle gate: from Medieval to Renaissance*, London & New York, Routledge.

Johnson, M. (2010). *Archaeological theory: an introduction* (2. ed.). Chichester: Wiley-Blackwell.

Karlholm, D. (2017). När konsten blev subject. In A. Burman & L. Lennerhed (Eds.), *Samtider. Perspektiv på 2000-talets idehistoria*. Gothenburg: Daidalos.

Kirsch, P. (1990). *The Galleon. The Great Ship of the Armada Era*. London: Conway. Maritime Press.

Knappett, C. & Malafouris, L. (Eds.) (2008). *Material agency: towards a non-anthropocentric approach*. New York: Springer.

Kroes, P. & Verbeek, P. (Eds.) (2014). *The Moral Status of Technical Artefacts. Springer Science & Business Media* (p. 89, 101). Springer.

Landström, B. (1964). *Vägen till Indien. Upptäcksresor till lands och sjöss från expeditionen till Punt 1493 f-Kr till upptäckten av Godahoppsudden 1488 e. Kr.* Forum.

Landin, M., Norman, P., Rönnby, J., Törnqvist, O. & Öberg, B. (2011). Arkeologiska undersökningar i Södermanlands skärgård: Rapport från projektet Förmoderna kustmiljöer. Naturresurser, klimat och samhälle vid östersjökusten före 1800 – ett miljöhistoriskt projekt. Arkeologi, Södertörn University.

Landström, B. (1980). *Regalskeppet Vasan från början till slutet*. Stockholm: Interpublishing.

Lange, F. A. (1913). *Materialismens historia: jämte en kritik av dess betydelse i våra dagar*. Stockholm: Bonnier.

Latour, B. (1994). On technical mediation. *Common Knowledge, 3*(2), 29–64.

Latour, B. (2005). *Reassembling the social: an introduction to actor-network-theory*. Oxford: Oxford University Press, UK.

Law, J. (1986). On the Methods of Long Distance Control: Vessels, Navigation, and the Portuguese Route to India. In J. Law (Ed.), *Power, Action and Belief: A New Sociology of Knowledge?* (p.p. 234–263), Sociological Review Monograph 32, Routledge, Henley.

Law, J. (2002). Objects and Spaces. *Theory, Culture & Society, 19*(5–6), 91–105.

Lemée, C. (2006). *The Renaissance Shipwrecks from Christianhavn. An archaeological and architectural study of large carvel vessels in Danish waters 1580–1640*. Ships and Boats of the North, Volume 6. Viking Ship Museum Roskilde.

Liedman, S-E. (1991). *Från Platon till Gorbatjov: de politiska idéernas historia*. [Ny utg.] Stockholm: MånPocket.

Lindkvist, T. & Sjöberg, M. (Ed.) (2013). *Det svenska samhället 800–1720: klerkernas och adelns tid*. 4., [rev. och uppdaterade] uppl. Lund: Studentlitteratur.

Macheridis, S., Hansson, M. & Foley, B. (2020). Fish in a barrel: Atlantic sturgeon (Acipenser oxyrinchus) from the Baltic Sea wreck of the royal Danish flagship Gribshunden (1495). *Journal of Archaeological Science, 33*, 102480.

Machiavelli, N. (1513) (2008). *The Prince*. Oxford: Oxford University Press.

Malmer, M. (1984). Arkeologisk positivism. *Fornvännen* 79. Stockholm.

Marsden, P. (Ed.) (2009). *Your Noblest Shippe: Anatomy of a Tudor Warship, Archaeology of the Mary Rose: vol. 2*, Portsmouth: Oxbow/Mary Rose Trust.

Mauss, M. (1972). *Gåvan*. Uppsala: Argos.

McCarthy, D. R. (2017). *Objects in Motion: Marx, Latour, and the Historical Processes of Powerful Things* (draft). https://ecpr.eu/Filestore/Paper Proposal/13aad5c9-04f8-4906-Media.

Middeke M. & Reinfandt C. (Eds.). (2016). *Theory Matters*. Palgrave Macmillan, London. DOI: https://doi.org/10.1057/978-1-137-47428-5_6

Milton, G. (2001). *Muskotkriget: kampen om de ostindiska kryddöarna*. Lund: Historisk.

Møller Jensen, J. (2007). *Denmark and the crusades, 1400–1650*. Leiden: Brill.

Moberg, C.-A. & Arbman, H. (1969). *Introduktion till arkeologi: jämförande och nordisk fornkunskap*. Stockholm: Natur och kultur.

Monié Nordin, J. (2020). *The Scandinavian early modern world: a global historical archaeology*. New York: Routledge.

Mortensen, M. (1999). *Dansk artilleri indtil 1600*. Copenhagen: Tøjhusmuseet

Mortensen, M. H. (2002). Early Danish naval artillery c. 1500–1523. The beginning of a new era. In A. Nørgård Jørgensen (Ed.), *Maritime warfare in northern Europe: technology, organisation, logistics and administration 500 BC–1500 AD: papers from an international research seminar at the Danish National Museum, Copenhagen, 3–5 May 2000*. Copenhagen: National Museum.

Mortimer, W. (1954). *Archaeology from the Earth*. Oxford: Clarendon Press.

Mozejka, B. (2019). *Peter von Danzig. The Story of a Great Carvel 1462–1475*. The Northern World, Volume: 86. Leiden: Brill.

Muckelroy, K. (1978). *Maritime archaeology*. Cambridge: Cambridge U. P.

Müller, M. (2015). Assemblages and Actor-networks: Rethinking Socio-material Power, Politics and Space, *Geography Compass*, 9, 27–41. DOI: 10.1111/gec3.12192.

Neuding Skoog, M. (2018). *I rikets tjänst: krig, stat och samhälle i Sverige 1450–1550* (Dissertation). Stockholm: Stockholm University.

Nordin, J. M. (2010). Det emblemiska silvret. Sverige i den atlantiska världen vid 1600-talets mitt. In: A. Lihammer & J. M. Nordin (Ed.), *Modernitetens materialitet: arkeologiska perspektiv på det moderna samhällets framväxt*. Stockholm: Statens historiska museum.

Noys B. (2016). Matter Against Materialism: Bruno Latour and the Turn to Objects. In: Middeke M., Reinfandt C. (Eds.), *Theory Matters*. Palgrave Macmillan, London. DOI: https://doi.org/10.1057/978-1-137-47428-5_6

Nyström, P. (1983). *I folkets tjänst: historikern, journalisten och ämbetsmannen Per Nyström*: artiklar 1927–83 i urval av Anders Björnsson i samarbete med författaren: utgivna till Per Nyströms 80-årsdag den 21 november 1983. 1. uppl. Stockholm: Ordfront.

Nussbaum, M. (1995). Objectification. *Philosophy & Public Affairs*, 24(4), 249–291. DOI: 10.1111/j.1088-4963.1995.tb00032

Olsen, B. (2006). Ting-mennesker-samfunn. Introduksjon till en symmetrisk arkeologi. *Arkeologisk Forum, 14*.

Olsen, B. (2012). *Archaeology: the discipline of things*. Berkeley: University of California Press.

Parker, G. (1988). *The Military Revolution: Military innovation and the rise of the West 1500–1800*. Cambridge.

Pitt, J. C. (2014). "Guns Don't Kill, People Kill"; Values in and/or Around Technologies. In P. Kroes & P.-P. Verbeek (Eds.), *The Moral Status of Technical Artefacts* (pp. 89, 101). Springer Science & Business Media.

Querini, P., De Michiele, N. & Fioravante, C. (P. Nelli, Ed.) (2007). *Il naufragio della Querina. Veneziani nel circolo polare artico*.

Rodger, N. A. M. (1996). The Development of Broadside Gunnery 1450–1650. *Mariner's Mirror, 82,* 301–24. DOI: 10.1080/00253359.1996.10656604

Rogers, C. J. (Ed.) (1995). *The military revolution debate: readings on the military transformation of early modern Europe.* Boulder: Westview Press.

Rubenstein, J. M. (2002). *The Cultural Landscape. An introduction to Human Geography.* Oxford, Ohio.

Rönnby, J & Adams, J. (1994). *Östersjöns sjunkna skepp. En marinarkeologisk tidsresa.* Höganäs. Tiden.

Rönnby, J. (2013). The Archaeological Interpretation of Shipwrecks. In J. Rönnby & J. Adams (Eds.), *Interpretating shipswrecks. Maritime Archaeological Approaches* (pp. 9–24). Southampton Monographs in Archaeology NS nr 4 and Södertörn Academic Studies 56. Southampton: Highfield Press.

Rönnby, J. & Björdal, C. (2023). *Kronholmskoggen: marinarkeologiska undersökningar: L1975:6999 Västergarn, Kronholmen 1:3, Gotland (Västergarn RAÄ-nr 116).* Huddinge: Södertörns University.

Rönnby, J & Sjöblom, I. (2015). Havsguden från Västervik – om skeppet Neptunus och vasakungarnas nya stora kravlar. Red Palm, V. *Västerviks historia II.* Västerviks Museum.

Rönnby, J. & Sjöblom, I. (2025). *Furstarnas fartyg. De nya stora skeppen. Vasakungarnas skepp 1.* Västerviks Museum. Book manuscript January 2025.

Rönnby, J. (1995). *Bålverket. Om samhällsförändring och motstånd med utgångspunkt från det tidigmedeltida Bulverket i Tingstäde träsk på Gotland. Riksantivaroeämbetet Arakeologiska undersökningar.* Skrifter nr 10. Stockholm.

Rönnby, J. (Ed.) (2019). *On War on Board: archaeological and historical perspectives on early modern maritime violence and warfare.* Huddinge: Södertörn University

Rönnby, J. (2021). *Grifun/Gribshund (1495): marinarkeologiska undersökningar.* Huddinge: Södertörn University.

Rosborn, S. (2009). *Att använda krut. Det tidiga artilleriet i Sydskandinavien.* Accessed online: https://www.academia.edu/3349702/Att_anv%C3%A4nda_krut_Det_tidiga_artilleriet_i_Sydskandinavien_2009_

Shanks, M. (2007). Symmetrical archaeology. *World Archaeology, 39*(4), 589–596. DOI: 10.1080/00438240701679676.

Sjöblom, I. (2003). Makalös motgång. Öland 1564. In L. Ericson et al., *Svenska slagfält.* Stockholm: Wahlström & Widstrand.

Sjöblom, I. (2009). Det första stora sjökriget – Nordiska sjuårskriget 1563–70. In L. Ericson Wolke & M. Hårdstedt (Eds.), *Svenska sjöslag.* Stockholm: Medströms förlag.

Sjöblom, I. (2015). Identifiering och historiska sammanhang. In J. Rönnby (Ed.), *Gribshunden (1495): Skeppsvrak vid Stora Ekön, Ronneby, Blekinge. Marinarkeologiska undersökningar 2013–2015.* Blekinge museum rapport 21. Blekinge museum/Södertörn University.

Sjöblom, I. (2016). *Svenska sjöofficerare under 1500-talet.* Malmö: Universus Academic Press.

Sjöblom, I. (2016b). Sjökrig och örlogsflottan. In S. Ekström, L. Müller, T. Nilson (Eds.), *Sjövägen till Sverige: från 1500-talet till våra dagar.* Malmö, Universus Academic Press.

Sjöblom, I. (Forthcoming). *Fästningskriget till sjöss 1555–1565.*

Sjöblom, I. (2019). Unionskrig och maktkamp: Gribshunden i källorna. *Gribshunden 1495: medeltidens modernaste skepp*, Karlskrona: Blekinge museum.

Sjöblom, I. (2021). Bösstock till handbössa/halvrör från Gribshunden. In J. Rönnby (Eds.). *Grifun/Gribshund (1495): marinarkeologiska undersökningar.* Huddinge: Södertörn University.

Sleeswijk, A. W. (1990). The Engraver Williem A. Cruse and the development of the Chain- Wale. *The Mariners Mirror, 76*(4), 345–361.

Sleeswijk, A. W. (1989). Carvel-planking and carvel ships in the North of Europe. *Archaeonautica, 14*, 223–228.

Soop, H., 1992. *The Power and the Glory.* Vitterhets historie och antikvitets akademin.

Tallett, F. & Trim, D. J. B. (Eds.) (2010). *European warfare, 1350–1750.* Cambridge: Cambridge University Press.

Thorelli, J. (2023). *De tjänstvilliga vännernas samhälle. Abraham Brahe och den svenska eliten 1590–1630* (Dissertation). Gothenburg Studies in History 3. Gothenburg.

Tilly, C. (1975). *The formation of states in Western Europe.* Princeton.

Ullidtz, P. (2016). *Hertugerna af Bourgogne 1363–1477.* Copenhagen: Books on Demand.

Ullidtz, P. (2017). *Medici, Columbus og kong Hans. Renæssance, Oppdagelserejser, Unionskonge.* Copenhagen: Books on Demand GmbH.

Unger, R. (Ed.) (1994). *Cogs, Caravels and Galleons.* London: Conway Maritime Press.

Wallace. S. (2013). The Sovereign's Cabin: Material Culture and Symbolic Expression: A case study of the wooden sculptures and wall panelling in the great cabin and stern gallery of the warship Vasa of 1628. In J. Adams & J. Rönnby (Eds.), *Interpreting Shipwrecks, Maritime Archaeological Approaches* (pp. 110–118). Southampton Monographs New Series 4 & Södertörn Academic Studies 56. Southampton: Highfield Press.

Wallerstein, I. M. [1974] (2011). *The modern world-system 1. Capitalist agriculture and the origins of the European world-economy in the sixteenth century.* Berkeley, California: University of California Press.

Warming, R. & Rönnby, J. (2024). *Gripen/Griphund. Marinarkeologisk dokumentation av ett senmedeltida kravellskepp.* Huddinge: Södertörn University.

Warming, R. (2014). Towards an Archaeology of Boarding: Naval Hand-to-hand Combat Tactics of Northwestern Europe in 16th Century. MA dissertation. University of Southampton.

Warming. R. (2019). An Introduction to Hand-to-Hand Combat at Sea: General Characteristics and Shipborne Technologies from c. 1210 BCE to 1600 CE. In J. Rönnby (Ed.), *On War on Board: Archaeological and Historical Perspectives on Early Modern Maritime Violence and Warfare* (pp. 99–124). Södertörn: Södertörn University.

Warming, R. (2020). Notes on the Guns and Gun Carriages onboard GRIBSHUNDEN (1495). *Society for Combat Archaeology*. http://combatarcha eology.org/guns-and-gun-carriages-aboard-gribshunden-1495/? fbclid=IwAR3eSs_JU3OMIG4cX3mgFg-sETf7ehvZXF0AQK7OMVpD noojDX9slnvC5ZI (05/10/2020)

Warming, R. (2020b). The Loss of the King's flagship GRIBSHUNDEN (1495): An Unknown Historical Source Surfaces. *Society for Combat Archaeology*. http://combatarchaeology.org/the-loss-of-the-kings-flagship-gribshunden-1495-an-unknown-historical-source-surfaces/ (2020-11-22).

Warming, R. (2021). Ringbrynja och armborst från Gribshunden. In: Rönnby, J. 2021. *Grifun/Gribshund (1495): marinarkeologiska undersökningar*. Huddinge: Södertörn University.

Warming, R. (in prep.). *Soldiers at Sea, c.1450–1650* (Dissertation). Department of Archaeology and Classical Studies. Stockholm University.

White, H. (2013). Materiality, Form, and Context: Marx contra Latour. *Victorian Studies, 55*(4), 667–682. DOI: 10.2979/victorianstudies.55.4.667

Wigforss, E. (1970/1908). *Materialistisk historieuppfattning. Industriell demokrati.* [Ny utg.] Stockholm: Tiden.

Witmore, C. L. (2007). Symmetrical archaeology: excerpts of a Manifesto. *World Archaeology, 39*(4), 546–562. DOI: 10.1080/00438240701679411

Witmore, C. L. (2014). Archaeology and the New Materialisms. *Journal of Contemporary Archaeology, 1*(2), 203–246. DOI: 10.1558/jca.v1i2.16661

Wold, H. (2004). *Querinis reise – historier om en historie.* Oversatt til italiensk av Lucio Lombardi og Enrica Sollaino Querinis og mannskapets beretning oversatt til norsk av Marie L. Aalen. Orkana Forlag 2004. ISBN 82-8104-000-9.

Zwick, D. (2016). Bayonese cogs, Genoese carracks, English dromons and Iberian carvels: Tracing technology transfer in medieval Atlantic shipbuilding. *Itsas Memoria. Revista de Estudios Marítimos del País Vasco, 8*, 647–680. Donostia-San Sebastián: Untzi Museoa-Museo Naval.

Åkerlund, H. (1951). *Fartygsfynden i den Forna Hamnen i Kalmar.* Almqvist & Wiksells Stockholm: Sjöhistoriska Samfundet.

Østerberg, D. (1977). *Makt och materiell: samhällsteoretiska essäer.* Gothenburg: Korpen.

Østerberg, D. (1989). *Tolkande sociologi.* Gothenburg: Korpen.

Östman, P. (1985). *Geografi som vetenskap. En introduktion.* Stockholm: Liber Förlag.

Money and War: The Contribution of Numismatics and Monetary History to the Study of Conflict

Jens Christian Moesgaard

'Money makes the world go around'. From a European and Western perspective, this is as true in peace time as it is in the context of conflicts. In war, money is a prerequisite! World War II was largely won because of the immense economy of the United States that fuelled the war effort of the allies. Often money is the source of a conflict. The thirst for gold and silver was one of the main drivers behind the Spanish expansion into the New World at the dawn of the modern era. The result can be seen in a concrete (archaeological) manner in the thousands of silver coins at the arms of Spain struck in Peru and Mexico between the sixteenth and eighteenth centuries and found today in the wrecks of ships that brought wealth to Europe. Conflict and war also often brought disorder into finances and monetary systems, which in turn may have huge social consequences on society. Consider the hyperinflation in post–World War I Germany when, between November 1918 and November 1923, one dollar rose from 7,43 to 4,200,000,000,000 marks (Kromann & Jensen, 1976:59). This, in turn, was part of the socio-political unrest that led to the rise of Nazism. It also induced an inherent fear of inflation in the German society that partly explains the anti-inflation policy of the strong Deutschmark in the post-World War II period, on which the Euro was modelled. Consequences can be long-standing!

The phrase 'Follow the money' is a widespread maxim that highlights the usefulness of studying money to understand other aspects of society. Several academic disciplines, like economics, anthropology and sociology, have all contributed to understanding this relationship, but in this chapter, the focus will be on the two sister disciplines, Numismatics and Monetary History. Indeed, they study money and its relation to society, and provide tools for the scholar who wants to investigate the various roles of money in conflicts. Numismatics has its origins in coin collecting and traditionally studies the coin as an artefact: its dating, issuing power, iconography and places of production as well as the classification of main types and varieties. In recent decades, it has however developed more into the field of monetary history, and now it is also concerned with the monetary policy of the coin issuer (e.g., study of variations in weights and alloys, study of mint outputs, etc.), as well as the role of coins in society. In this latter part, the archaeological approach to coins plays a major role. Indeed, the find spot and the find circumstances as well as the wear and tear on the coins say a lot about how they were handled by people in the past. Both the official monetary policy and how people handled money in practice were key features of society. As we shall see below, both aspects were heavily affected by conflict and war, which in turn was affected by monetary affairs.

This paper will present a string of small cases illustrating how these disciplines can provide knowledge and insights about the interaction between conflict and society. Rather than theorization, the cases provide a bottom-up and materialistic perspective on money and war. This brings us closer to the very real causes and consequences of war. Each case will highlight a different approach, source material or aspect. The cases are mainly taken from France and Scandinavia during the Middle Ages and the Early Modern Period. They treat various aspects, such as: how to finance warfare through debasement of the currency; monetary war between belligerents; the difficult logistics of money supply; coping with the social unrest within the army, as well as within the civil society that debasement provoked; the disruption of everyday life caused by war and war-related monetary disorders, and finally how people sought to avoid being plundered by the troops. The aim of the paper is not to provide a full overview – for example, the choice of cases implicitly restricts the scope to the Western world – but rather to give appetizers to the broad field of possibilities of this material. Hopefully, this will inspire scholars to include this material in their studies of war and conflict. Money is such a substantial part of society that it cannot be left aside without running the risk of missing important insights.

Income from Coinage

A central concern of any sovereign power is how to maintain its defence in a stable manner. The monetary system itself could contribute to the crucial question of financing this effort. Up to a few generations ago, coins in the western tradition were struck in precious metals. However, their face value was generally slightly higher than the intrinsic value of the precious metal they contained. The difference partly covered the production cost, called *brassage*, but also provided income to the issuing power, the so-called *seigneuriage*. This can be seen as a fee to the issuing power for providing a convenient means of exchange. As such, coinage was an important source of income for sovereigns of the Middle Ages and the Modern Period. The amount of the income varied a lot for various reasons, such as the number of coins issued and the variation in the market price of the metal used for minting. In England between the thirteenth and sixteenth centuries, the royal income is well-attested in surviving accounts. During some years, the *seigneuriage* accounted for more than 10 % of the total annual income of the crown. At other times, when the bullion was expensive, the sovereign had to mint at a loss. On average, the income from coinage counted for a few per cent of the royal income. Consequently, while it was not the most important source of revenue, it remained a steady source year after year (Allen, 2012:201–210).

Wartime Debasement

There were ways of ensuring a quick and substantial increase of the *seigneuriage* through manipulation of the intrinsic value of the coins, providing several advantages in relation to financing war. One such advantage was that less precious metal was needed to strike one coin, so more coins could be struck with the same amount of silver. Another advantage was that inflation itself dramatically increased production volumes. When the content of precious metal decreased (a so-called debasement), the issuing power could increase the nominal price paid for the silver, resulting in it becoming profitable for people to bring their hoarded silver to the mint. This meant increased coin production and consequently increased income from the *seigneuriage*.

This was an opportunity that sovereigns regularly used but most frequently and intensively in wartime when the need for money became urgent. Thus, during the Hundred Years' War (1337–1453), the French King John II (1350–1364) made a series of rapid devaluations and revaluations that maximized income. This was a convenient way to quickly obtain money for the expenses of warfare, instead of raising taxes which was very unpopular. France was at a military disadvantage in the war, and the country was ravaged by the *chevaucées* of the English King Edward III. Moreover, John II was made prisoner at the Battle of Poitiers in 1355 and France subsequently had to pay a large ransom to free him. The debasement played a major role in improving the difficult financial situation.

The monetary manipulations are known from surviving written documents from the royal administration, as well as from the coins themselves. To take one of the more extreme cases, on 3 June 1359 a new coin type, the *gros aux trois lis*, was introduced at a face value of 15 pence of Tours. It contained 0.98 g of silver. During the next four months, the silver content was reduced six times, and on 18 October the same year it was at 0.32 g. As a result, people had lost confidence in this coin, and thus on 22 November a new and better type was introduced: the *gros à l'étoile* at 30 pence of Tours, containing at first 1.63 g of silver. However, only four months later, after seven successive reductions, it was at a mere 0.23 g of silver (Duplessy, 1988: nos 307–308)! At first, this procedure worked. In 1349, for example, the income of the French king was 782,000 pounds of Tours with 522,000 pounds (or 67 %) derived from coinage (Spufford, 1988:305)! Of course, it was not a practice that could work forever because people would simply not use coins and find other ways of trading. The inflation of the 1350s was so disturbing that it became a major topic of debate within the assembly of the Estates General. The royal monopoly was consequently challenged both by the nobility, wanting strong money, and the common people. The monetary manipulations of the Hundred Years' War thus provides a telling example of how war-provoked inflation can have implications on the power structure of society.

Monetary Competition

During conflict, debasement could be a means of competition between enemies. If one of the belligerents lowered the silver content in his coins, he could pay a higher nominal price for the bullion and thus drain all the available silver on the market towards his mints. The other competitors would be forced to close their mints – or to debase their own coinage. This could provoke a rapid inflationist spiral with serious consequences for society.

An illustrative example is found in the civil war in France between the successive dukes of Burgundy, John the Fearless (1404–1419) and Phillip the Good (1419–1467) and the crown prince (Dauphin) Charles (VII). The conflict was further fuelled by Henry V of England's (1413–1422) invasion of Normandy in 1417. The coinage had been relatively stable for more than 50 years, but the political instability led to renewed monetary volatility. The duke of Burgundy took control of some of the royal mints, so too did the crown prince and the English king. In May 1417, the *florette*, a royal silver coin of 20 pence of Tours, contained 1.95 g of silver, which was soon lowered to 1.30 g. Then, the duke of Burgundy devaluated the coins at the mints in his possession further still. Consequently, crown prince Charles (VII) and Henry V had to follow suit to be able to attract the silver and continue their coin production. A rapid downward spiral of debasement had begun. This was monetary warfare. In June 1422, the Dauphin struck a *florette* with only 0.05 g a silver, a decrease of 97 % in just five years (Duplessy, 1988: nos 387, 405, 417, 435)! These extremely debased coins were deliberately exported to the enemy lands to gain extra income to the Dauphin and to disturb the economy of his enemies (Beaune, 1990:§ 346).

The debasement cycle of 1417–1422 illustrates two phenomena linked to coinage and warfare. Coinage meant income, and it was a priority for the belligerents to assure bullion for their mints. But it was also beneficial to bar enemies from running their mints. Thus, coinage could be a weapon in the warfare.

The Social Consequences

No one really benefitted from the forced competition described in the previous section, even though the competing parties each in their turn managed to leverage some short-terms advantages from the increased *seigneuriage*. Society at large paid the price of the war-induced monetary disorder. Notwithstanding these disadvantages for civil society, the return to good money could in turn cause problems for a long time after the war-time debasement spiral had stopped. Starting from late 1420 until mid-1422, a process of restauration of sound money occurred in France (Lardin, 1998; Moesgaard, 1999:92–94). A new two-pence coin was struck and the face value of the old *florette* was gradually reduced, first from 20 to 5 pence and then to 2.5 pence. This caused rising prices and much discussion that even sometimes led to murder, as shown by a pardon letter from the court in Rouen (Le Cacheux, 1907–08:doc. 129). More serious for the issuing power was the popular unrest. Debts contracted in bad money sometimes had to be paid in sound money. Indeed, the aim of the reform was to restore the incomes of people receiving rents and fixed revenues, but this was of course to the disadvantage of the poor. In Paris in 1421, a chronicler tells us that 'ordinary people were very unhappy and gathered in the town hall to discuss, and when the town officials saw them, they were so afraid [that they had to let people pay at the old rate concerning the upcoming payment term]' (Beaune, 1990:§ 314), and the authorities had to urge the merchants to ask fair prices (Ordonnances XI:122–125). Some years later, when better money had been put into circulation, and one of the varieties of the reform two-pence had its face value reduced, many people lost a lot of money. One chronicler even tells us that people in Paris threw their coins into the Seine River in despair (Beaune, 1990:§ 443 & 445)! Paradoxically, as the above example shows, the restauration of sound money after the disorders of war was not straightforward and could cause serious social problems.

Manipulation of Dates and Names of Issuing Powers

It is said that the truth is the first victim of war. This is also true with coinage. As the following examples will show, coins sometimes show a false year or the wrong issuing power. This is done to accommodate the concerns of various social groups who would be unhappy with the truth.

Coin minting in the aftermath of the Count's Feud (1534–1536), which was a civil war in Denmark that was won by Christian (III), son of the former King Fredrick I (1523–1533) and Duke of Schleswig-Holstein, provides an example of how this could be done. As usual, the coinage had suffered during the conflict and the currency was heavily debased. The bad war-time coins were very unpopular among the population. On 6 April 1536, when the war was almost won, Christian made a solemn promise to restore sound money. The fact that monetary affairs were brought into political negotiations shows the importance of coinage in society and the disruption that war had brought to it. At first, Christian only partially fulfilled his promise. Some of the very bad coins were indeed withdrawn from circulation but the mint accounts clearly show that other types of debased coins continued to be produced in large quantities until 1540/1541. However, if we look at the coins themselves, they do not carry the real year of striking. Instead, they show the pre-peace dates of 1535 (Figure 1) and 1536. Only a few large full-value silver coins carry the real year 1537 (Galster, 1934; Moesgaard, 2006). This procedure of ante-dating the coins was done to hide the broken promise to the population to avoid popular unrest and was necessary because Christian III did not have the resources to restore coinage at first. Only in 1540–1541 was new sound money finally introduced, which incidentally, in the Danish numismatic tradition, marks the transition from the Middle Ages to the modern period. Accordingly, the aftermath of the Count's Feud shows the significance of an effective handling of post-conflict coinage and that issuing powers sometimes judged 'false' coin minting as necessary means by which to attain and maintain power. Coinage was an important political and societal issue, and war-induced disruption could cause dissatisfaction among the coin users.

The Count's Feud also offers insights into the different actors involved in the war financing and the international relations of the time. A particular series of coins stands out among the coins in the name of Christian III with the year 1535. The mint master usually put a mint master's mark on the coins. The purpose was to be able to identify the person responsible of the production and, if appropriate, punish them if the coins were under-value.

Figure 1: Denmark, Christian III, 4 skilling, struck in Copenhagen. It carries the year 1535, but Christian did not conquer Copenhagen before 29 July 1536 (Bruun Rasmussen Auction 791, 17 June 2008, no 5115).

However, in the case of the coins under consideration here, they do not carry the usual trefoil of Christian's mint master, Reynold Junge, but the symbols of the contemporary Stockholm mint masters, Anders Hansson and Morten Jönsson (Figure 2). The reason is that King Gustav Vasa (1521–1560) of Sweden backed Christian III in the civil war and sent troops to Halland and Scania to support him. To pay for the troops, Gustav Vasa struck coins in the name of Christian III at the mint of Stockholm because Swedish coins were not legal tender in Denmark, but the troops wanted Danish money (Bentsen, 1994; Rye & Märcher, 2013). By putting one's own name on the coins, the issuing power guaranteed the value of the coin – a fundamental principle in minting. On face value, Gustav Vasa is a forger, and in peace time Christian would never have tolerated this manifest breach of his minting right. But, because of war-time necessity, it was accepted.

Previously, Gustav Vasa had successfully struck other Danish coins. In 1521–1522, he struck false Danish *klipping* (coins struck hastily on roughly square flans). The *klipping* was originally issued in 1518–1522 by Christian II, King of Denmark (1513–1523).

Figure 2: 8 skilling 1535 struck in Stockholm by Gustav Vasa of Sweden the name of Christian III of Denmark (The Royal Collection of Coins and Medals, Copenhagen, inv. KP 635).

It was an underweight coin in debased silver tending towards pure copper. Christian struck them in huge quantities to finance his conquest of Sweden which had broken away from the Danish-led Kalmar Union. Following the massacre of the anti-Danish noblemen in Stockholm in November 1520, Gustav, then a nobleman, led a Swedish uprising and ousted the Danes. The Danish *klippings* were very unpopular, and by striking false ones, purporting being genuine Danish coins, Gustav Vasa achieved three objectives: adding to the anti-Danish sentiment in Sweden, gaining money and undermining the Danish economy (Hemmingsson, 1973; Moesgaard, 2020). This is not to say that the false *klippings* alone helped Gustav win the war, but they contributed to the victory. One should not underestimate the damage to the economy, and to the trust in currency, that an arrival of many debased forgeries issued by the enemy can cause. The two examples of Danish coins struck by Gustav Vasa illustrate how issuing powers can effectively make use of monetary manipulation to both support and oppose foreign powers in international relations.

Money Supply in Wartime

In the Late Medieval–Early Modern period, a professionalisation of warfare took place which involved hiring trained mercenaries. Paying for these freelance soldiers was one of the largest posts in the state spending and was a considerable drain on the finances of kings and princes. Later on, the national armies of the seventeenth and eighteenth centuries were costly. Having the necessary funds was not the only problem, however. There were also the logistic aspects of having the right money at the right place and time.

The Wrong Money

After being ousted from Sweden (see above), Christian II faced a revolt in Denmark led by his uncle, Fredrick (I), Duke of Schleswig-Holstein. Christian's debased *klippings* were part of the reason for his defeat and are an example of how monetary affairs can influence the result of an armed conflict (Figure 3). According to the historian Michael Venge, Christian II's mercenaries showed little resistance when Fredrick's troops landed on the island of Zealand on 31 May 1523 because they were busy negotiating their salary! They asked to be paid only half in the despised copperish *klippings*. For the other half, they wanted 'thick silver coins', i.e., good silver coins. On this occasion they accepted payment in *klippings* after several days of negotiations. In the meantime, Fredrick's troops had gained a foothold on Zealand (Venge, 1994). This was the beginning of the end of Christian II's reign, and soon Fredrick took over the throne from his nephew. In this case, the soldiers' dissatisfaction with coins changed the course of the war. Even if he had wanted to, Christian was probably not able to pay the soldiers in good coins. Production of good coins all but stopped, and the old good quality coins had vanished from circulation, either hoarded as savings or melted down to be restruck as debased war money.

This example highlights that the outcome of a war depends on more than military skill. Finances influence the course of events. This is true at all times, but especially in the age of mercenaries who fought not out of loyalty to an employer or commitment to a cause but solely for money!

The 'Field Mint'

The need for a constant and substantial money supply for paying the mercenaries becomes visible in a concrete way when the mint followed the army, as was the case during the Danish civil war, the Count's Feud (1534–1536).

Figure 3: Denmark, Christian II, klipping, struck in Malmö 1518–1522 (The Economy Museum/Royal Coin Cabinet, Stockholm).

As we saw above, one of the belligerents was Christian (III), son of the former King Fredrick I (1523–1533) and Duke of Schleswig-Holstein. In June 1534, there was fighting in Holstein and around Lübeck. Minting took place at its usual peace time location at Christian's residence at Gottorp Castle in Schleswig. In December, Christian's army moved north into western and northern Jutland to fight a popular uprising. In January 1535, the mint followed suit and moved north to Aarhus in Central Jutland. When the uprising was crushed, the army prepared for the next step. In March, the army moved on to the Island of Funen, and in July it pushed east to the central part of the kingdom and besieged the cities of Copenhagen and Malmö. The mint of Aarhus was temporarily shut down in August and a new mint was set up in Roskilde in September, nearer to the besieged cities and the mercenaries who were to be paid with the newly struck coins. After a year of siege, Copenhagen surrendered on 29 July 1536. On 12 August 1537 Christian III was officially crowned (Galster, 1934; Moesgaard, 2006). All three locations of the mint were within range of combat, far enough from the front to be secure yet close enough to produce money for the troops. This moving of the mint in the footsteps of the army shows the degree to which society had become militarized. The needs of the army took over this institution.

The Logistics of Money Supply

The war treasury also had a logistic aspect since money had to be transported to the zones of combat. Failing to manage this could potentially influence the course of the war. If money was not at the right place, the war effort could be forced to be downscaled or, at worst, halted. Of course, money transfers were not always enough. Other factors, such as insufficient military skill, were also important. Despite successful large-scale transfers of funds – literally sacks of coins – from England to the Continent, the English King John Lackland lost all his French possessions north of the Loire (Normandy, Maine, Anjou, etc.) to the French King Philipp August in 1204. These transfers were so large the English sterling was introduced into the general coin circulation on the Continent, which lastingly changed the composition of currency. Thus, war financing did not always win wars but could nonetheless modify civil society's money supply regardless of who won on the battlefield (Moesgaard, 2002).

It was risky to transport valuables during war time, and the consequences of losing large money supplies could be devastating. Ships were the main transports for both troops and valuables over long distances but were at risk of both sinking or capture by enemy fleets. Several warships are known to have sunk with substancial treasures as well as personal possessions, the remains of which can sometimes be found archaeologically on wreck sites. One example is the Danish King John I's flagship, *Griffin/Gribshunden*, which sank after a devastating fire aboard in 1495 along with many of John I's treasures – and among them gold, silver and currency, according to the Sture Chronicle. Following the loss of the ship, King John, who was not aboard, continued his journey but abandoned his expensive German mercenaries and left them to find their own way home, according to Reimar Kock's Lübeckian chronicle (Sjöblom, 2015:47–48; I thank Rolf Warming for making me aware of this case). Several coins, possibly from a high-ranking military officer, have been recovered from the wreck (for archaeological finds, see Rönnby, 2021:59; Ingvardson, et al. 2022). Another example is the wreck of the Swedish warship *Mars Makalös*, which sank in the Battle of Öland (1564). Following her surrender, the ship exploded and sank along with c. 800 people and a great treasure of golden and silver coins (2000 goldgulden and 200 0000 thaler), which had been brought to recruit mercenaries in Rostock (de Crèvecour, 1959:95; Rönnby, 2012; Ingvar Sjöblom, pers. com.:11.07.2024).

Recently, the theory has been promoted that Christian II's final defeat, when he tried to reconquer the Danish and Norwegian thrones in 1531–1532, was caused by the loss of his war treasury that was on board his flag ships, which sank off the Norwegian coast (Kristensen & Flinthöj, 2023). As such, the long-distance transport of valuables often entailed a continuous risk of sudden loss, especially along maritime routes.

The transport of valuables created lucrative possibilities both for the enemy and for others wanting to enrich themselves. In seventeenth-century Sweden the dearth of silver led to striking coins in pure copper. During the Scanian War (1675–1679), the one thaler 'coin' was a copper plate of 1.36 kg and the common denomination of the double thaler weighed 2.72 kg! This should be compared to an ordinary silver thaler that weighed 0.03 kg. This made management of money more complicated. As the Swedish army needed money, loads of heavy copper plates were transported south in a convoy of carriages to the war scene in Scania. On 24 July 1676, in Loshult, at the border of Småland and Scania, the war treasury was robbed by Danish soldiers and local peasants who stole as much as they could carry. After the war a juridical process recovered much, but not all of what was stolen. Some of the spoils were hidden away and are still regularly found today and deemed a treasure trove by the State (Hammarberg, 1997). Ultimately, these practical kinds of logistical issues could have important repercussions on the military possibilities on the ground.

War also led to serious logistical problems for civil society. Besieged cities could lack everything, including coins. They often then struck very base emergency money to meet the need of small change in everyday life. For instance, the Scanian city of Kristianstad was occupied by the Danish army during the Scanian War and blockaded by the Swedes. Emergency coins were struck in copper and lead (Figure 4), and their intrinsic value was far below their face value (Hede, 1976). This example highlights that coinage was a core institution that had to be at hand for society to function. It also says something about the adaptability of the monetary system during military conflicts.

Disruption to Civil Society

We now turn away from the perspective of the state to take a closer look at the impact of war on society. During times of war, armies came by plundering and heavy taxes were levied. Naturally, people hid their savings. This is documented both in historical sources and by archaeology. We learn that all levels of society suffered disruption brought by war and made various attempts to cope with it.

Burying savings was common but not always a successful counter-measure plundering. The English chronicler Simeon of Durham tells us that when the troops of Henry I, King of England (1100–1135) and duke of Normandy (1106–1135), had taken and burnt down the Norman town of Pont-Audemer (dép. Eure), some of his soldiers dug the soil and found gold, silver, clothes, pepper, ginger that townsfolk had buried (Arnold, 1885:274). The riches were retrieved by soldiers, so hiding them had been in vain! The hoards also contained perishable items like clothes and spices that would not have survived in the ground until today, unlike gold and silver.

As well as individuals, entire institutions buried their treasures during war. For instance, during the civil warfare in France between Catholics and Protestants, the monks of Jumièges (dép. Seine-Maritime) fled their Abbey in 1562. Before leaving they hid the treasury in the ground in two different places to avoid losing everything if one of the caches was discovered. This proved fruitless, however, because when the Protestant Calvinists arrived at the Abbey, they found and tortured a lay brother until he revealed where the treasury was hidden (Loth, 1882–1885:287).

There are many examples of people hiding valuables during times of war. Some were successfully retrieved by their owners after the hostilities ended, others were less lucky, like the two previous cases. Written sources provide a lot of details about the circumstances of the concealment and those involved – details that archaeology seldom illustrates. Thus, the different categories of sources are complementary.

Figure 4: 8 skilling emergency money, struck in lead by the Danes in the besieged city of Kristianstad, Scania (Bruun Rasmussen, auction 901, 3 May 2021, no. 136)

Contrary to the cases mentioned earlier, the hoards that we find archaeologically today – at least for the areas and periods dealt with in this paper – represent the ones that were not found by the enemy or retrieved by their rightful owners but left in the soil. Hoarding also took place during peace time but clusters of hoards are often seen during times of unrest. For instance, there are relatively few hoards in Sweden (within the borders of the epoch) from the sixteenth century but one decade stands out: the 1560s, coinciding with the Nordic Seven Years' War between Denmark and Sweden (1563–1570). More than thirty hoards are recorded from this decade (Gerdin, 2009), which is as many as from the four-decade long reign of Gustav Vasa (Jonsson, 2019). Moreover, if one looks at the find spots of these hoards, they closely relate to the route taken by the Danish commander Daniel Rantzau in Västergötland in 1566 and in Östergötland in 1567–1568. It seems clear that the cluster of hoards is linked to the insecurity caused by the war, and it is almost possible reconstruct the movement of the troops by plotting the hoard finds on a map. The amount of unretrieved coins is an indirect indication of the amount of destruction and human displacement that affected civil society during this time.

However, not every hoard should be interpreted as people hiding their riches away in a hurry as the enemy approaches. Banks as we know them did not exist in the sixteenth century. The way to keep one's savings safe was to hide them in a wall or in the ground nearby one's house. This was an everyday way of dealing with money during times of peace and war. It was commonplace for these savings to be recovered and spent (leaving nothing in the soil for us to find). However, during war, sometimes people were killed before telling their family where the savings were kept. More savings were therefore forgotten and left in the ground during war time. Other hoards probably represent savings more hastily hidden away because of the impending dangers of war. On the other hand, the more symbolic or social interpretations of hoards put forward by archaeologists in recent decades are probably not relevant for the period studied here. Consequently, it takes a careful archaeo-logical and numismatic analysis to interpret a hoard correctly and make it deliver all its potential information about people's fear of war and how they coped with it.

In addition to providing details regarding societies, coin finds can also provide specifics regarding individuals. One example is the iden-tification of soldiers fighting in the Battle of Visby (1361) which marked the Danish conquest of the island of Gotland. The mass graves of the slain soldiers have been excavated and several small purses were found close to some of the skeletons. The content of the purses allows us to identify some of the soldiers as Danish and others as locals (Thordeman, 1932). Coins found on battlefield sites also bring us close to the soldiers. These finds appear in increasing numbers due to metal detector surveys on the sites. Thus, a Swedish ½ öre 1563 was found at the site of the battle between the Danish army and Swedish militias at Getaryggen 1567, during the Nordic Seven Years' War, one of the best investigated battlefields in Sweden in archaeological terms (Jönköping läns museum, n.d.; Engkvist, Pettersson, Wennerberg, 2012:11).

Another example, which allows us to come even closer to a deceased soldier, comes from the wreck of the Confederate submarine Hunley, that sank in 1864 during the American Civil war. On board was found an 1860 gold 20 dollar piece. It carries a bullet impact, traces of lead and an engraved inscription: 'Shiloh/April 6th 1862/My life Preserver/G.E.D'. G.E.D. are the initials of captain Georges Dixon, who was saved by this coin during the Battle of Shilo. The coin is evidence of both the shot which possibly would have killed Dixon, if not for the coin, but also how he kept it as a token of good luck after the event (Friends of the Hunley, n.d.). The personal connections that people have to coins because of their monetary value – and sometimes sentimental or symbolic value – can thus provide rare insights into the individuals who fought or otherwise were affected during conflict.

Conclusion

To summarise, numismatics and monetary history can tell us a lot about many aspects of war and conflict and their interaction with society (Table 1). War is expensive, and financing war is a huge undertaking, and extraordinary means often have to be employed. War and conflict may cause disorder in the currency that can have immediate as well as long-standing social and political consequences. The financial disorders can also impact the conflict itself in the short-term, for instance by making the soldiers unhappy and not willing to fight. Coinage and currency can constitute an economic battlefield, where the opponents seek to harm each other, either by draining the available bullion away from the enemy towards one's own mints or by destabilizing the enemy's currency by issuing forgeries of their coins.

Changing perspective from the state to people, numismatics and monetary history can also illuminate important other features of society such as the consequences of war. The social disruption caused by the insecurity linked to war can be read through the increase in the hiding of savings or by the disturbances in the trade caused by debased war money. On a larger scale, it can also lead to social unrest that can affect politics.

The sources for studying these features are both historical and archaeological, each line of evidence providing us different valuable insights. Official documents inform us about finance and the official monetary policy, currency manipulations and about mint output and revenues from coinage. Narrative sources and legal archives can reveal details about the economic and social consequences of war economy.

Table 1: Summary of sources mentioned in the paper.

Place	Date	Case	Comment
France	1350s	Debasement of the silver coins	The king's method to meet the urgent need for money for warfare
France	1417–22	Debasement of the silver coins	The various belligerents' competition for the bullion for minting
France	1420s	Civil unrest led by holders of war-time coins after return to good money	Disruption of the economic life of the population can lead to political instability
Denmark	1536–40	Ante-dating of coins	Concealing the production of debased coins to the population to avoid popular unrest
Sweden	1534–36	Striking of Danish coins	The need to pay troops in the currency they wanted
Sweden	1521–22	Striking of debased Danish coins	Providing money for the war and destabilizing the enemy's economy
Denmark	1523	Problems getting the kind of coins that the soldiers wanted	Refusal to fight because of monetary dissatisfaction leading to defeat
Denmark	1534–36	Moving the mint from town to town following the army	Logistical demand of providing fresh coins in large amounts to pay the soldiers
NW France	1204	Massive transfers of funds from England to France	Failed attempt to win the war
Blekinge	1495	Fire and shipwreck of the king's flagship Gribshunden	Loss of treasury that led to dismissal of troops
Öland	1564	Loss of the warship Mars Makalös during battle	Loss of treasury for salary payment
Norway	1531–32	Hypothesis that Christian II's war treasury was lost in a ship-wreck	Hypothesis that this is the explanation for Christian's defeat
Sweden	1676	The attack of the war treasury during transport to the war scene	The difficulty of the logistics of transport of treasury
Scania	1675–79	Striking of emergency coins in the besieged city of Kristianstad	The disruption of everyday life during sieges
Normandy	1100–35, 1562	Emergency hiding of valuables during war	The population and institutions try to protect their belongings from looting
Sweden	1563–70	A concentration of recorded hoards during the Nordic Seven Year's war	Some hoards are everyday savings and some are emergency hidings. Their non recovery reflects the sudden death of their owner during war time
Gotland	1361	Purses found during excavation of mass grave	Personal belongings of the dead soldiers
Getaryggen	1567	Coin found on battlefield	Personal belongings of soldiers in action
Charleston	1864	Coin with bullet impact and engraved inscription	Soldier saved by coin and using it as a luck token showing an individual coping with war

The coins themselves can tell us about debasements and emergency issues. Coin finds also offer insights into the fear of looting, where fighting took place, and what kind of money the soldiers had in their pocket.

In conclusion, numismatics and monetary history have huge potential for contributing to war studies, along with other disciplines like economics, anthropology and sociology. They provide information and nuances on many aspects of the interaction of conflict and society. Information can be found both in written sources, in the coins themselves and in analyses of the coin finds, but this should not refrain scholars from integrating this material. Not all the aspects have been treated in this short essay, which has just given a series of examples – drawn from a European/Western perspective – as an appetizer.

References

Allen, M. (2012). *Mints and Money in Medieval England.* Cambridge University Press.

Arnold, T. (Ed.) (1885). *Symeonis Monachi Opera omnia, Historia Regum* (vol. 2). London.

Beaune, C. (Ed.) (1990). *Journal d'un bourgeois de Paris de 1405 à 1449.* Livre de Poche.

Bentsen, B. (1994). Gustav Vasa's danske 1 marck 1535. *Numismatisk Rapport, 41,* 115–121.

de Crèvecour, E. B. (1959). *Herluf Trolle: Kongens Admiral og Herlufsholm Skoles Stifter.* Copenhagen: C.A. Reitzels Forlag.

Duplessy, J. (1988). *Les monnaies françaises royales,* tome 1. Platt.

Engkvist, S. Pettersson, C. B. & Wennerberg, R. (2012). *Getaryggen 1567. Delrapport för år 2011.* Milisium (accesible https://jonkopingslans museum.se/wp-content/uploads/2012/04/rapport-getaryggen-2011.pdf, consulted 4 Dec 2023).

Friends of the Hunley (n.d). *Artifacts. Dixon's Coin.* https://www.hunley. org/artifacts/, consulted 15 Oct 2023.

Galster, G. (Ed.) (1934). *Reynold Junges møntmesterregnskaber 1534–1540.* Selskabet for udgivelse af kilder til dansk historie

Gerdin, V. (2009). *Död, pest och pina! Myntskatter och Nordiska sjuårskriget* (Bachelor essay). Stockholm University.

Hammarberg, I. (1997). Plåtmynt från snapphanarnes tid. *Svensk Numismatisk Tidskrift, 4,* 84–88.

Hede, H. (1976). *Danmarks og Norges mønter 1541–1814–1977.* Copenhagen. Dansk Numismatisk Forening.

Hemmingsson, B. (1973). Ett klippingfynd från Västerås. *Numismatiska Meddelanden, 31,* 61–74.

Ingvardson G. Muter, D. & Foley, B. (2022). Purse of medieval silver coins from royal shipwreck revealed by X-ray microscale Computed Tomography (μCT) scanning. *Journal of Archaeological Science: Reports, 43*.

Jönköping läns museum (n.d.). *Mynt.* https://digitaltmuseum.se/021028432505/mynt, consulted 4 Dec 2023.

Jonsson, K. (2019). Skatten från Sysslomansgården i Uppsala 1775 och myntcirkulationen under Gustav Vasa. In *Samlad glädje 2019* (pp. 167–177). Numismatiska klubben i Uppsala.

Kromann, A. & Jensen, J. S. (1976). *Inflation.* National Museum of Denmark.

Kristensen, P. K. & Flinthöj, M. (2023). *Mission har været hemmelig indtil nu: Dansk-krigsskib på-500 år jages på havets bund.* https://www.dr.dk/nyheder/indland/mission-har-vaeret-hemmelig-indtil-nu-dansk-krigsskib-paa-500-aar-jages-paa-havets, consulted 15 Oct 2023

Lardin, P. (1998). La crise monétaire de 1420–1422 en Normandie. In *L'argent au Moyen Âge* (pp. 101–143). Publications de la Sorbonne.

Le Cacheux, P. (1907–08). *Actes de la chancellerie d'Henri VI concernant la Normandie sous la domination anglaise (1422–1449).* Société d'historie de Normandie.

Loth, J. (Ed.) (1882–85). *Histoire de l'abbaye royale de Saint-Pierre de Jumièges* (3 vols). Rouen.

Moesgaard, J. C. (1999). La circulation monétaire au temps de Charles VI. In *La Normandie au XVe siècle, Art et Histoire, Actes du colloque organisé par les Archives départementales du 2 au 5 décembre 1998* (pp. 87–102). Archives départementales de la Manche.

Moesgaard, J. C. (2002). La circulation des monnaies anglaises en France et le financement de la guerre franco-anglaise 1193/1194–1203/1205. *Cahiers numismatiques, 154,* 49–76.

Moesgaard, J. C. (2006). Monnaie et armée pendant le Guerre civile danoise de 1534–1536. In D. Hollard (Ed.), *L'armée et la monnaie* (pp. 61–73, pl. VI). Société d'études numismatiques et archéologiques.

Moesgaard, J. C. (2020). I skyggen af 500-årsjubilæet for blodbadet i Stockholm: status i forskningen i Christian II's klippinge. *Svensk Numismatisk Tidskrift, 7,* 153–159.

Les Ordonnances des rois de France (1723–1849), 21 volumes.

Rönnby, J. (Ed.) (2012). *Skeppet Mars (1564). Marinarkeologisk fältrapport Etapp II 2012.* Södertörn University. Available at [accessed 03.11.2023]: https://www.diva-portal.org/smash/get/diva2:664328/FULLTEXT01.pdf

Rye, J. & Märcher, M. (2013). Nyt eksemplar af hidtil unik 8 skilling 1535 Stockholm. *Nordisk Numismatisk Unions Medlemsblad, 3,* 74–75

Sjöblom, I. (2015). Identifiering och historiska sammanhang. In J. Rönnby (Ed.), *Gribshunden (1495): Skeppsvrak vid Stora Ekön, Ronneby, Blekinge. Marinarkologiska undersökningar 2013–2015.* Blekinge museum rapport 21. Blekinge museum/Södertörns Högskola.

Spufford, P. (1988). *Money and its use in medieval Europe*. Cambridge University Press.

Thordeman, B. (1932). Myntfynden i Korsbetningens massgravar. *Fornvännen*, 27, 23–39, 65–87.

Venge, M. (1994). Oberstens møntproblemer og Christian II's klippinge. *Nordisk Numismatisk Unions Medlemsblad*, 4, 67–69.

Concluding Remarks: Reflections on Research into Conflict Archaeology

Lena Holmquist

In the permanent exhibition at the Army Museum in Stockholm, a few decades old by now, the visitor first meets the modern human's closest relative among the Primates – the chimpanzee – engaging in aggressive acts and wielding 'weapons'. It has been shown that chimpanzees organized patrols to guard their territory, sending out scouts to surveil hostile groups and to battle them if the chance arises (Goodall, 1990). When the exhibition opened, the suitability of employing primates as the starting point for an exhibition on human martial history was strongly questioned. But armed conflict is not a deviation from the norm; rather, as made clear in this volume, it is an active ingredient in social interaction and the development of societies (see Warming, this volume).

Today, it is generally accepted that war, conflicts and armed aggression have been humanity's constant companion (cf. Rönnby, 2019:257ff.). This has naturally varied over time and place. Equally, attitudes towards conflict research have varied throughout history. Armed conflicts could be toned down or their existence totally denied despite clear evidence to the contrary. War fatigue following on World War I and II has no doubt been a contributing factor to a reluctance for research in this field. Since the 1990s, and more so recently, a reaction can be observed to previous conflict research oriented towards military history with its sometimes-questionable reconstructions (cf. e.g., Armit et al., 2007; Bornefalk Back, 2016). Besides studies of weapons and war-hostages, some larger interdisciplinary attempts have been made showing the importance of examining all potential material and combining different methods, including special emphasis on technology and the natural sciences. This, together with the creation of new applicable analytical tools, has opened conflict research as an important source for understanding cultural history and the growth of societies. One of the greater challenges for the future is locating sites of conflict in the new field of conflict scenography.

In reviewing past archaeological literature and projects relating to conflicts, it is apparent that all countries and research communities have their own research biographies, preferences and shared paradigms. This is case in Sweden, where archaeological research on conflicts has seen both gradual and drastic shifts in focus over the years, often following general international trends (for an overview, see Carman, 2013) but also developing in its own right.

In the following pages, I will share some reflections based on my own field of research on conflict studies of an archaeological nature from a Swedish and partly Scandinavian perspective. Several examples will be drawn from research on fortifications, as their excellent preservation in Sweden has made them suitable for several important investigations. Over 1,000 hillforts have been identified across the country, most of them situated outside modern settlements, which has shielded them from exploitation. Additionally, they have remained untouched by the direct impact of warfare for at least 200 years (Figure 2). Their location, far from continental Europe, also presents a valuable opportunity for comparative studies of construction techniques, functions, and external influences.

Conflict research in the 20th century

Early challenges

A persistent issue with which conflict archaeological research in general has had to contend in many research communities – both in Sweden and abroad – is a certain neglect or downplay of violence in the past. As mentioned above, this attitude may to some extent be owed to a war fatigue and antimilitarism that arose after the two world wars and influenced research paradigms in the second half of the 20th century.

An example of how scholars have downplayed the martial element in past societies concerns the famous Bronze Age palace of Knossos in Crete where the legendary scholar Sir Arthur Evans, based on his excavations in the 1930s, reconstructed Minoan culture as the first flowering of Western civilization. It was seen as a golden childhood nurtured by a benevolent mother goddess, situated in an age of peace on a beautiful island protected by the sea (Gere, 2009). This interpretation was put forth at a time when all of Europe suffered from post-war fatigue and longed to hear of peaceful societies (Armit et al., 2007:3). Later investigations into the warlike aspects of Minoan culture nonetheless show that times were not nearly as peaceful as Evans believed. As Barry Molloy has shown, war, conflicts and violence were an integral part of this culture even if direct evidence of actual battlefields is lacking (Molloy, 2012).

In general, it can be stated that both in Europe and the rest of the world, conflict research has had to take a backseat in favour of more peaceful explanations. This was certainly the case in Sweden. The case of the more peaceful reading of Bronze Age Crete, which has since then been debunked, is seemingly paralleled in the Nordic Bronze Age. Although once believed to be peaceful, it is now generally understood that Nordic Bronze Age societies engaged in more violent activities and on a larger scale than previously thought, as evidenced by the Tollense battlefield site. Indeed, they appear to have been much more complex societies in which conflict and cooperation were intricately intertwined (Horn & Molloy, this volume). Another case in point is Viking Age studies. It is evident that there was a time when the image of the plundering and hot-tempered Viking warrior had to be accompanied by that of the peaceful merchant engaged in long-distance trade (Jansson, 1997).

Although this attitude may be said to have diminished over the years, a recent systematic review of literature on conflict archaeology indicate that papers of a conflict-related nature remain quantitatively underrepresented within Swedish research (Bornfalk Back, 2016).

The Late 20th Century

Notwithstanding such disciplinary challenges in this field, more recent research in the late 20th century was clearly able to demonstrate that armed conflict was a significant feature of Scandinavian societies.

An important find well worth mentioning in this context is the discovery of a boat and weapons sacrifice from Hjortspring on the island of Als in Jylland/Jutland in Denmark. It was found in a tiny bog and was excavated in the early 1920s. It is 19 m long boat with a crew of about 22 warriors/rowers and dates to the fourth century BC. The most likely interpretation is that it is the spoils of a defeated enemy army. The finds were re-examined and contextualized in the 1990s by Klavs Randsborg, who by exploring the topic of warfare and sacrifice paints a broad picture of the development of society during prehistoric times in Europe with ancient Greece as his starting point (Randsborg, 1995). According to Randsborg, "Hjortspring reflects not only social but also religious or cultic behaviour. In fact, ancient society, seemingly, took only limited intellectual and ritual interest in its own "economies… Rather the people of old were preoccupied with the triad of "politics", warfare and religion…" (Randsborg, 1995:14). Randsborg's work, although at times stretched thin in its interpretations, stands as an important and early effort in the broad social contextualization of a conflict archaeological find in Scandinavia.

Another important work published in the 1990s, a year after that of Randsborg is Lawrence H. Keeley's *War Before Civilization* (1996). Randsborg and Keeley can be said to be complementary to each other in terms of time and space. Until then, only a few overarching works had been written in the field. Keeley combined archaeological and anthropological data, arguing that the latter would help fill a knowledge gap. His study showed that "Still the overwhelming majority of known societies have made war. Therefore, while it is not inevitable, war is universally and common and unusual" (Keeley, 1996:32).

The publishing dates of the works of Randsborg (1995) and Keeley (1996) are hardly a coincidence and reflect a shifting trend in the archaeological research community on an international level. These works, as well as several other notable publications that appeared around that time (see below) indicate a greater interest in conflict studies, not least a push towards more socially contextualized understandings of past conflicts and weaponry.

New Currents in Conflict Research

During the late 20th century, new currents in conflict research in Scandinavia began to emerge, indicating tendencies towards new orientations. Weapons finds in graves and so-called war-booty sacrifices have been the primary foci of such studies.

A revealing example of how information on armed conflict can be gleaned is the case of Illerup Ådal in Denmark, where researchers have gained a detailed knowledge of a battle fought in Jutland during the Roman Iron Age. The exact location of the battlefield is unknown, but an associated sacrificial deposition of weapons was discovered in 1950. This was in a peat bog which at the time formed a lake. The deposition produced 15,000 finds, including many weapons sacrificed on four occasions. The equipment has been shown to have been mainly manu-factured in what is now western Sweden and Norway, but there are also imported weapons from the Roman Empire. These imported weapons are considered to have equipped soldiers of lower rank in contrast to the high-ranking soldiers who bore Scandinavian weapons (Ilkjær, 2000). In 2009, human remains, estimated to be those of 1,000 individuals, were found in the river valley at Alken Enge, close to the sacrificial bog (Løvschal et al., 2020). This is interpreted as the remains of an army on its way to or from the Roman Empire that was overcome by the local population. Here, a large unit of at least 1,000 soldiers was sacrificed or killed in a major battle. Valuable knowledge has been obtained about the size and composition of this unit and how they were armed.

To name a few other studies, important research on Iron Age weapon categories and fighting equipment have been made by Anne Nørgård Jørgensen (1999) who has studied weapon asscmblages in Scandinavian graves AD 520/30–900. Scholars have eagerly pursued studies into weaponry technologies in Scandinavia, also in relation to various social aspects, for example, Fedir Androshchuk (2014) who has described, dated and studied the social aspects of 832 Scandi-navian Viking Age swords.

Iron Age fortifications – the BMS project

Yet with such success in research into war booty sacrifices and weap-ons, several other aspects received considerably less attention. One such area of research in Sweden was fortifications.

However, in 1998, a new project was initiated with the title "Hill-forts and fortifications in central Sweden 400–1100" (*Borgar och befästningsverk i Mellansverige 400-1100*", or BMS, 1998–2001) (Holmquist, 2016). The timeliness of this project was confirmed by the initiation that same year in Denmark of the project "Warfare and Society from the Perspectives of Archaeology and European Communities" (under the direction of Helle Vandkilde), which dealt with conflict during the Bronze Age (Vandkilde, 2006).

The BMS project was based on a study of the hillforts in central Sweden and Birka's fortifications on Björkö in Lake Mälaren (Figure 1). The research focused on the role of armed conflicts in terms of martial technology together with sociopolitical and architectonic aspects (Holmquist Olausson & Olausson, 2009). It embraced existing investigations but also carried out new surveys and exploratory research excavation within the auspices of the project. The project attracted a fair degree of attention and its relevance was discussed. The appropriateness of having a female project leader (the present writer) was raised on several occasions. One critique that was often expressed was the need for a male leader/researcher who would have better insight and understanding of the topic. This same viewpoint is reflected in attitudes to women's involvement and participation in the actual act of armed conflict in past societies (see below).

Hillfort research in Sweden

It is my perception that relatively little has happened in fortification research in Sweden after the completion of the BMS project. One exception is the study of hillforts, a category of ancient monuments that has enjoyed stable scholarly attention in the past two decades.

Since the beginning of the 20th century, hillforts had been traditionally seen as hilltop sites of defence or refuge during the Migration Period of the sixth century AD. In his dissertation *Det inneslutna rummet* ("The Enclosed Space") from 1995, Michael Olausson, took up this category of ancient monument for renewed discussion.

Figure 1: An early excavation of Birka's garrison in 1934 with Alf Nordström (left), prof. Holger Arbman (center) and prof. Greta Arwidsson (right). Photo: Unknown, Riksantikvarieämbetet/Kulturmiljöbild.

He initiated a research project on stone- and earthen forts in general, showing their great variation in date and function. For example, his research excavations of hillforts in central Sweden produced dates ranging from the Bronze Age to the Viking Age and can be divided into four functionally different groups. Following the presentation and discussion of this dissertation, a few related dissertations have emerged from Stockholm University, all of which question previously imagined functions of these ancient forts by presenting alternative interpretations. Birgitta Johansen (1997) adopted a metaphorical perspective and Kerstin Cassel (1998) interpreted them as "intellectual defence works" erected in the interests of the whole local community. In 2002, Åsa Wall coined the concept of the "enclosed hill", interpreting these sites as part of a mythical geography. In this context mention can also be made of the work of Anders Carlsson (2001:58 ff, 2015:106) who sees ancient forts as places for ritual activities during both the Bronze Age and the Migration Period, the so-called "clas–

sical" fort-building phase (cf. Bornefalk Back, 2016). In the autumn of 2023, ancient forts were again the centre of attention, this time focusing on their construction to "define the development over time and space of the fort and fortification tradition employing the dry-stone walling technique"; a secondary aim was to use "this chronology to explore the needs and concepts that formed the basis for and continued development of the fort and fortification tradition" (Bornefalk Back, 2023:4).

Conflict Research in the 21st century and Onwards

Battlefield and Combat Archaeology

Battlefield archaeology, a type of study which emerged in the 2000s can be briefly mentioned here. A team of researchers led by Bo Knarrström searched the landscape for former battlefields. This specialisation is relatively young in Sweden. While aimed at the excavation of located battlefields and field surveys, this research is largely fixed on scrutinizing local maps and historical sources. Archaeological research topics usually span over long periods of time, but with the investigation of battlefields one is dealing with a matter of days or at best months (Knarrström, 2006:13–21). Another important source of new knowledge in this field concerns detailed bone investigations of the fallen victims found at battlefield sites and other scenes of conflict. An example of this among many is a study of the scene of the "Good Friday Battle" in Uppsala (1520), examining the patterns of injuries and how the dead were treated at the scene (Kjellström, 2005).

Combat archaeology has developed as a related subfield that directs attention to the use of weapons and the practice of warfare. Its rise can be seen as a response to the call for greater emphasis on the actions of people in combat within conflict archaeological research in general (Nielsen & Walker, 2009). Studies of this sort were conducted early on within Bronze Age research (e.g., Kristiansen, 1984), seeing increased attention in recent years (e.g., Kristiansen, 2002; Horn, 2013). Now it is also more widely featured in research into the Iron Age and Medieval period (e.g., Pauli Jensen, 2007; Warming, 2018).

Figure 2: One of the many hillforts in Sweden, Skoftesta hillfort in Västmanland. Photo: Gunnar Forsberg, Riksantikvarieämbetet/Kulturmiljöbild.

Such studies need not confine themselves to the actions of individuals but can highlight a broad variety of societal, political, economic and social aspects, especially through a practice approach. Studies of the material remains, historical sources and experimental archaeology can make a strong contribution to this (Warming, 2018). The Society for Combat Archaeology was formed in Denmark in 2014 as an international and interdisciplinary organization to advance such contributions, as well as conflict-related studies of the past in general.

Women and Conflicts

Another area of research that has recently gained momentum is the role of women in conflicts. The relevance of women to conflict-studies has previously been unclear, so much so that it was questioned if women were present at all!

Clearly women have followed alongside warriors and soldiers throughout the ages as the camp followers who provided the combatants with essential supplies (e.g., Jesch, 1991:204). During the

Viking Age, the warrior ideal dominated society. One female researcher who embraced this subject early on is Judith Jesch. Based on mostly written sources, and partly archaeological, from the Northern Isles, she studied how women perceived and were perceived in relation to armed conflicts. Jesch argues that the warrior ideal was also embraced by women and children (Jesch, 1991:176–202). From the Icelandic saga literature, we know that women were important in the maintenance of honour. They guarded it and could, for example, initiate conflicts and seek out revenge in the name of honour, even sometimes taking matters into their own hands by enacting the mortal revenge (Magnúsdóttir, 2014).

In this context, it is impossible to avoid mentioning the discussion concerning the so-called Warrior Woman from Birka on Björkö in Lake Mälaren. Birka grave Bj.581 was carefully excavated by the renowned scholar Hjalmar Stolpe at the end of the nineteenth century. It was subjected to renewed study within the Atlas Project (2014–2020) at Stockholm University – a DNA study of hundreds of people over thousands of years, aimed at tracing how Scandinavia had become populated. The paper attracted worldwide attention and was a hot topic in scientific papers and the press in general. Bj. 581 contained an individual buried with a complete assemblage of weaponry, who in independent studies has been judged to be female. The discussion centred around whether the woman had fought in battle (Hedenstierna-Jonson, 2017). More comprehensive works on women and weapons in the Viking Age have since been published (e.g., Gardeła, 2021).

Where are we going?

In reflecting on past research, it is appropriate to ask what is the future of conflict archaeology. Detailed predictions are futile, but one way forward is to engage more in current debates and research topics. This means dealing with various questions relating modern-day conflicts and society at large, something which has become increasingly relevant due to the war in Ukraine. As asserted by previous writers (e.g., Carman, 1997), conflict archaeology can then say something more relevant instead of anchoring itself to the chronicling of events of the past.

The project *"Crisis, Conflict and Climate"* at the Archaeological Research Laboratory, Stockholm University, reflects this sentiment, and the state of conflict research today. Beginning in 2023, this project concerns the prominent ringforts on Öland (Lidén et al., 2023). The ringforts were previously the subject of individual investigations, but no overall study had been made. This project, however, ties in with previous hillfort research. Its aim is to reconstruct local divergences, and, in an era (mainly Migration Period) of climate change and pandemics, to investigate the local impact of such events on the economy, material culture and religion of the region. Here is a unique opportunity to study conditions that are not significantly different from the situation in many countries today: a time of climate change, pandemics and internal conflicts.

To advance this kind of conflict, archaeological research requires the development of a more mature theoretical foundation and commitment to a form of dialogue that goes beyond individual case studies and chronological boundaries. In many ways, this volume seeks to foment just that by bringing together a variety of archaeological and historical papers.

Overall, the anthology makes an important contribution to the field of conflict research, which has been overshadowed by other, more prominent areas of study within archaeology. However, this publication indicates that this is beginning to change. The subject has great untapped potential and can both deepen and broaden in scope, as many of the articles demonstrate. Several of the articles are specialized and cover limited areas; hopefully, in the future, we will see more comprehensive overviews of how conflicts have played an important role in societal development over time and space. These overviews should also highlight the extensive impact of conflicts on society from multiple perspectives. Questions such as why wars and conflicts arise are central, but so are questions about how and why societies can coexist peacefully for extended periods. The situation of women and children is important to integrate into the discussion. In the future, we will likely see more of this integration as well as a broader variety of both subjects and researchers.

Conclusion

These few selected examples of studies on armed conflict in prehistory show that conflict research follows trends in archaeology as well as prevailing values in society and current events. It does not serve research to deny the existence of armed conflicts or the major role they have played in the development of human society. To gain a correctly nuanced and in-depth picture of armed conflict throughout prehistory, it is important to work on a broad front across disciplines, to combine a multitude of methods and techniques, make use of all available source material and finally, but not least, to create new pertinent analytical tools. The present publication should be seen as a contribution this endeavour. It is also very important today when large-scale wars and armed conflicts are continuing all over the world.

References

Androshchuk, F. (2014). *Viking swords. Swords and social aspects of weaponry in Viking Age Societies.* The Swedish History Museum, Studies 23. Stockholm.

Armit, I. Knüsel, C. Robb, J. & Schulting, R. (2007). Warfare and Sacrifice. An Introduction. In T. Pollard & I. Banks (Eds.), *Studies in Archaeology of Conflict. Warfare and Violence in Prehistoric Europé* (pp. 1–11). Leiden/Boston.

Bornefalk Back, A. (2016). Konflikt i den arkeologiska rekonstruktionen: en pacificerad förhistoria? *Fornvännen, 111,* 184–191.

Carlsson, A. 2001. *Tolkande arkeologi och svensk forntidshistoria (med senneolitikum och förromerska järnåldern).* Stockholm Studies in Archaeology 22. Stockholm University.

Carlsson, A. (2015). *Tolkande arkeologi och svensk forntidshistoria: från stenåldern till vikingatid.* Stockholm Studies in Archaeology 64. Stockholm University.

Carman, J. (1997). Giving Archaeology a Moral Voice. In J. Carman (Ed.), *Material Harm: Archaeological Studies of War and Violence* (pp. 220–239). Glasgow: Cruithne Press.

Carman, J. (2013). *Archaeologies of Conflict.* London/New York: Bloomsbury.

Cassel, K. (1998). *Från grav till gård. Romersk järnålder på Gotland.* Stockholm Studies in Archaeology 16. Stockholm University.

Gardeła, L. (2021). *Women and Weapons in the Viking World: Amazons of the North*. Oxford & Philadelphia: Oxbow Books.

Gery, C. (2009). *Knossos and the Prophets of Modernism*. Chicago.

Goodall, J. (1990). *Through a Window: My Thirty Years with the Chimpanzees of Gombe*. Boston/New York: Houghton Mifflin Company.

Hedenstierna-Jonson, C. Kjellström, A. Zachrisson, T.& Krezewinska, M. (2017). A female Viking Warrior confirmed by genomics. *American Journal of Physical Antrophology. 164*(4), 853–860.

Holmquist, L. (2016). Birka's Defence work and Harbour – linking one recently ended and one newly begun Research project. In L. Holmquist S. Kalmring & C. Hedenstierna-Jonson (Eds.), *New Aspects on Viking-age Urbanism c. AD 750–1100* (pp. 35–46). Theses and Papers in Archaeology B:12.

Holmquist Olausson, L. & Olausson, M. (Eds.) (2009). *The Martial society. Aspects of warriors, fortifications and social change in Scandinavia*. Theses and Papers in Archaeology B:11. Stockholm.

Horn, C. (2013). Harm's Way: An Approach to Change and Continuity in Prehistoric Combat. *Current Swedish Archaeology, 21*(1), 93–116.

Ilkjær, J. (2000). *Illerup Ådal: et arkæologiskt tryllespejl*. Moesgård.

Jansson, I. 1997. The rural Viking in Russia and Sweden. In P. Hansson (Ed.), *Conference 19–20 October 1996 in the manor of Karlslund, Örebro. Lectures* (pp. 9–64). Örebro.

Jesch, J. (1991). *Women in the Viking Age*. Woodbridge.

Johansen, B. (1997). *Ormalur. Aspekter av tillvaro och landskap*. Stockholm Studies in Archaeology 14. Stockholm University.

Keely, L. H. (1996). *War before civilization*. Oxford.

Kjellström, A. A Sixteenth-Century Warrior Grave from Uppsala – the Battle of Good Friday. *International Journal of Osteoarchaeology, 15*, 23–50.

Knarrström, B. (2006). Slagfältsarkeologi. *Borgbrevet*. Sällskapet för borgstudier. 2006:1.

Kristiansen, K. (1984). Krieger und Häuptlinge in der Bronzezeit Dänemarks. Ein Beitrag zur Geschichte des bronzezeitlichen Schwertes. *Jahrbuch des Römisch-Germanischen Zentralmuseums Mainz, 31*, 187–208.

Kristiansen, K. (2002). The tale of the sword: Swords and swordfighters in Bronze Age Europe. *Oxford Journal of Archaeology, 21*(4), 319–332. DOI: 10.1111/1468-0092.00166.

Løvschal, M. Iversen, R. B. & Holst, M. K. (Eds.) (2019). *De dræbte krigere i Alken Enge: Efterkrigsritualer i ældre jernalder*. Højbjerg: Jysk Arkæologisk Selskab.

Magnúsdottir, A. (2014). Kvinnorna i sagorna. In N. Coleman & N. Løkka (Eds.), *Kvinner i vikingatid/Vikingatidens kvinnor*. Oslo.

Molloy, B. P. C. (2012). Martial Minoans? War as social process, practice and event in Bronze Age Crete. *The Annual of the British School at Athens, 107*, 87–142.

Nielsen, A. & Walker, W. (Eds.) (2009). *Warfare in Cultural Context: Practice, Agency and the Archaeology of Violence.* Arizona: University of Arizona Press.

Lidén, K. Eriksson, G. Isaksson, S. Kalmring, S. Papmehl-Dufay, L.& Victor, H. (2023). New Research Programme: Crisis, Conflict and Climate. Societal Change in Scandinavia 300–700 CE. *Current Swedish Archaeology, 31*, 213–218.

Løvschal, M. Birch Iversen, R. Kähler Holst, M. (2020). *De dræbte krigere i Alken Enge: Efterkrigsritualer i ældre jernalder.* Jysk Arkæologisk Selskabs Skrifter 108. Aarhus: Aarhus Universitetsforlag.

Olausson, M. (1995). *Det inneslutna rummet – om kultiska hägnader, fornborgar och befästa gårdar i Uppland från 1300 till Kristi födelse.* Studier från UV Stockholm. Arkeologiska undersökningar. Skrifter nr 9. Stockholm.

Pauli Jensen, X. (2007). The Use of Archers in the North Germanic Armies: Evidence from the Danish war booty sacrifices. In T. Grane (Ed.), *Beyond the Roman Frontier: Roman Influences on the Northern Barbaricum* (pp. 143–152). L'Erma di Bretschneider.

Randsborg, K. (1995). *Hjortspring: warfare and sacrifice in early Europe.* Aarhus.

Rönnby, J. (Ed.) (2019). *On War on Board: Archaeological and historical perspectives on early modern maritime violence and warfare.* Södertörn University.

Vandkilde, H. (2006). *Warfare and Society from the perspectives from Archaeology and European Communities.* Aarhus.

Wall, Å. (2003). *De hägnade bergens landskap. Om den äldre järnåldern på Södertörn.* Stockholm Studies in Archaeology 27. Stockholm University.

Warming, R. F. 2018. The Practice Approach og vikingetidens krigeriske praksisser. *Arkælogisk Forum, 38*, 15–23.

The Archaeological Contribution
to the Study of War and Its Future Directions

Rolf Warming

> …weapons have a life of their own, emerging from terrains of war that extend deep into the fabric of our societies while also exerting their own generative powers within the worlds of violence they beget. The geological strata of humanity's passage on this planet will most certainly be shot through with countless fossils of our implements for war and killing. Should we thereupon leave it to a future species of archaeologists to ponder the role these artefacts played in the constitution of our own being and the unfolding of its brief history? (Bousquet et al.; 2017:7)

To an archaeologist, the question posed above is anything but rhetorical. While the answer may surprise the authors, whose work is primarily intended for an International Relations (IR) audience, they commendably (and interestingly) acknowledge a shared disciplinary interest with archaeology, particularly in exploring socio-technical relations between human societies and artefacts – in this case, weapons. However, contrary to what the authors suggest, it should be noted that although archaeology is often perceived as focusing solely on (pre)historical investigations, it is also about addressing contemporary issues and contributing to the modern world (Sabloff, 2008; Dawdy, 2009; Rockman & Flatman, 2012). Therefore, to offer an archaeological response to the above question, the study of the role of artefacts, including weapons, is not a matter to be left to future archaeologists alone; it firmly falls into the purview of Conflict Archaeology and material culture studies.

Given the social questions raised in this volume and the current geopolitical climate, this anthology invites readers to consider how archaeological perspectives can enrich our understanding of both historical and contemporary forms of violence and warfare. As mentioned in the introduction, many of the themes covered in this volume and the broader social implications of the chapters are relevant to research of both (pre)historic and contemporary conflicts: the social role of violence (Armit), the ontology of war (Solfeldt), civil-martial relations (Lundström), war as a productive and destructive force (Horn & Molloy), the conceptualization of fighting (Ijäs), human–thing relationships in conflicts (Rönnby), economy and war (Moesgaard), the influence of research paradigms (Holmquist) etc. As highlighted by Professor J. J. Widen (Department of War Studies, Swedish Defence University) in the foreword, there is significant potential for cross-pollination between War Studies and Conflict Archaeology. They study the same social phenomena, after all. However, while contemporary studies of war, supported by a vast body of preceding literature, evidently can aid archaeological investigations by serving as a form of 'ethnographic' literature (Bleed & Scott, 2011:49), the question arises: Does archaeology have anything to offer in return?

While archaeology has yet to make a serious contribution to contemporary discourses and the modern study of war, it is evident that its disciplinary locus should not be a hindrance. In fact, related disciplines are habitually incorporated into modern studies of war or commonly inform them. It is generally acknowledged, for instance, that Military History can make valuable contributions – both for academic researchers and military commanders – through the lessons that they can teach us about successes and failures in war. Similarly, sociology and anthropology are frequently featured as part of War Studies literature (Malešević, 2010; Price, 2011; Rubinstein, Fosher & Fujimura, 2013). Conflict Archaeology[1] has hitherto been comparatively mute in these debates, a situation no doubt partly owing to the relative newness of the field and its fragmented state (see the introduction chapter). However, as the contributions from these related fields in the humanities and social science fields suggest, there is ample opportunity for Conflict Archaeology to also engage more robustly in interdisciplinary dialogues that concern the study of war. Undoubt-

---

[1] For a definition and overview, see the introduction chapter.

edly, the rhetorical question posed by Bousquet et al (2017), cited at the beginning of this chapter, is an acknowledgement of the same.

In what way, then, can Conflict Archaeology make an original contribution to contemporary debates in the study of war? This pertinent question has recently been addressed by John and Patricia Carman (2020), who cogently argue for archaeology's relevance to Critical Military and Security Studies in virtue of its inherent capacity to position modern practices in relation to different cultures and different times. Previously, John Carman (2013:68) has also stressed archaeology's capacity to add to a 'wider, long-term understanding of how conflict contributes to the structure and development of society and culture, and how humans respond to situations of threat and danger'. Elsewhere, he highlights the ways in which such studies can add to contemporary moral debates about human behaviour and thought, preeminently through its focus on context, materialism and long-term differences (Carman, 1997b:220). Other archaeologists, such as Rönnby (2019:8ff.), Fernández-Götz and Roymans (2018:5), and Wileman (2009), have also emphasized the comparative value of examining systematic violence across different cultural contexts and the importance of studying the materiality of conflict over long time scales.

To synthesize these arguments, and to develop them further, Conflict Archaeology (and archaeology at large) may be said to embody three key strengths through which it can make an original and valuable contribution to the study of war and contemporary discourses, namely its (1) materialist, (2) anthropological, (3) longterm perspectives. As will be shown below, these perspectives result in deep contextualisation of the complexities of human conflict, making Conflict Archaeology well-suited to provide new dimensions to the contemporary discourses in studies of war, particularly within War Studies, International Relations, and Political Science.

Materialist Perspective

As a subdiscipline of archaeology, a field that is inherently devoted to the study of material, Conflict Archaeology draws upon a vast array of theories and methodologies for the study of material conditions. Fundamentally, as argued by Olsen (2012:22), 'archaeology is the foremost discipline of things', and it is the task of archaeologists to study material (Van Dyke, 2015:5ff.; Young-Wolfe, 2015:151). The empirical data within Conflict Archaeology studies are not only drawn from direct physical traces of combat – such as weaponry and battle-fields – but more subtle empirics that indirectly relate to conflict, in particular its causes and effects, are also considered, such as material commemorations in the form of monuments or changes in settlement patterns and trading networks (Carman, 1997a; Wileman, 2009). These lines of evidence generally fall into five main strands, as sum-marized by Armit et al. (2006:6ff.): (1) Skeletal, (2) iconographic, (3) artefactual (primarily arms and armour), (4) architectural (e.g., forti-fications), (5) written (conventionally the domain of historians but through which material culture also can be studied). The material phenomena, their appertaining practices and general contexts are studied using micro (individual), meso (group) and macro (institu-tional) approaches through both quantitative and qualitative analyses (e.g., Dolfini et al., 2018). The analyses range from classical artefact studies of weaponry and the reconstruction of battlefield tactics through metal detecting surveys to osteological analyses, surveys of violent scenes in iconography and geospatial analyses of settlement patterns. These tools provide archaeology with the rare ability to provide a forensic narrative that is unavailable from other sources, and which can challenge and transform dominating narratives, as for instance demonstrated through excavations of World War I and II battles and mass graves of former-Yugoslavia (e.g., Juhl, 2005; Leonard, 2016; Saunders, 2012). As can be gained from the above, and as noted by Carman (2013:12ff.)

> …the field goes beyond a direct concern with the directly violent aspects of conflict not only to its more insidious but also positive impacts on society at large, and by taking such studies into the past, the field offers insights into how things came to be as they are that other studies do not provide.

The methodologies and approaches are many and varied in the field, but the shared commonality throughout is the central concern with conflict-related material.

The intrinsic focus on material conditions can conduce to valuable and unique contributions to contemporary discourses in the study of war. Most importantly, they provide a useful vantage point in a discourse otherwise primarily of a non-materialist character in which war is examined through more detached and conceptual approaches, often focused upon leaders and policies. As Carman (1997c:12) observes, war 'is *par excellence* the province of the student of politics and international relations, the strategic theorist and the military historian.' For international-relations expert Hedley Bull (1977:184), for example:

> War is organized violence carried on by political units against each other. Violence is not war unless it is carried out in the name of a political unit; what distinguishes killing in war from murder is its vicarious and official character, the symbolic responsibility of the unit whose agent the killer is.

Nonetheless, Bull also acknowledges a need to distinguish 'between war in the material sense, that is actual hostilities, and war in the legal or normative sense, a notional state of affairs brought into being by the satisfaction of certain legal or normative criteria.' (Bull, 1977:85). While the latter sense of war has been subject to great scholarly interest, the former remains significantly less explored. The importance of such material studies in discourses of war are nonetheless highlighted by influential works within both military history and anthropology that have brought stimulus to more emic (or experience-near) approaches within war studies (e.g., Hanson 2009; Keegan 1987; Linger 2001; Nordstrom & Martin 1992; discussed in Carman 1997c). Complementing this line of research, archaeology could make significant contributions towards human-centred perspectives on war that do not lose sight of material conditions (for perspectives, see Hulterström & Widen, 2019). In so doing, and as this volume demonstrates, it provides a more bottom-up way of studying past conflicts than is conventional among many other scholars (Carman, 2013:177).

A valuable theoretical direction of the study of material conditions is that of the 'material-cultural turn', as dubbed by Hicks (2010), which has brought added vitality to archaeology in manners that should also be of interest in relation to the study of war. While various understandings of the concept of material culture and related terms – most notably 'materiality' – have been widely debated within both anthropology and archaeology (Fahlander & Oestigaard, 2004; Ingold, 2007; Hicks, 2010; Knappett 2012, 2014), it may generally be conceived as referring to the culturally dependent socio-material relations in the interactions between humans and physical things. Material culture studies thus offer a socio-cultural perspective on the material aspects of warfare and is featured in several works dealing with conflict archaeological material (e.g., Rönnby, this volume; Horn, 2013; Adams & Rönnby, 2019). Some authors from the emerging branch of 'Modern Conflict Archaeology', which focuses on 20th and 21st century conflicts, also highlight the importance of material culture for understanding modern wars (Saunders, 2004, 2005, 2012). As Nicholas J. Saunders (2005:1ff.) notes, 'The fact that modern conflicts are defined by their technologies as wars of material is an unequivocal invitation for such an approach…'. The material culture studies of anthropology and archaeology thus provide an alternative view to the widespread perspective of technological determinism by recognizing the social and cultural dimensions of technologies.

Relatedly, the embrace of new materialism as a theoretical direction within archaeology has increased recognition of the agentic powers of material within human–thing relationships. As such, it effectively acts as a corrective to the dominance of anthropocentric studies in which material components in social interactions are trivialized or regarded as epiphenomenal (Olsen, 2010; Van Dyke, 2015). This 'materialist turn' in archaeology, while intellectually indebted to philosophy and anthropology, has also led to the development of distinctive archaeological methodologies that operationalize these theories. In many ways, the 'materialist turn' has had a collaborative effect on the discipline, bringing together many methodological and theoretical efforts (Jones, 2002, 2004; Knappett, 2012). A particular strength of this strand of materialism is the development and application of methodologies that are not confined to lofty theorization and can zoom in and out between material and social theory. Worthy of special mention are studies relating to the analysis of the various technical and social components or steps that unfold in technological sequences, such as behavioural chains, *chaîne opératoire* and fragmentation (Knappett, 2012:196ff.). Their application to research outside prehistorical contexts could, with the necessary adjustments, prove useful and analytical tools for conflict scholarship in general. While material culture studies adopting a new materialist perspective offer an important approach to understanding war through sociomaterial relationships, they have not been explicitly connected to relevant discourses within War Studies to any significant extent.

The lack of interdisciplinary interaction is surprising considering that issues directly relating to materiality and new materialism have emerged in literature within International Relations (IR) and Critical War Studies, finding common ground in an attempt to establish a concept of materiality beyond the 'boundaries of positivist social science' (Lundborg & Vaughan-Williams, 2014:3; e.g., Bousquet, 2017; Bousquet et al., 2017; van Liere & Meinema, 2022; Pretorius, 2008). As outlined by Meiches (2017), these include critical analyses of specific weapon assemblages (Larrinaga, 2016; Vucetic, 2016; Shapiro, 2015; Beier, 2011; Stavrianakis, 2011), the role of weapons in complex social systems (Bousquet, 2008; DeLanda, 1997; De Landa, 1991; McNeill, 1984) as well as deconstructions of conventional understandings of weapons whereby gender, race, coloniality and power are examined (Rappert, 2013; Santana, 2009; Booth, 2008; Verwimp, 2006; Diken & Laustsen, 2005). Notwithstanding the materialistic nature of such studies, only relatively few authors extend their analyses to examine the agentic powers of objects. Instead, such issues are explored more fully in literature that critically consider the ontologies of war and the technical and social aspects of targeting as directed by weaponry use (Dill, 2015; Nordin & Öberg, 2015; Holmqvist, 2013; Grayson 2012; Meiches 2017; Weber 2005) as well as in materialist analyses of weapons in nuclear politics, militarization and warfare (Bourne, 2016, 2012; Cooper & Mutimer, 2011). This strand of studies stimulates critical thinking about how mutually essential object–human relationships influence our ontologies of war and our actions in conflict, both in terms of the discursive social history of objects as well as their intrinsic physical properties. In so doing, they tackle materialistic dimensions in ways that are otherwise largely unaccounted for in traditional security studies and Clausewitzian readings of war. The above listed examples are by no means exhaustive but will suffice as an illustration of the range of contemporary discourses that also qualify for archaeological inquiry.

As can be gathered from the above, the theoretical lens of materialism and material focus of Conflict Archaeology provides ample opportunity to contribute to contemporary discourses pertaining to materiality with the added benefit of analysing and testing hypotheses against historical cases and the archaeological record. However, as cited in the beginning of this paper, that connection has yet to be made.

Anthropological Perspective

The anthropological perspective on material culture is another key strength of Conflict Archaeology, defining a standpoint that provides a wide comparative lens for the study of war. Rooted in close disciplinary ties between anthropology and archaeology, this standpoint emphasizes cross-cultural comparisons and the contextual understanding of violence in its specific settings. With the beginnings of processual archaeology in the 1950s it became something of a maxim that 'archaeology was anthropology – or it was nothing', emphasizing that the archaeological endeavour should be geared towards understanding cultures and societies instead of just artefacts. Consequently, an anthropological reading of violence and warfare entails an examination of the phenomena in their social and cultural variations, a perspective also embraced in contemporary studies of war, for instance within War Studies (e.g., Price, 2011; Rubinstein et al., 2013). The overarching aim of this common enterprise between archaeology and anthropology has been to identify differences and similarities in violent and conflict-related practices across territorial, cultural and chronological boundaries. Moreover, given the relatively early beginnings of an anthropology of war (as early as c. 1850–1920), archaeologists often draw upon this specialized core of anthropological theory and methods to inform their interpretations about past conflicts (for a brief overview, see Vandkilde, 2014; Scott & McFeaters, 2011). This has entailed, among other things, the adoption of interpretive strategies such as 'thick description', examining the social life of things, mapping interactions between human and material actants within complex networks, etc. (Geertz, 1973; Appadurai, 1986; Latour, 2005). Several examples of such use of anthropology are also evident in this volume (see, for example, chapters by Armit, Solfeldt, Horn & Molloy and Rönnby).

The relationship between anthropology and archaeology is complex, however. In this context, it is significant that some archaeologists have critiqued the influence of anthropology on the study of war as becoming too narrowly focused on the institutional nature of war to the detriment of its more material manifestations and too detached or experience-distant (etic) rather than experience-near (emic) (Nordstrom & Martin, 1992:4; Carman, 1997c). Relatedly, as discussed by Helle Vandkilde (2014), the anthropology of war contains relatively little reference to the agents of war, notably warriors, who remain under-theorized. In their archaeological and material culture manifestations, however, such studies can be said to inherently circumvent this dilemma owing to the emphasis on material conditions, as outlined above. By examining material cultures through an anthropological perspective in this manner, Conflict Archaeology provides a useful basis from which we can critically approach the manifold sociocultural relationships of warfare and violence without losing sight of the participants or the material conditions.

An anthropologically oriented Conflict Archaeology aligns particularly well with interpretivist efforts within War Studies that aim at understanding war as cultural phenomena (e.g., Biddle, 2006; Adamsky, 2010). With close ties to Military History, cultural approaches towards understanding war and its transformations especially came into the purview of War Studies in connection with the 'cultural turn' in the 1990s as part of the broader 'new military history' (Hoffenaar, 2021:3ff.; see also, Shy, 1993; Black, 2011). A central tenet in this understanding is that the nature of warfare is largely determined by culture, for which reason it should be studied to understand its role in military effectiveness (Hoffenaar, 2021: 3ff.; Keegan, 1993:12; Lee, 2011; Lynn, 2003:xvi; Rosen, 1995; see also, Gabriel, 1990; Hanson, 2007; Van Creveld, 2008). More generally, however, these cultural approaches inevitably provide an improved recognition of how violence and conflict are expressed within different social structures as well as the different conditions acting upon such practices and their transformations, not least the existing discourses within research.

One particularly significant benefit in this regard is the critical reassessment of different ontologies of war and the underlying ethnocentric assumptions, such as the overarching governance of pragmatism and rationality in conflict. As highlighted by Carman and Carman (2020:6f, 231), the investigations into the phenomena of war, violence and conflict in past cultures contribute to a process of defamiliarization in which present-day assumptions are unsettled through comparisons (Tarlow & West, 1999; Harrison & Schofield, 2010). By making these underlying assumptions explicit, such an approach helps to critically interrogate and problematize the underlying foundation of military practices, revealing them as neither universal or inevitable but as historically contingent constructs open to change and potentially dangerous. For instance, Nordin and Öberg (2015) observe that adhering to a certain ontology of war – such as war as 'fighting' – may lead to a reiterative process and seriously blind us to other things that can make 'war'. Anthropological approaches, broadly conceived, can therefore bring valuable perspectives to bear on modern discourses on violence and conflicts by exploring alternative ontologies and practices of other cultures.

The exceptionally diverse range of cultures and societies accessible through archaeological study offers lucrative opportunities for investigating the complexities of conflict and warfare. As observed by Carman and Harding (1999:6ff.), the evolving threats of the post-Cold War era and the changing concept of war require scholars to reconsider the nature of modern conflicts:

> …traditional theories of strategy and war are of little help when faced with the complexities and apparent irrationality of ethnic or religious conflict, which would seem (at least on the surface) to share some of the attributes of war prior to the emergence of the nation-state, and certainly the modern super power.

This argument is echoed by 'new war' theorists, who emphasize how the modern concept of war has lost its analytical value in a world in which sovereign states are no longer the main belligerents and the distinction between international and domestic conflicts have become increasingly blurred (Barkawi, 2016; Bartelson, 2016; Stoker & Whiteside, 2020). In the search for analytical tools to better understand modern low-intensity warfare and conflicts beyond the narrow conception of 'battles', the rich body of archaeological research on various manifestations of conflict constitute a relevant yet underutilized resource.

Given the compatibility discussed above, Conflict Archaeology should be viewed as a complementary approach to existing anthropological and cultural discourses within War Studies, especially those associated with the 'new military history.' On a fundamental level, as Armit et al. (2006) note, 'cultural analyses reveal social environments where violent responses are enculturated into people – in other words, socialisation for aggression.' Insights from Conflict Archaeology, especially those gleaned from studies in non-Western areas (e.g., Solfeldt, this volume), prehistoric societies (e.g., Armit, this volume), and early states at the time of their formation (e.g., Rönnby, this volume), offer a broader understanding of the diverse ways in which warfare and societies have influenced and shaped each other (Allen & Arkush, 2008:1). This approach enriches the analysis of how cultural and social factors contribute to the development of conflict and warfare, providing a more nuanced perspective on the global and historical variations in these phenomena.

Long-term Perspective

A third strength of Conflict Archaeology that can conduce to unique contributions for the study of war and conflict is its long-term perspective and its capacity for diachronic analyses. In dealing with both the deep human past and modern-day issues, archaeology has developed into a discipline operating with widely different temporal scales in its enquiries, each of which require different forms of analyses. However, in line with *longue durée* in historical parlance (Braudel, 1980), archaeology, owing to its typical great time depth, frequently emphasizes social processes and practices in long-term temporal scales. By examining conflict-related material culture across extended periods – such as centuries or millennia – archaeologists can identify the emergence as well as changes and consistencies in violent practices.

A major advantage of this approach is its capacity to reveal the physicality of long-standing causes and consequences of war as well as the complex ways in which inherited value frameworks, beliefs and dispositions are recursively reflected or transformed through warfare or conflict resolution on a multi-generational level (e.g., Nielsen & Walker, 2009). This temporal depth allows for the exploration of how both technological advancements – such as weaponry and fortifications, both on land and at sea (Rönnby, this volume) – as well as social factors – such as warriorhood (Vandkilde, 2006), paradigms of war (Sipilä & Lahelma, 2006), etc. – influence conflict and warfare dynamics as well as society at large. Even long-lasting consistencies or conservatism – for instance in military technology, where certain weapons or fortifications remain in use for centuries or millennia – offer insights into the deeper reasons behind violent practices (Finkel, 2019). These studies may focus on either direct or indirect traces of warfare and conflicts. An interesting application of diachronic analyses on indirect traces of violent practices is Esther López-Montalvo's (2018) investigation into depictions of violence in Levantine rock art, arguing that the diachronic changes in the design and frequency of acts of interpersonal and group violence can help discern isolated tensions and deeply rooted conflictive dynamics between communities. These may in turn allow the identification of hotspots of conflict and political instability. From this long-term perspective, the actual incidents of violence and battles are seen as complex sequences of events and processes, rather than single micro-events. As Wileman (2009) makes clear, warfare can be identified from a series of antecedents and consequences which can be found in the archaeological record on different temporal scales (short-, medium- and long-term). In the absence of historical sources, the long-term symptomatic traces of war-related violence are crucial for identifying the social dynamics and development of societies (Horn & Molloy, this volume).

Beyond tracing the broader patterns of warfare, Conflict Archaeology has also incorporated temporal scales to the study of specific battles and other violent acts and their aftermath. For instance, Roymans and Fernández-Götz (2018:5) propose a four-phase interpretative framework for analysing combat events: (1) pre-battle activities, (2) activities related to actual combat, (3) post-battle looting and cleaning of the battlefield and (4) post-battle ritual deposition and the erection of commemorative structures. While the final phase may seem like a mere epilogue, the significance of commemoration of war and conflict has been highlighted in recent years. Twentieth century conflict studies have stressed how the aftermath, and the associated material culture as well as the bibliography of the landscape, continue to play an important role for society and management of future conflicts (Saunders, 2012; Saunders & Cornish, 2021). Prehistoric studies have also remarked that the symbolic dimensions of ancient battlefields as 'memoryscapes', or *lieux de mémoire*, may even have entailed that they were culturally designated as battle sites and boundary markers, thus constituting sites for recurring military action but not necessarily holding strategic significance (Carman, 1999; Pérez Rubio, 2018). The archaeology of commemoration reveals how societies continue to engage with their violent pasts, whether through monuments, battlefields preservation, or the reinterpretation of historical narratives (Carman & Carman, 2020). In tandem, these temporal scales in Conflict Archaeology contextualize specific instances of conflict within larger frameworks, providing insights into the long-term causes and consequences of warfare as well as its dynamics that might be overlooked in more short-term studies.

These temporal perspectives, particularly the long-term, are crucial for modern discourses and the study of war as they reveal enduring patterns and transformations in warfare and society and enable critical reassessments of prevailing narratives and the clarification of key concepts. *The Western Way of War: Infantry Battle in Classical Greece* (2009) by military historian Victor Davis Hanson, is an oft cited and debated study that posits that the classical Greeks established the parameters for war and a distinctive style of warfare, characterized by decisive battles and a heavy reliance on infantry, which have lasted into modern times. John A. Lynn (2003) argues against the existence of such a long-lasting tradition but acknowledges that Greek and Roman cultures have profoundly influenced modern ideas, myths and vocabulary related to war. The issue here is the 'culture of war' and to what extent certain cultural assumptions that guide war-making are inherited across generations (see also Keegan, 1993; for an archaeological perspective, see Carman, 1999). Importantly, this includes combat but also the rules of surrendering, which, although often overlooked, may be said to be the biggest contributor to the containment of violence in warfare (Afflerbach & Strachan, 2012). Moreover, the diachronic approach can also challenge and refine enduring conceptualizations and narratives – such as war itself (Nordin & Öberg, 2015; Bartelson, 2016) or the notion of warriorhood (Vandkilde, 2014, 2018) – which often go unexamined and appear to be unchanging when, in fact, they are not.

Accordingly, by examining violence and warfare – including technologies, narratives, and concepts – across different temporal scales, Conflict Archaeology provides critical insights into how societies construct, sustain, and transform conflict-related practices. Its long-term perspective allows for the identification of enduring patterns, historical precedents, and long-range consequences that might be overlooked in short-term analyses. As a methodological framework, it offers tools for analysing how past conflicts shape present security dynamics, how military innovations emerge and propagate over time, and how cultural perceptions of war evolve across generations.

Conclusion

As demonstrated, Conflict Archaeology holds significant yet untapped potential for contributing to contemporary discourses on war. This field intersects with key themes in modern War Studies, such as the culture of war, norms in warfare, warrior identities, the ontology of war, the agency of weaponry technologies and much else. Although Military History and anthropology have regularly provided insights into these areas, Conflict Archaeology has yet to fully establish itself as a serious interdisciplinary partner.

At the same time, interdisciplinary collaboration between Conflict Archaeology and modern studies of war may present significant challenges and limitations. Archaeologists may struggle to engage with contemporary military discourses, as their expertise is often (but not always) grounded in historical and material analyses rather than modern concerns. Moreover, archaeology's reliance on physical evidence inherently limits its ability to address non-material aspects of modern warfare, such as cyberwarfare, psychological operations, and economic coercion – elements that are increasingly central to contemporary conflicts but largely fall outside the scope of traditional archaeological inquiry. However, as this afterword demonstrates, archaeology's theoretical and methodological tools still provide valuable insights into the material dimensions of war. By embracing interdisciplinary dialogue and adapting their approaches to incorporate more recent material culture studies, archaeologists can make meaningful contributions to broader discussions on warfare, security, and conflict in both historical and modern contexts.

Three key strengths of Conflict Archaeology stand out in this regard: its materialistic, anthropological and long-term perspectives. While these perspectives are not unique in and of themselves, their combination within archaeology offers a distinctive materialistic, bottom-up approach that enriches our understanding of violence and warfare. The materialistic perspective provides concrete data that can challenge and complement the narratives and theoretical frameworks predominant in other disciplines, particularly by shedding light on human-material relationships. The anthropological perspective within Conflict Archaeology deepens our understanding of the cultural and social dimensions of conflict, while the long-term perspective offers insights into change and continuities in practices over time. The three perspectives position archaeology as a valuable but underutilized tool for research into more contemporary forms of war and conflict.

These disciplinary strengths should encourage archaeologists to further explore the possibilities of enhancing our understanding of both historical and contemporary warfare beyond traditional disciplinary boundaries. Given its potential to offer fresh perspectives on modern conflict, is there not also an ethical responsibility for archaeologists to engage more actively in these critical debates?

References

Adams, J. & Rönnby, J. (2019). The consequences of new warships. Medieval to modern and our dialectical relation with things. In J. Rönnby (Ed.), *On War on Board. Archaeological and Historical perspectives on Early Modern Maritime Violence and Warfare*. Huddinge: Södertörn Academic Studies.

Adamsky, D. (2010). *The Culture of Military Innovation: The Impact of Cultural Factors on the Revolution in Military Affairs in Russia, the US, and Israel*. Redwood City, United States: Stanford University Press.

Afflerbach, H. & Strachan, H. (Eds.). (2012). *How Fighting Ends: A History of Surrender*. Oxford: Oxford Academic.

Appadurai, A. (1986). *The Social Life of Things: Commodities in Cultural Perspective*. Cambridge: Cambridge University Press

Arkush, E. N. & Allen, M. W. (2008). *The Archaeology of Warfare: Prehistories of Raiding and Conquest*. Gainesville, Florida: University Press of Florida.

Armit, I. Knüsel, C. Robb, J. & Schulting, R. (2006). Warfare and Violence in Prehistoric Europe: An Introduction. *Journal of Conflict Archaeology, 2*(1), 1–11.

Barkawi, T. (2016). Decolonising War. *European Journal of International Security, 1*(2), 199–214.

Bartelson, J. (2016). Blasts from the Past: War and Fracture in the International System. *International Political Sociology, 10*(4), 352–368.

Beier, J. M. (2011). Dangerous Terrain: Re-Reading the Landmines Ban through the Social Worlds of the RMA. *Contemporary Security Policy, 32*(1), 159–175.

Biddle, S. (2006). *Military Power: Explaining Victory and Defeat in Modern Battle*. Princeton, N.J: Princeton University Press.

Black, J. (2011). *War and the Cultural Turn*. Cambridge, UK: Polity Press.

Bleed, P. & Scott, D. D. (2011). Contexts for Conflict: Conceptual Tools for Interpreting Archaeological Reflections of Warfare. *Journal of Conflict Archaeology, 6*(1), 42–64.

Booth, K. (2008). *Theory of World Security*. Cambridge: Cambridge University Press.

Bourne, M. (2012). Guns Don't Kill People, Cyborgs Do: A Latourian Provocation for Transformatory Arms Control and Disarmament. *Global Change, Peace & Security, 24*(1), 141–163.

Bourne, M. (2016). Invention and Uninvention in Nuclear Weapons Politics. *Critical Studies on Security, 4*(1), 6–23.

Bousquet, A. J. (2008). *The Scientific Way of Warfare: Order and Chaos on the Battlefield of Modernity*. New York: Columbia University Press.

Bousquet, A. (2017). A Revolution in Military Affairs? Changing Technologies and Changing Practices of Warfare'. In *Technology and World Politics: An Introduction*. Routledge.

Bousquet, A. Grove, J. & Shah, N. (2017). Becoming Weapon: An Opening Call to Arms. *Critical Studies on Security*, 5(1), 1–8.

Braudel, F. (1980). *On history*. Chicago (IL): The University of Chicago Press.

Bull, H. (1977). *The Anarchical Society: A Study of Order in World Politics*. London: Macmillan.

Carman, J. (Ed.) (1997a). *Material Harm: Archaeological Studies of War and Violence*. Glasgow: Cruithne Press.

Carman, J. (1997b). Giving Archaeology a Moral Voice. In J. Carman (Ed.), *Material Harm: Archaeological studies of war and violence* (pp. 220–39). Glasgow: Cruithne Press.

Carman, J. (1997c). Introduction: Approaches to Violence. In J. Carman (Ed.), *Material Harm: Archaeological studies of war and violence* (pp. 1–23). Glasgow: Cruithne Press.

Carman, J. (1999). Beyond the western way of war: ancient battlefields in comparative perspective. In J. Carman & A. Harding (Eds.), *Ancient Warfare: Archaeological Perspectives* (pp. 39–55). Stroud: Sutton.

Carman, J. (2013). *Archaeologies of Conflict*. London: Bloomsbury Academic, an imprint of Bloomsbury Publishing Plc.

Carman, J. & Carman, P. (2020). *Battlfields: from Event to Heritage*. Oxford: Oxford University Press.

Carman, J. & Harding, A. (Eds.) (1999). *Ancient Warfare: Archaeological Perspectives*. Stroud: Sutton.

Cooper, N. & Mutimer, D. (2011). Arms Control for the 21st Century: Controlling the Means of Violence. *Contemporary Security Policy*, 32(1), 3–19.

Dawdy, S. L. (2009). Millennial Archaeology: Locating the Discipline in the Age of Insecurity. *Archaeological Dialogues* 16(2): 131–42.

De Landa, M. (1991). War in the Age of Intelligent Machines. New York: Zones Books.

DeLanda, M. (1997). A Thousand Years of Nonlinear History. New York: Zone Books.

Diken, B. & Laustsen, C. B. (2005). Becoming Abject: Rape as a Weapon of War. *Body & Society*, 11(1), 111–128.

Dill, J. (2015). *Legitimate Targets? Social Construction, International Law, and US Bombing*. Cambridge: Cambridge University Press.

Dolfini, A., Crellin, R. J., Horn, C. & Uckelmann, M. (Eds.) (2018). *Prehistoric Warfare and Violence: Quantitative and Qualitative Approaches*. London & New York: Springer.

Fahlander, F. & Oestigaard, T. (Eds.) (2004). *Material Culture and Other Things: Post-disciplinary Studies in the 21ˢᵗ Century*. Vällingby: Elanders Gotab.

Fernández-Götz, M. & Roymans, N. (Eds.) (2018). *Conflict archaeology: materialities of collective violence from prehistory to Late Antiquity*. London: Routledge.

Finkel, M. (2019). Conservatism by Choice (Stability) – a Necessary Complement to Innovation and Adaptation in Force Design. *Defence Studies, 19*(4), 392–409.

Gabriel, R. A. (1990). *The Culture of War: Invention and Early Development*. Westport: Greenwood Publishing Group.

Geertz, C. (1973). *The Interpretation of Cultures: Selected Essays*. New York: Basic Books

Grayson, K. (2012). Six Theses on Targeted Killing. *Politics, 32*(2), 120–128.

Hanson, V. D. (2007). *Carnage and Culture: Landmark Battles in the Rise to Western Power*. Westminster, United States: Knopf Doubleday Publishing Group.

Hanson, V. D. (2009). *Western Way of War: Infantry Battle in Classical Greece*. University of California Press.

Harrison, R. & Schofield, J. (2010). *After Modernity: archaeological approaches to the contemporary past*. Oxford: Oxford University Press.

Hicks, D. (2010). The material-cultural turn: event and effect. In D. Hicks & M. C. Beaudry (Eds.), *The Oxford Handbook of Material Culture Studies* (pp. 25–98). Oxford: Oxford University Press.

Hoffenaar, J. (2021). 'New' Military History. In A. M. Sookermany (Ed.), *Handbook of Military Sciences* (pp. 1–14). Cham: Springer International Publishing.

Holmqvist, C. (2013). Undoing War: War Ontologies and the Materiality of Drone Warfare. *Millennium: Journal of International Studies, 41*(3), 535–552.

Horn, C. (2013). Harm's Way: An Approach to Change and Continuity in Prehistoric Combat. *Current Swedish Archaeology, 21*, 93–116.

Ingold, T. (2007). Materials against materiality. *Archaeological Dialogues, 14*(1), 1–16.

Jones, A. (2002). *Archaeological theory and scientific practice*. Cambridge: Cambridge University Press.

Jones, A. (2004). Archaeometry and materiality: materials-based analysis in theory and practice. *Archaeometry, 46*(3), 327–338.

Juhl, K. (2005). *The Contribution by (Forensic) Archaeologists to Human Rights Investigations of Mass Graves*. Stavanger: Arkeologisk museum i Stavanger.

Keegan, J. (1993). *A History of Warfare*. New York: Alfred A. Knopf.

Knappett, C. (2012). Materiality. In I. Hodder (Ed.), *Archaeological theory today*, (2nd ed., pp. 188–207). Cambridge: Polity.

Knappett, C. (2014). Materiality in Archaeological Theory. In C. Smith (Ed.), *Encyclopedia of Global Archaeology* (pp. 4700–4708). New York, NY: Springer.

Leonard, M. (2016). *Beneath the Killing Fields: Exploring the Subterranean Landscapes of the Western Front.* Pen and Sword Archaeology. Barnsley: England.

Lévi-Strauss, Claude. 1963. *Structural Anthropology.* New York: Basic Books.

van Liere, L. & Meinema, E. (Eds.) (2022). *Material Perspectives on Religion, Conflict, and Violence: Things of Conflict.* Leiden: BRILL.

Larrinaga, M. D. (2016). Tear Gas. In M.B. Salter (Ed.), *Making Things International 2: Catalysts and Reactions* (pp. 313–326). Minneapolis: University of Minnesota Press.

Latour, B. (2005). *Reassembling the Social: An Introduction to Actor-Network-Theory.* New York: Oxford University Press.

Lee, W. E. (Ed.) (2011). *Warfare and Culture in World History.* New York: New York University Press.

Linger, D. T. (2001). *Dangerous Encounters: Meanings of Violence in a Brazilian City.* Nachdr. Stanford, California: Stanford University Press.

López-Montalvo, E. (2018). War and Peace in Iberian Prehistory: The Chronology and Interpretation of the Depictions of Violence in Levantine Rock Art. In A. Dolfini, R. Crellin, C. Horn, & M. Uckelmann, (Eds.), *Prehistoric Warfare and Violence. Quantitative Methods in the Humanities and Social Sciences* (pp. 87–107). Springer, Cham.

Lundborg, T. & Vaughan-Williams, N. (2015). New materialisms, Discourse Analysis, and International Relations: A Radical Intertextual Approach. *Review of International Studies, 41*(1), 3–25.

Lynn, J. (2003). *Battle: A Cultural History of Combat and Culture.* Colorado: Westview.

Malešević, S. (2010). *The Sociology of War and Violence.* Cambridge University Press.

McNeill, W. H. (1984). *The Pursuit of Power: Technology, Armed Force, and Society since A.D. 1000.* Chicago: University of Chicago Press.

Meiches, B. (2017). Weapons, Desire, and the Making of War. *Critical Studies on Security, 5*(1), 9–27.

Nielsen, A. E. & Walker, W. H. (2009). *Warfare in Cultural Context: Practice, Agency, and the Archaeology of Violence.* Tucson: The University of Arizona Press.

Nordin, A. H. M. & Öberg, D. (2015). Targeting the Ontology of War: From Clausewitz to Baudrillard. *Millennium: Journal of International Studies, 43*(2), 392–410.

Nordstrom, C. & Martin, J. (Eds.) (1992). *The Paths to Domination, Resistance, and Terror.* Berkeley: University of California Press.

Olsen, B. (2013). *In Defense of Things: Archaeology and the Ontology of Objects.* Lanham New York Toronto Plymouth, UK: AltaMira Press.

Pérez Rubio, A. (2018). Singing the deeds of the ancestors: the memory of battle in Late Iron Age Gaul and Iberia. In M. Fernández-Götz & N. Roymans (Eds.), *Conflict archaeology: materialities of collective violence from prehistory to Late Antiquity* (pp. 89–102). London: Routledge.

Pretorius, J. (2008). The Security Imaginary: Explaining Military Isomorphism. *Security Dialogue, 39*(1), 99–120.

Price, D. H. (2011). *Weaponizing Anthropology: Social Science in Service of the Militarized State.* Petrolia and Oakland, California: CounterPunch and AK Press.

Rappert, B. (2013). *Controlling the Weapons of War: Politics, Persuasion, and the Prohibition of Inhumanity.* New York: Routledge.

Rockman, J. & Flatman, J. (Eds.) (2012). *Archaeology in Society: Its Relevance in the Modern World.* Springer.

Rosen, S. P. (1995). Military Effectiveness: Why Society Matters. *International Security, 19*(4), 5–31.

Rubinstein, R. A. Fosher, K. B. & Fujimura, C. K. (2013). *Practicing Military Anthropology: Beyond Expectations and Traditional Boundaries.* West Hartford, CT: Kumarian Press.

Rönnby, J. (Ed.) (2019). *On War on Board. Archaeological and Historical perspectives on Early Modern Maritime Violence and Warfare.* Södertörn Academic Studies 78 & Södertörn Archaeological Studies 15. Huddinge: Södertörn University.

Sabloff, J. A. (2008) *Archaeology Matters: Action Archaeology in the Modern World.* Walnut Creek: Left Coast Press.

Santana, A. H. D. (2009). Nuclear Weapons as the Currency of Power. *The Nonproliferation Review, 16*(3), 325–345.

Saunders, N. J. (2004). *Matters of Conflict: Material Culture, Memory and the First World War.* London: Taylor & Francis Group.

Saunders, N. J. (2005). Culture, Conflict and Materiality: The Social Lives of Great War Objects. In B. Finn & B. C. Hacker (Eds.), *Materializing the Military* (pp. 77–94). London: Science Museum.

Saunders, N. J. (Ed.) (2012). *Beyond the Dead Horizon: Studies in Modern Conflict Archaeology.* Oxbow Books.

Saunders, N. J. & Cornish, P. (Eds.) (2021). *Conflict Landscapes: Materiality and Meaning in Contested Places.* Abingdon: Routledge.

Scott, D. D. & McFeaters, A. P. (2011). The Archaeology of Historic Battlefields: A History and Theoretical Development in Conflict Archaeology. *Journal of Archaeological Research, 19*(1), 103–132.

Shy, J. (1993). The Cultural Approach to the History of War. *Journal of Military History, 57,* 13–26.

Stavrianakis, A. (2011). Small Arms Control and the Reproduction of Imperial Relations. *Contemporary Security Policy, 32*(1), 193–214.

Stoker, D. & Whiteside, C. (2020). Blurred Lines: Gray-Zone Conflict and Hybrid War – Two Failures of American Strategic Thinking. *Naval War College Review, 73*(1), 1–37.

Tarlow, S. and West, S. (Eds.) (1999). *The Familiar Past? archaeologies of later historical Britain.* London: Routledge.

Van Creveld, M. (2008). *The Culture of War.* New York: Presidio.

Van Dyke, R. M. (Ed.) (2015). *Practicing Materiality.* Tucson: The University of Arizona Press.

Vandkilde, H. (2006). Warriors and warrior institutions in the European Copper Age. In T. Otto, H. Thrane & H. Vandkilde (Eds.), *Warfare and Society: Archaeological and Social Anthropological Perspectives* (pp. 393–422). Aarhus: Aarhus University Press.

Vandkilde, H. (2014). Archaeology, theory, and war-related violence: theoretical perspectives on the archaeology of warfare and warriorhood. In A. Gardner, M. Lake & U. Sommer (Eds.), *The Oxford handbook of archaeological theory* Oxford University Press.

Verwimp, P. (2006). Machetes and Firearms: The Organization of Massacres in Rwanda. *Journal of Peace Research, 43*(1), 5–22.

Vucetic, S. 2016. The F-35 Joint Strike Fighter. In M. B. Salter (Ed.), *Making Things International 2: Catalysts and Reactions* (pp. 3–19). Minneapolis: University of Minnesota Press (forthcoming).

Weber, S. (2005). *Targets of Opportunity: On the Militarization of Thinking.* New York: Fordham University Press.

Wileman, J. (2009). *War and Rumours of War: The Evidential Base for the Recognition of Warfare in Prehistory.* BAR International Series 1984. Oxford: Archaeopress.

Young-Wolfe, H. (2015). The Work They Do. In R. M. Van Dyke (Ed.), *Practicing Materiality* (pp. 149–75). Tucson: University of Arizona Press.

Professor **Ian Armit** (University of York) is an authority on the European Iron Age and the archaeology of conflict and violence. He studied for both his undergraduate degree and PhD in the Department of Archaeology at the University of Edinburgh and was Senior Lecturer at Queen's University Belfast before moving to the University of Bradford as Professor of Archaeology in 2006. He took up his current post of Chair in Archaeology at the University of York in 2019. His current research centres on the cultural archaeology of the European Later Bronze and Iron Ages, the role of conflict and violence in non-state societies, and the demographic and genetic prehistory of European populations. He has directed fieldwork projects in Scotland, France and Sicily and has worked extensively in south-east Europe. He currently runs the ERC-funded COMMIOS Project.

Lena Holmquist is an Associate Professor at the Archaeological Research Laboratory (Stockholm University) and works with issues relating to the Viking age with focus on Viking Age towns especially Birka. The projects in 1995–2004 were about Birka's fortifications and garrison. They were part of the project *Hill- forts and fortifications in Central Sweden 400–1100*. Since then, she has researched Birka's harbour facilities, which concerned trade contacts in Northern Europe and around the Baltic Sea. She has also led excavations of fortifications in North Macedonia and Germany. Today she is employed in the project *Crisis, Conflicts and Climate* as conservator.

Christian Horn is an Associate Professor specialised in the prehistory of Europe and digital archaeology, with a particular focus on conflict during the fourth to the first millennium BC and 3D documentation methods. Furthermore, he is co-director of the Swedish Rock Art Research Archives (https://shfa.dh.gu.se/). He has published extensively on prehistoric warfare and violence from the Neolithic to the Bronze Age, wear analysis on flint and metal weaponry, Nordic Bronze Age rock art and local societies. He has led rock art documentation campaigns in Sweden and geomagnetic surveys in Sweden, Germany, and Israel and conducted metalwork wear analysis in many European museums.

Antti Ijäs earned his doctorate in Latin Language and Roman Literature at the University of Helsinki. His main fields of interest are Classical and Medieval philology, with a particular focus on Medieval Latin, manuscript studies, and book history. His research revolves around pragmatic and technical literature and language, particularly questions related to the history and semantics of technical terminology and the transmission of knowledge and technique through text and image. He is currently a researcher with the University of Helsinki, working on a new edition, translation, and commentary of Konrad Kyeser's *Bellifortis*.

Fredrik Lundström is a PhD candidate at the Archaeological Research Laboratory, Department of Archaeology and Classical Studies, Stockholm University. He researches hunting techniques in relation to environmental and societal change during the Mesolithic through geometric morphometrics, continuum mechanical simulations, ecological psychology and dynamic systems theory and experimental archaeology.

Professor **Jens Christian Moesgaard**, born in Aarhus, Denmark, in 1963, holds a Cand. phil. in History from the University of Copenhagen (1992). He managed the numismatic collection at the Musée des Antiquités in Rouen, 1992–1995, then served as a research associate at the Fitzwilliam Museum, Cambridge, in 1997. From there, he was a curator and researcher at the National Museum of Denmark, 1997–2019. Since 2020, he has held the Gunnar Ekström Chair as Professor at the Stockholm Numismatic Institute, Stockholm University. Moesgaard's research focuses on coinages and coin use in France, England, and Scandinavia, spanning the Viking Age, Middle Ages, and Renaissance. He explores coins as state expressions, the relationship between coins and the population, and the impact of metal detecting on coin finds. He has published extensively, including two books and numerous articles, and frequently engages with the public through talks and edited works.

Barry Molloy is an Associate Professor specialised in the prehistory of Europe and the Mediterranean, with a particular focus on crises driven social change during the later third to early first millennia BC. He has published widely on conflict and violence in the Bronze Age, the archaeometallurgy of tools and weapons, experimental archaeology and landscapes of defensible sites. He has directed excavations and surveys in Greece and Serbia and conducted museum research on metalwork across Europe.

Professor **Johan Rönnby** earned his PhD from Stockholm University in 1995. He began his career as a senior curator and marine archaeologist at the National Heritage Board UV Stockholm, 1994–1997, before transitioning to Södertörn University, where he has been a dedicated teacher and researcher since 1997. Rönnby was appointed Associate Professor (Docent) in Archaeology at Stockholm University in 2000, and in Maritime Archaeology at Helsinki University in 2008 and Professor in Archaeology at Södertörn University 2009. He also served as the head of Södertörn University's Higher Education Development Unit from 2003 to 2008 and has held visiting professorships at Skidmore College and Middlebury College in the USA. His research has focused on different shipwrecks in the Baltic Sea, but have also concerned lake dwellings, harbours and prehistoric landscapes under water, coastal landscapes and human cultural and social interaction with water.

Erik Solfeldt is a PhD candidate at the Department of Archaeology and Classical Studies at Stockholm University. Combining archaeology and museum ethnography, he specializes in the study of animism and material culture among hunter-gatherers and hunter-herders of northwestern Eurasia. His research explores ethnographic materials (ethnographic artefacts and visual ethnography) from northwestern Siberia, with a particular focus on the Nenets. By employing theoretical perspectives of new animism in combination with critical and deconstructive ethnographic analogies his work challenges conventional archaeological theories and interpretations that rely on Western ontological preconceptions. His current PhD project, "Material Spirits of the Past and Present," delves into these themes, following his Master's thesis titled "En arkeologi av det animistiska" (An Archaeology of Animism), which received the "Highly Commended, Master's Thesis Prize" from the International Society of Hunter-Gatherer Research (ISHGR).

Rolf Fabricius Warming is a PhD candidate at the Department of Archaeology and Classical Studies, Stockholm University, and is a part of the Centre for Maritime Studies (CEMAS). His doctoral research project, titled "Soldiers at Sea, c. 1450–1650", explores the topic of close-quarter combat at sea between c. 1450–1650 through a selection of notable shipwrecks like *Griffin/Gribshunden* (1495), *Mary Rose* (1545), *Mars* (1564) and *Vasa* (1628) as case studies. With an academic background that includes an MA (with distinction) in Maritime Archaeology (University of Southampton) and another MA in Prehistoric Archaeology (University of Copenhagen), his amphibious interests stretches both prehistoric and historical periods, with particular focus on conflicts and warfare (both on land and at sea). Currently, he is also a visiting scholar at the Department of War Studies (Maritime Operations Division), Swedish Defence University, and is a founding member of the Society for Combat Archaeology.

J. J. Widen is Professor of War Studies at the Swedish Defence University. He is also Docent/Associate Professor in Nordic History at Åbo Akademy University, a member of the Swedish Society for Maritime History and the Royal Swedish Society of Naval Sciences. His research mainly focuses on military and naval theory. Widen is the author of "Theorist of Maritime Strategy – Sir Julian Corbett and his Contribution to Military and Naval Thought" (Routledge, 2016) and co-author of "Contemporary Military Theory – The Dynamics of War" (Routledge, 2015). He has published in *Journal of Strategic Studies, Defence Studies, Terrorism and Political Violence, Diplomacy & Statecraft, History – The Journal of the Historical Association,* and *Studies in Conflict and Terrorism.* Professor Widen is currently writing a monograph on naval tactical theories, principles and applications.

Stockholm Studies in Archaeology
(ISSN 0349-4128)

Series editor: Andrew M. Jones

1. KYHLBERG, Ola 1980. Vikt och värde. Arkeologiska studier i värdemätning, betalningsmedel och metrologi. I. Helgö. II. Birka.
2. AMBROSIANI, Kristina 1981. Viking Age Combs, Comb Making and Comb Makers, in the Light of the Finds from Birka and Ribe.
3. SÄRLVIK, Ingegärd 1982. Paths Towards a Stratified Society. A Study of Economic, Cultural and Social Formations in South-West Sweden during the Roman Iron Age and the Migration Period.
4. BLIDMO, Roger 1982. Helgö, Husgrupp 3. En lokalkorologisk metodstudie. Helgöstudier 2.
5. CARLSSON, Anders 1983. Djurhuvudformiga spännen och gotländsk vikingatid. Text och katalog.
6. DURING, Ebba 1986. The Fauna of Alvastra. An Osteological Analysis of Animal Bones from a Neolithic Pile Dwelling.
7. BERTILSSON, Ulf 1987. The Rock Carvings of Northern Bohuslän. Spatial Structures and Social Symbols.
8. CARLSSON, Anders 1988. Vikingatida ringspännen från Gotland. Text och katalog.
9. BURSTRÖM, Mats 1991. Arkeologisk samhällsavgränsning. En studie av vikingatida samhällsterritorier i Smålands inland.
10. VARENIUS, Björn 1992. Det nordiska skeppet. Teknologi och samhällsstrategi i vikingatid och medeltid.
11. JAKOBSSON, Mikael 1992. Krigarideologi och vikingatida svärdstypologi.
12. RINGSTEDT, Nils 1992. Household economy and archaeology. Some aspects on theory and applications.
13. Withdrawn.
14. JOHANSEN, Birgitta 1997. Ormalur. Aspekter av tillvaro och landskap.
15. ZACHRISSON, Torun 1998. Gård, gräns, gravfält. Sammanhang kring ädelmetalldepåer och runstenar från vikingatid och tidigmedeltid i Uppland och Gästrikland.
16. CASSEL, Kerstin 1998. Från grav till gård. Romersk järnålder på Gotland.
17. CARLSSON, Anders 1998. Tolkande arkeologi och svensk forntidshistoria. Stenåldern.

18. GÖRANSSON, Eva-Marie 1999. Bilder av kvinnor och kvinnlighet. Genus och kroppsspråk under övergången till kristendomen.

19. BOLIN, Hans 1999. Kulturlandskapets korsvägar. Mellersta Norrland under de två sista årtusendena f. Kr.

20. STRASSBURG, Jimmy. 2000. Shamanic Shadows. One hundred Generations of Undead Subversion in Southern Scandinavia, 7,000–4,000 BC.

21. STORÅ, Jan 2001. Reading Bones. Stone Age Hunters and Seals in the Baltic.

22. CARLSSON, Anders 2001. Tolkande arkeologi och svensk forntidshistoria. Bronsåldern.

23. HAUPTMAN WAHLGREN, Katherine 2002. Bilder av betydelse. Hällristningar och bronsålderslandskap i nordöstra Östergötland.

24. ADAMS, Jonathan 2003. Ships, Innovation and Social Change. Aspects of Carvel Shipbuilding in Northern Europe 1450–1850.

25. HED JAKOBSSON, Anna 2003. Smältdeglars härskare och Jerusalems tillskyndare. Berättelser om vikingatid och tidig medeltid.

26. GILL, Alexander 2003. Stenålder i Mälardalen.

27. WALL, Åsa 2003. De hägnade bergens landskap. Om den äldre järnåldern på Södertörn.

28. STENBÄCK, Niklas 2003. Människorna vid havet. Platser och keramik på ålandsöarna perioden 3500–2000 f. Kr.

29. LINDGREN, Christina 2004. Människor och kvarts. Sociala och teknologiska strategier under mesolitikum i östra Mellansverige.

30. LAGERSTEDT, Anna 2004. Det norrländska rummet. Vardagsliv och socialt samspel i medeltidens bondesamhälle.

31. von HEIJNE, Cecilia 2004. Särpräglat. Vikingatida och tidigmedeltida myntfynd från Danmark, Skåne, Blekinge och Halland (ca 800–1130).

32. FERNSTÅL, Lotta 2004. Delar av en grav och glimtar av en tid. Om yngre romersk järnålder, Tuna i Badelunda i Västmanland och personen i grav X.

33. THEDÉEN, Susanne 2004. Gränser i livet – gränser i landskapet. Generationsrelationer och rituella praktiker i södermanländska bronsålderslandskap.

34. STENSKÖLD, Eva 2004. Att berätta en senneolitisk historia. Sten och metall i södra Sverige 2350–1700 f. Kr.

35. REGNER, Elisabet 2005. Den reformerade världen. Monastisk och materiell kultur i Alvastra kloster från medeltid till modern tid.

36. MONIÉ NORDIN, Jonas 2005. När makten blev synlig. Senmedeltid i södra Dalarna.

37. FELDT, Björn 2005. Synliga och osynliga gränser. Förändringar i gravritualen under yngre bronsålder – förromersk järnålder i Södermanland.

38. RUNER, Johan 2006. Från hav till land eller Kristus och odalen. En studie av Sverige under äldre medeltid med utgångspunkt från de romanska kyrkorna.
39. STENQVIST MILLDE, Ylva 2007. Vägar inom räckhåll. Spåren efter resande i det förindustriella bondesamhället.
40. BACK DANIELSSON, Ing-Marie 2007. Masking Moments. The Transitions of Bodies and Beings in Late Iron Age Scandinavia.
41. SELLING, Susanne 2007. Livets scener och dödens platser. Om bronsålder i södra Bohuslän utifrån en gravläggning i Faxehögen, Kareby socken.
42. ARNBERG, Anna 2007. Där människor, handling och tid möts. En studie av det förromerska landskapet på Gotland.
43. BERGERBRANT, Sophie 2007. Bronze Age Identities: Costume, Conflict and Contact in Northern Europe 1600–1300 BC.
44. FRANSSON, Ulf, SVEDIN, Marie, BERGERBRANT, Sophie & ANDRO-SCHUK, Fedir (Eds.) 2007. Cultural interaction between east and west. Archaeology, artefacts and human contacts in northern Europe.
45. MYRBERG, Nanouschka 2008. Ett eget värde. Gotlands tidigaste myntning, ca 1140–1220.
46. BRATT, Peter 2008. Makt uttryckt i jord och sten. Stora högar och makt-strukturer i Mälardalen under järnåldern.
47. BACK DANIELSSON, Ing-Marie, GUSTIN, Ingrid, LARSSON, Annika, MYRBERG, Nanouschka & THEDÉEN, Susanne (red.) 2009. Döda personers sällskap. Gravmaterialens identiteter och kulturella uttryck. (On the Threshold. Burial Archaeology in the Twenty-first Century).
48. REGNER, Elisabet, von HEIJNE, Cecilia, KITZLER ÅHFELDT, Laila & KJELLSTRÖM, Anna (Eds.) 2009. From Ephesos to Dalecarlia: Reflections on Body, Space and Time in Medieval and Early Modern Europe.
49. LINDEBERG, Marta 2009. Järn i jorden. Spadformiga ämnesjärn i Mellan-norrland.
50. JONSSON, Kristina 2009. Practices for the Living and the Dead. Medieval and Post-Reformation Burials in Scandinavia.
51. von HACKWITZ, Kim 2009. Längs med Hjälmarens stränder och förbi – relationen mellan den gropkeramiska kulturen och båtyxekulturen.
52. MONIKANDER, Anne 2010. Våld och vatten. Våtmarkskult vid Skede-mosse under järnåldern.
53. FAHLANDER, Fredrik & KJELLSTRÖM, Anna (Eds.) 2010. Making Sense of Things. Archaeologies of Sensory Perception.
54. FAHLANDER, Fredrik (red.) 2011. Spåren av de små. Arkeologiska per-spektiv på barn och barndom.
55. SJÖSTRAND, Ylva 2011. Med älgen i huvudrollen. Om fångstgropar, häll-bilder och skärvstensvallar i mellersta Norrland.

56. BURSTRÖM, Nanouschka M. & FAHLANDER, Fredrik (Eds.) 2012. Matters of scale. Processes and courses of events in archaeology and cultural history.

57. BACK DANIELSSON, Ing-Marie, FAHLANDER, Fredrik & SJÖSTRAND, Ylva (Eds.) 2012. Encountering Imagery: Materialities, Perceptions, Relations.

58. BACK DANIELSSON, Ing-Marie & THEDÉEN, Susanne (Eds.) 2012. To Tender Gender. The Pasts and Futures of Gender Research.

59. MC WILLIAMS, Anna 2014. An Archaeology of the Iron Curtain: Material and Metaphor.

60. LJUNGE, Magnus & RÖST, Anna (red.) 2014. I skuggan av solen. Nya perspektiv på bronsåldersarkeologier och bronsålderns arkeologiska källmaterial.

61. RUNESSON, Gunilla 2014. Bronsålderns bosättningsområden och boplatser på Gotland. Många syns inte men finns ändå.

62. KLEVNÄS, Alison & HEDENSTIERNA-JONSON, Charlotte (Eds.) 2015. Own and be owned. Archaeological perspectives on the concept of possession.

63. ENGSTRÖM, Elin 2015. Eketorps veckningar. Hur arkeologi formar tid, rum och kön.

64. CARLSSON, Anders 2015. Tolkande arkeologi och svensk forntidshistoria. Från stenålder till vikingatid.

65. LJUNGE, Magnus 2015. Bortom avbilden. Sydskandinaviska hällbilders materialitet.

66. NIKLASSON, Elisabeth 2016. Funding Matters: Archaeology and the Political Economy of the Past in the EU.

67. LJUNG, Cecilia 2016. Under runristad häll. Tidigkristna gravmonument i 1000-talets Sverige.

68. ANDERSSON, Helena 2016. Gotländska stenåldersstudier. Människor och djur, platser och landskap.

69. BERG, Ingrid 2016. Kalaureia 1894: A Cultural History of the First Swedish Excavation in Greece.

70. SPANGEN, Marte 2016. Circling Concepts. A Critical Archaeological Analysis of the Notion of Stone Circles as Sami Offering Sites.

71. RÖST, Anna 2016. Fragmenterade platser, ting och människor. Stenkonstruktioner och depositioner på två gravfältslokaler i Södermanland, ca 1000–300 f Kr.

72. NILSSON, Per 2017. Brukade bilder. Södra Skandinaviens hällristningar ur ett historiebruksperspektiv.

73. EIKJE RAMBERG, Linn 2017. Mynt er hva mynt gjør. En analyse av norske mynter fra 1100-tallet: produksjon, sirkulasjon og bruk.

74. AUDY, Florent 2018. Suspended Value: Using Coins as Pendants in Viking-Age Scandinavia (AD 800–1140).

75. SÖRMAN, Anna 2018. Gjutningens arenor: Metallhantverkets rumsliga, social och politiska organisation i södra Skandinavien under bronsåldern.

76. FAHLANDER, Fredrik 2018. Bildbruk i mellanrum. Mälarvikens hällbilder under andra årtusendet fvt.

77. QVISTRÖM, Linda 2020. Rum utan utsikt. Fönster och ljus i medeltida byggnader.

78. ARNSHAV, Mirja 2020. De små båtarna och den stora flykten. Arkeologi i spåren av andra världskrigets baltiska flyktbåtar.

79. ODEBÄCK, Kerstin 2021. Vikingatida sköldar. Ting, bild och text som associativt fält.

80. GÜNTHER, Helena 2022. The Rhythm of Rock Art Animals. Picturing Reindeer, Elk and Bear around the Seasonal Cycle in Stone Age Alta.

81. FAHLANDER, Fredrik (red.) 2023. Tredimensionell dokumentation av hällar och hällbilder i Uppland. Rapport från ett FOU-projekt: Digitala bilder för forskning och publik.

82. LARSSON, Anton 2023. Landslide Archaeology: Past hazards and disasters in the Göta River Valley and beyond.

83. FAHLANDER, Fredrik och VINBERG, Ann (red.) 2023. Arkeologiska undersökningar i Jordbro 2017–2019. Gravar och aktivitetsytor från bronsålder och äldre järnålder på Jordbrogravfältet (L2014:3046) i Österhaninge sn, Haninge kn.

84. WARMING, Rolf och RÖNNBY, Johan (red). 2024. Grifun/Gribshund (1495) Marinarkeologisk dokumentation 2023 av ett senmedeltida kravellskepp.

85. LINDSTRÖM, Tobias. 2024. Människor, djur och varelser i miniatyr. Flerartliga förbindelser i den gropkeramiska kulturen.

86. FALCK, Tori. 2024. The Becoming of Boats. Craft Practices in Southern Norwegian Boatbuilding (1050–1700 CE).

87. NYBERG, Jenny. 2024. Förgängligheten och evigheten. Samhällselitens förhållande till döden genom omhändertagandet av de döendes och dödas kroppar i det tidigmoderna Sverige (ca 1500–1800).

88. SJÖGREN, Anna Andréasson 2025. Från Kål till Paradis. Medeltidens trädgårdar inom dagens Sverige.

89. WARMING, Rolf (red.). 2025. Violence and Warfare in Social Context: Archaeological and Historical Studies.